DISABILITY IN FILM
AND LITERATURE

D1596194

DISABILITY IN FILM AND LITERATURE

Nicole Markotić

McFarland & Company, Inc., Publishers
Jefferson, North Carolina

LIBRARY OF CONGRESS CATALOGUING-IN-PUBLICATION DATA

Names: Markotić, Nicole, author.
Title: Disability in film and literature / Nicole Markotić.
Description: Jefferson, North Carolina : McFarland & Company,
    Inc., Publishers, 2016 | Includes bibliographical references
    and index.
Identifiers: LCCN 2016011942 | ISBN 9780786496495 (softcover :
    acid free paper) ∞
Subjects: LCSH: People with disabilities in motion pictures. |
    People with disabilities in literature. | Human body in motion
    pictures. | Human body in literature. | Sociology of disability.
Classification: LCC PN1995.9.H34 M37 2016 | DDC
    791.43/6527—dc23
LC record available at https://lccn.loc.gov/2016011942

ISBN 978-0-7864-9649-5 (softcover : acid free paper) ∞
ISBN 978-1-4766-2466-2 (ebook)

BRITISH LIBRARY CATALOGUING DATA ARE AVAILABLE

Cover photograph © 2016 Debi Bishop (IStock)

Printed in the United States of America

McFarland & Company, Inc., Publishers
    Box 611, Jefferson, North Carolina 28640
    www.mcfarlandpub.com

For Louis Cabri

Table of Contents

Acknowledgments

Chapter 1 previously appeared in *Different Bodies: Essays on Disability in Film and Television* © 2013, Edited by Marja Evelyn Mogk, by permission of McFarland & Co., Inc., Box 611, Jefferson, NC 28640; Chapter 3 first appeared in the *Journal of Literary & Cultural Disability Studies* (Vol. 1, no. 1, 2007); a version of Chapter 5 appeared as "Re/Presenting Disability and Illness: Foucault and in 20th Century Fiction" in *Disability Studies Quarterly* (Vol. 23, no. 2, 2003); a shorter version of Chapter 6 appeared in *Open Letter* (14th Series, no. 8, 2012); a much reduced version of Chapter 7 was published in *Review of Education, Pedagogy, and Cultural Studies* (Vol. 34, nos. 3–4, 2012); a small portion of Chapter 8 appeared in the Vancouver Festschrift, *Tracing the Lines: in Honour of Roy Miki* (Talon Books, 2011); and Chapter 9 first appeared in the *Canadian Journal of Disability Studies* (Vol. 1, no. 2, 2012). I thank the editors of these journals and book publications: Marja Mogk, David Bolt, David Pfeiffer, Frank Davey, Nancy Gillespie, Peter Jaegar, Sarah Brophy, Janice Hladki, and Jay T. Dolmage. I presented small selections of this text at various academic conferences; I am grateful to the organizers of the conferences and individual panels, as well as my co-panelists and the audience members who generously listened, and often provided helpful and necessary queries about my work. These conferences include: Society for Disability Studies (SDS), the Health, Embodiment, and Visual Culture conference (Sarah Brophy and Janice Hladki), an invited talk at Deakin University in Melbourne (Debra Dudek), a presentation as part of VERSeFest (Rob McLennan), and I was invited to present at the Social Bond lecture series on Lacan and poetry (Nancy Gillespie and Nikki Reimer).

I am also grateful to Amy Hasbrouck for permission to reprint her germane political cartoon, which appears in the afterword.

I passionately thank and appreciate Louis Cabri, Sally Chivers,

Michael Davidson, Mike Gill, Ingrid Hofmann, Susan Holloway, Eunjung Kim, Suzette Mayr, Robert McRuer, David Mitchell, Marja Mogk, Rosemary Nixon, Peter Quartermain, Tobin Siebers, Sharon Snyder, and Cynthia Wu for lively and pertinent conversations, for invaluable comments and opinions, and/or for outstanding critical feedback, all of which has helped me develop and shape the ideas in this book. Extra, extra gratitude goes to Louis Cabri and Eunjung Kim for multiple readings of multiple chapters: thanks, thanks, thanks for the constant criticism and advice! A profound thank-you to Martin Boyne, Indexer extraordinaire.

When I first started working as an assistant professor, my interests focused on Canadian literature, specifically disjunctive poetry and nonlinear narrative. I was lucky to find colleagues and writers, across Canada and in my own English department, who shared my interests and encouraged me along odd and surprising paths. Subsequently, my parallel interest in disability studies brought me in contact with more amazing and dedicated scholars, and I am grateful for the intelligence and engagement that I continue to discover in this productive and splendid research field. Now working in a department where I am the sole disability scholar in Humanities brings joys and frustrations. I sometimes envy scholars at other institutions who share ideas and conversations with colleagues down the hall, or who reside within a department wholly dedicated to this field. But that frustration is fleeting; I am immensely lucky to teach and research within a department as supportive as the Department of English Language, Literature, and Creative Writing at the University of Windsor. My colleagues remain a truly unique bunch: brilliant teachers and enthusiastic scholars, dutiful to administrative duties, often overworked yet always open and helpful to every student, dedicated to their own work, and yet consistently supportive of others' research interests. I am lucky to teach a variety of courses and subject matters, to meet undergraduate students who—though they may have known little or nothing about disability studies before taking this one course—become enamored with studying representations of disability. Colleagues in tangential research fields also get swept up in this wide-reaching subject area, and I have participated in immensely lively and satisfying conversations about the current and future states of disability research. Some of these colleagues and my graduate students at the University of Windsor—many now fascinated with this exciting field of enquiry—send off papers, attend conferences, and often shift their research area to include (or entirely encompass) disability theory.

To those emerging scholars, I give a hearty "thank you!"

Introduction:
The [adj.] Body

In March 2012, the Internet was flooded with pictures of a six-legged calf, Lilli, raised by its Swiss owner Andreas Knutti. It is unclear whether people were more fascinated by a calf boasting six legs, or that the two surplus appendages decorated its left shoulder rather than operated as a third set of load-bearing limbs.

The comments people posted beneath the websites carrying this story intrigue me. For example, from Yahoo News, "mpup" writes: "Any decent vet would have removed that at birth. Cruel and ignorant to let this happen, and get media coverage as well. FFS." And "Marilyn" writes: "That's not a six-legged calf. That's a calf with an appendage that should have been removed at birth. Are they THAT poor in Switzerland?" And finally, one Yahoo!User writes: "Come on animal rights people, if this guy doesn't have the money for surgery then this is where you should be helping. If this were a human being it would be done as soon as possible (Associated Press)." Not only, in this discussion loop, is the physically proficient body associated with the idea of normality, but the assumption here is ubiquitous that surgery will and should "correct" any physical body. Commenters equate this calf with children who may have physical disabilities and leap to the assumption that physical difference is automatically worse than invasive and painful surgery (although one user, "Guy," did quip: "Poor calf—people will make fun of him [sic] all his life. They may call him legs"). The photo of this calf standing on the Swiss Alps outraged website visitors by its apparently trouble-free, "natural" posture. By all accounts the calf's owner should have found a way to standardize the body of this domesticated animal; the calf should either have been "destroyed," "cured," or subjected to cosmetic surgery, depending on the discussion thread.

1

That many commenters equate the calf (originally destined to work as a milking cow) with a child or anthropomorphized pet is telling.[1] The automatic response to "save" Lilli through corrective bodily measures speaks to how vital most people feel it is to present to the world a "normal" body. Indeed, Knutti eventually sold Lilli to an "animal lover" who paid £1,420 for surgery to remove her extra limbs (Watson).

Rather than argue (at length, as there are a plethora of examples) about the numerous ways that film, literature, and other media consistently present disability as a "problem" best solved through surgery (and sometimes death), this book is about overwhelming impulses—to regulate, normalize, and regiment the (human) body—and literary representations in fiction, poetry, and film to identify, label, and mark the body. What seemed to upset most commenters on the six-legged calf story was not the disability as such, but the visual reminder of disability on this calf. The site proffered presumably non-disabled people commenting on their own desires to remove evidence of perceived disability.

The desire to regard bodies—all bodies—as beholden to an ideal standard of what Erving Goffman calls an "unspoiled identity,"[2] on the understanding that bodies failing the norm must be subject to physical modifications, upholds conventional notions of ableism. To quote a definition of ableism crafted by Laura Smith, Pamela Foley, and Michael Chaney: "Ableism is a form of discrimination or prejudice against individuals with physical, mental, or developmental disabilities that is characterized by the belief that these individuals need to be fixed or cannot function as full members of society." This is an encompassing definition that embraces what most disability activists and scholars refer to as the social model of disability.[3] In 1983, Michael Oliver and Bob Sapey coined the term "social model" to argue that "adjustment" for people with disabilities, then, is "a problem for society, not for disabled individuals" (37). The social model, then, effectively challenges readings of disability as damage or imperfection.[4] "As a result of these assumptions," they continue, "individuals with disabilities are commonly viewed as being abnormal rather than as members of a distinct minority community." Considering disability to be socially equivalent to other minority cultures, Smith et al. take the distinction further: "Because disability status has been viewed as a defect rather than a dimension of difference, disability has not been widely recognized as a multicultural concern by the general public as well as by counselor educators and practitioners" (304). Lawrence Carter-Long, media personality and executive director of the Disabilities Network, aligns disability with multiplicity: "Polite society often tells us that we need to take the 'dis' out of disability, but maybe … just maybe, we should spend some time putting it back in. Take the 'dis' out of disability and you remove the core of what has shaped my life. Disability puts the 'D' in diversity" (*Ollibean*).

Impulses to regulate, normalize, and regiment the (human) body construct disability narratives and accompany their critical reception in popular media. Overwhelmingly, depictions in popular culture of disability are conveyed by way of narratives of heartbreak, misfortune, or tragedy (or what Michael Davidson calls "triumphalist" parables in *Concesto*, 14). Even when stories (such as the novel *Good Kings Bad Kings* by Susan Nussbaum) favorably present the lives of disabled characters, or depict them in plots that have little or nothing to do with their disability (such as frequently occurs with the cheerleader character, Becky, in the 2009–15 FOX network show *Glee*), reviewers often remark upon the brave or noble protagonists. As an example, many reviewers writing about the Oscar-winning film *Forrest Gump* (1994) offer praise such as "awe-inspiring" (Wine), an "extraordinary story" (Thompson), and that Tom Hanks brings a "touching gravity to the role of an idiot savant" (Travers). While Kenneth Turan, writing for the *Los Angeles Times*, allows that the film is an example of "Hollywood's fascination with the mentally challenged," he nevertheless praises its protagonist as a "kind of holy fool." What reviewers seem to admire most is Tom Hanks's portrayal of "an innocent on a colorful odyssey" (Thompson). The film makes a point of announcing Forrest Gump's IQ as 75, and reviewers accept the protagonist as both a representative of anyone with a mental disability and as "celebration and satire" (Thompson) of American culture: he is childlike (his favorite book is *Curious George*), he only discovers his superb speed when his leg braces fall apart as he runs from bullies, and he is a vital catalyst around which historically significant events unfold (as one example, Elvis learns to dance by observing the "gimpy" dance Gump performs wearing his leg braces). Because he plays a stock character, the "idiot savant," Gump, much like Chauncey Gardiner (Peter Sellers) in *Being There* (1979), can only convey simple and gentle emotions and ambitions (though *Being There* is much more biting satire about American popular media than *Forrest Gump*'s blithe acclamation). Gump falls in love as a child and is unwavering in that love. He greatly influences the American story of the individual who triumphs on merit alone, but inadvertently, without intention. He is meek and unpretentious, naïve and unsophisticated and, in Hollywood terms, mentally challenged. In many ways, the film is an extended punch line, one in which a "creature supremely naïve yet mystically wise" (Wirt) not only commands the fate of an entire generation, but where the (presumably non-mentally disabled) actor who plays him wins an Academy Award for his performance.[5]

In an episode of *Seinfeld*, George Costanza, upon realizing that someone has been shining a laser-pointer at his face, cries out in trepidation, "I can't be blind, Jerry, the blind are courageous!" The punch line sums up one of the many stock reactions to disability: that disabled people must be noble or especially spirited in order to cope with what "normal" people would find too difficult or overwhelming to handle. To critique such attitudes, Ellen Painter Dollar admonishes: "Admire me for what I do—for writing well, raising decent kids or having a lovely garden. But don't admire me just for existing, just because I live a mostly unremarkable life with scars and a limp and a history of dozens of broken bones. Admiration of this sort is really just pity in disguise. The implication? 'If I had a body like yours, I would hide myself at home all day. You must have huge reserves of courage, to bring this body out into public every day.'" (Dollar). Such assumptions arise from what comedian and activist Stella Young calls "inspiration porn," videos or posters that praise disabled people for accomplishing everyday tasks. "I use the term porn deliberately because they objectify one group of people for the benefit of another group of people." Referring to the media slogan, *The only disability in life is a bad attitude!*, Young cleverly protests: "No amount of smiling at a flight of stairs has *ever* made it turn into a ramp." With "inspiration porn" comes the flip side of such admiration: pity. An especially pertinent parody but in a similar vein, is posted by *The Onion* (via ClickHole). In it, sighted people try to describe what food tastes like to blind people. One woman says, "I guess it tastes strawberry-y." And in a perfect inversion of the usual synesthesia descriptions, one of the men claims: "Ice cream is like the taste version of the color blue" ("These People Describe"). Most of the satire lies in the transposing of one sense for another (why not just let the other person bite into the food?), but the skit also parodies sentimental videos that circulate about how to describe color to someone who is blind, or how to "explain" music to a deaf person. At the basis of such schmaltzy "celebrations" is the public demand for universal experience: *you* must experience the world as *I* do (as the rest of "us" do). The constant assertion being to urge disabled people to be more "like the rest of us."

The *Seinfeld* scene succinctly evidences how people with disabilities are likely to be viewed on screen: not just as disabled people, but also as stereotypes. Can an unschooled audience embrace the disabled protagonist?[6] Martin Norden has shown that disabled characters on film seemingly *must* reveal a "spiritual" attribute that makes their disability tragic because of their "suffering" (e.g., the "Tragic Victim" or the "Saintly Sage"), or somehow heightens their dignity and goodness (e.g., the "Sweet Innocent" or the "Noble Warrior") (Norden 26, 121, 131, 221). In discussing how one defines who is—or is not—disabled, Mary Johnson writes, "The real clue as to whether someone is truly disabled is if we feel sorry for them being that way; if we secretly are horrified at the prospect of being like that ourselves" (59). According to the ableist prejudice Johnson outlines in her book *Make Them Go Away*, disability is measured by how much an able-bodied viewer pities or admires characters for "enduring" their disabilities. George Costanza's panic—not only at the possibility of losing his sight but also at the possibility of expectations for him to start acting as a brave soul—reinforces normative assumptions about the frightening demands the disability places on a blind person's actions and attitudes.

Within narrative convention, novels and poems traditionally portray disabled characters as either pathetic victims (Alan Lightman's *The Diagnosis*, which I address in Chapter 5), courageous or daring protagonists (Jean-Do Bauby and Ramón Sampedro, which I address in Chapter 7), avenging villains (the malevolent antagonist in virtually any superhero story; the characters in the 1932 Tod Browning film *Freaks*, who murder and mutilate the treacherous antagonists; I speak a bit about that film in Chapter 4), or minor metaphorical glosses to a more important "normal body" narrative (the eponymous "hero" in Earle Birney's "David" poem, which I examine in Chapter 3). These strict categories are not always so strict in that, more and more, contemporary media tend to acclaim untraditional "heroes" (including historical figures such as Harriet Tubman, Terry Fox, or Helen Keller) whom audiences often relate to as underdogs, and who both encompass and challenge notions of a "superior" hero. I am particularly interested in how the disabled body is often invoked, in various media, as the automatic negative container against some ideal positive. David Mitchell and Sharon Snyder, in their pivotal book *Narrative Prosthesis: Disability and the Dependencies of Discourse*, point out that "negative representations" of disabled characters is "proof" that discrimination against disabled people is furthered by "images consumed by readers and viewers" (20). The persistent idea that there exists such a thing as a "normal" body reveals itself in the plethora of adjectives that proceed the noun.

Rather than simply demarcating and championing what may appear to be yet another identity category, in this book I wish to investigate the very impulses that lead to marking the body with particular qualifiers. I wish to examine the language that encodes disability and that surrounds (and sometimes supports) it. This is language that metaphorically elides, shapes, or *adjectivizes* disability. I wish to look at egregious depictions of disability, but also some that are marvelous, intriguing, even fun. I wish to parse as well as deconstruct. The book speaks to the layered ways in which writers, filmmakers, scholars, activists, journalists, and some members of the general public construe the body via its parts and its adjectives, naming identity through divergences from a supposedly fixed "norm." These cultural media offer representations of disabled bodies I wish to explore (in poetry, narrative, and film): the edgy body, the mediated and constructed body, the "problem" body. Elsewhere, I use the term "problem body" to address the variable determining factors defining the problematic relationship between "normal" and "abnormal" bodies, and I argue that, in terms of a chronological narrative of recent progressive social change, the disabled body cannot merely operate as the next added adjective (after class, after gender, after race, etc.) to the burgeoning critical writing on the body.[7] Disability entails multiple forms and modes of difference at once, as many theorists and activists recognize, including racialization, gender, age, and queerness. The disabled body, then, is not merely another add-on as the next overlooked critical frame; I wish to expand the discussion beyond a focus on either *this* [adjective] body or *that* [adjective] body. Rather, the disabled body encompasses that shifting and vexing identity marker that includes "spoiled" bodies (Goffman), "extraordinary" bodies (Garland-Thomson), "silent" bodies (Murphy), "defamiliar" bodies (Davidson), "rejected" bodies (Wendell), bodies "solitaire" (Mitchell and Snyder), and bodies "politic" (Linton). In other words: *bodies*, in all their exasperating, unruly, problematic, and magnificent variations. My book responds to the problematics of representations and the constructions of the body's "edges" and its social roles, especially as disability theory reimagines those edges. The problem body is the [adj.] body: people and fictional characters who fluctuate across a range of differences, presumed to require that compulsory adjective to allocate a *kind* of body, a *type* of body.

Classic books and films have for a long time depicted the social outcast who is either highly esteemed or deplored for his character. There is an equally long association of disabled characters and of specific physical traits tied to the role of a societal outcast promoted as a model of evil, as depicted in films and classic books, such as Captain Hook in *Peter Pan*, Quasimodo in *The Hunchback of Notre Dame*, Erik in *Phantom of the Opera*, or the creature (so named by the narrator) in *Frankenstein*. Almost as frequently, texts portray the opposite, depicting "ordinary characters" whose disabilities—in and of themselves—transform them into noble and dignified people, such as Tiny Tim in *A Christmas Carol* or John Merrick in *The Elephant Man*. In the late 1980s and early 1990s science fiction films which featured disabled and "genetically altered" characters began to proliferate. Set in a time markedly different from the present, such sci-fi narratives invariably propose "alternative" bodily categories as abundant examples of the "norm" gone deviant. In David Cronenberg's film *Dead Ringers* (1988), twin male gynecologists Beverly and Elliot Mantle (both played by Jeremy Irons) liken themselves to the famous conjoined twins Chang and Eng, thereby enhancing, so the film suggests, both their titillating actions (unbeknownst to the women they date, they often pretend to be one person) and their horrific actions (Beverly violently operates on women he considers to have "mutant genitalia"). By contrast, independent Winnipeg filmmakers Shawna Dempsey and Lorri Millan, in their short film *The Headless Woman* (1998), display the circus freak not only as metaphoric of the contemporary status of women and especially lesbians, and also reveal the haven that the sideshow world has traditionally offered people whose bodies and bodily desires did not always fit into societal ideals. In *The Headless Woman*, then, disability and deviation remain associated with each other, but valued positively.

In what has now become a well-known examination of metaphorical language, Mark Johnson and George Lakoff, in their 1980 *Metaphors We Live By*, suggest that metaphor is not only a rhetorical device of ornamentation; it shapes and defines everyday "reality": "Our concepts structure what we perceive, how we get around in the world, and how we relate to other people" (3). One palpable example they use is that "argument is war," a metaphor perpetuated in everyday conversations: "He *attacked every weak point* in my argument," and, "He *shot down* all of my arguments" (4). Metaphor, they write, is of central concern to "how language can reflect the conceptual system of its speakers" (xi). This systemic conceptualization structures discourse. Metaphorical language perpetuates ideas about social norms, especially as pertaining to minority groups. So for example, media coverage about "broken families" plays into ideas about the nuclear family as paramount, as well as associating such "brokenness" with poorer families who may need welfare assistance. Further, shifting the emphasis from noun to adjective often allows deleterious meanings imbedded in particular terms to remain covert. As Simi Linton points out in *Claiming Disability: Knowledge and Identity*, "*Cripple* as a descriptor of disabled people is considered impolite, but the word has retained its metaphoric vitality, as in 'the exposé in the newspaper crippled the politician's campaign'" (16). The term "cripple," used here as a verb, gains neutral political weight ostensibly because it is not aimed a person; yet its "metaphoric vitality" comes from the image of an economic system crumbling inexorably the way a disabled body is presumed to inexorably decline. The metaphor functions at a larger social level through implicit imagery that has been transferred from a person subject to a political subject. Textual and corporeal "meaning," in such ways, exist as a repository for cultural evaluations and judgments.

Physical "anomalies" are often attributed to a "natural" or essential link between how the body operates and what such operations *mean*. In the introduction to their 1997 edited essay collection *The Body and Physical Difference: Discourses of Disability*, David Mitchell and Sharon Snyder assert: "The current popularity of the body in critical discourse seeks to incorporate issues of race, gender, sexuality, and class while simultaneously neglecting disability" (5). They point to a lack of critical analysis of the disabled body, without such prioritizing coming at the expense of the other equally critical factors determining the body. Mitchell and Snyder note in their anthology introduction: "Analyses of disability in art, popular media, and history have much to teach us about the role of disability in culture than the assumption that lives defined as disabling (and hence unlivable or unworthy) go unrepresented and un(der)appreciated by audiences and cultures" (12). My book intends to explore these larger cultural themes within which disability is figured, not figured, and disfigured.

Rosemarie Garland-Thomson, in her book that designates disabled bodies "as extraordinary rather than abnormal" (137), points out that "the meanings attributed to extraordinary bodies reside not in inherent physical flaws, but in social relationships" (*Extraordinary Bodies*, 7). Garland Thomas goes on to say that "gender, ethnicity, sexuality, and disability are related products of the same social processes and practices that shape bodies according to ideological structures" (*Extraordinary*, 136). Within the cultural inheritance of conceptual-metaphorical discourse, negative terms are frequently drawn from disability (for example, the ubiquitous term "lame" to designate everything from an unpleasant idea to a deteriorating political campaign). With every year that passes since the early 1980s, literary scholars in the U.S., Canada, and the U.K. increasingly acknowledge disability studies as a significant dimension of social critique. Thus, disability critics have taken up the political dimension of Lakoff's work, which is to figure ways of changing how constitutive conceptual metaphors exploit negative representations of disability. Widespread metaphorical uses, in the media and literature, of bodily depravity and unfitness perpetuate not only images of disability (or any body configured as deviating from an established norm) as fitting examples for moral correction, but also erase the actual physical body from representational visibility. My aim in this book, then, is to celebrate those texts that attempt to confront actual physical existence, as well as those that resist or challenge societal customs with respect to how to respond to people who are deemed to have "lesser" bodies, bodies apparently deficient or lacking in some fundamental way.

Back in February 2000, CTV National News carried a story relating to the then–Reform Party's (which subsequently became the ruling Conservative Party) charge against the Liberal Party concerning imprudent spending of federal funds. During Parliamentary session, MP Diane Ablonczy demanded explanations from then–Prime Minister Jean Chrétien. Not satisfied with Chrétien's response, Ablonczy sarcastically remarked that, perhaps "the Prime Minister has a hearing problem." Interestingly, Chrétien's reply—that yes indeed he's had a hearing problem since childhood—takes Ablonczy's metaphorical reference to his hearing disability and reads it literally. The deliberate humor of his doing so shifted attention away from the attack on his party's economics, and onto the "rude" remark made by a political opponent. After the session, reporters asked if Ablonczy's question was "inappropriate." She told them that "since I have the same problem [she herself wears two hearing aids], it wasn't meant as a personal attack, but rather as a political one" (CTV News).

The line between the literal and the metaphorical became blurred in that comment by Ablonczy to Chrétien, in that she states that she had not *meant* to comment on her opponent's disability, but she *had* meant to designate his *metaphorical* lack of hearing as disgusting—to her party, to the people of Canada, and to truth itself. Such is the nature of bodily metaphors that their use invokes the very stakes of truth and decency. Such is the constitutive nature of our metaphorical language that even someone who has a hearing problem and is a political rhetorician is not fully aware of the implications of her own language. When her attack was reconstructed as a literal one, Ablonczy hastily ensured her alliance with all people who cannot *literally* hear well (and, therefore, should not *actually* be perceived as inviting disgust, despite her accusing tone and the rhetorical context of her disparaging question in the House), by revealing one of her own bodily "problems." At the same time she gave herself permission to make such an attack out of an essentializing identification she shared with Jean Chrétien. That she herself also had a hearing disability apparently gave her license to use a physical reality as a metaphor for political unreliability. And thus physical disability remains the faultless simile conveniently imposed onto political fabricators.

By reading Ablonczy's political attack as a personal one, Chrétien reversed the rhetorical coding to expose the lived reality hidden behind such metaphorical language (and, of course, to squirm out of a political reproach). "Hard of hearing," in Chrétien reconfiguration, immediately ceased to be a code for the politically unfit and becomes an insensitive insult made by one politician to another. Although reporters allowed her words as a defense for what they have just deemed an inappropriate attack, the TV audience's sudden awareness of both Ablonczy's and Chrétien's hearing difficulties complicates "hearing problem" as *merely* metaphorical political stance. For viewers, then, two political "figures" became literally corporeal.

What interests me most about this political anecdote is the convenient metaphorical *use* it makes of differently abled bodies. The anecdote reveals the availability, within normative discourse, of the so-called challenged body in order to enact a public notion of corruption. Linton also argues against well-meaning terms such as "physically challenged" that merely patronize people whose main obstacles are social, rather than physical. She describes a bookstore with a section for Children with Special Needs as having one shelf devoted to "Misc. Challenges," indicating, as she ironically notes, its use as a convenient and universalizing organizing category (*Claiming Disability*, 15). The body-corrupt presents the mind or soul as essence-corrupt. Garland-Thomson, in *Extraordinary Bodies*, says of the physically disabled body: "Constructed as the embodiment of corporeal insufficiency and deviance, [it] becomes a repository for social anxieties about such concerns as vulnerability, control, and identity" (6).

As Susan Wendell notes, in *The Rejected Body*, that architectural designs that make it difficult for people who are ill or disabled also "cause problems for pregnant women, parents with strollers, and young children. This," she says, "is no coincidence" (40). As buildings are planned for "young adult, non-disabled male paradigms of humanity," so, too, is the world split into a public (male and abled) one, and a private (female, children, ill, disabled), neglected, world. The writing that engages me the most is that writing which challenges, resists, and transgresses an interpellated norm, whether that norm be social, physical, cultural, or aesthetic. How bodies get read, assessed, and interpellated through literature continues to inform, determine, regulate, and govern how bodies get treated in the world. Michael Davidson notes in his book *Concerto for the Left Hand* that "the question of what bodies mean for a social covenant is paramount" (xv). And what bodies *mean* gets imitated and copied and reworked and redefined by the artistic and social worlds that embrace them. With this book, I join those dialogues that continue to transform the conversations.

1

Razzle Dazzle Heartbreak

Disability Promotion and Glorious Abjection in Guy Maddin's The Saddest Music in the World

> We don't know if he's in a coma or just very, very sad.
> —Contest Announcer, *The Saddest Music in the World*

What is it about sadness that is so very, very funny? Winnipeg director Guy Maddin purportedly explores this question in his "big production"[1] film, *The Saddest Music in the World*. In this chapter, I shall examine the contrast Maddin establishes between the commercial exploitation of human suffering and the unruly joy of the fragmented and disabled body, which capitalism stages and displays. More than simply its titular sadness, his film develops and exploits notions of grief, melodrama, and the commodification and marketing of emotions as ways of exploring how these characters enact agency and embody representations of a persuasive market ideology. Maddin's characters display a striking variety of disabilities, at times feeding a contemporary audience's desire for post–Freudian, psycho-biographical explanations for behavior, often decontextualized from a larger socio-cultural rhetoric. Within a familiar narrative of the capitalist exploitation of emotion for profit, *The Saddest Music in the World* singularly depicts disabled characters as protagonists who exhibit their disabilities on their own terms, while paradoxically acknowledging that one cannot stage disability without at the same time enabling its excess. Ultimately, I argue, Maddin's film articulates a new positioning for disability in contemporary film and mass culture: commodified and packaged in a film that both invokes and mocks deliberately convoluted and layered disability tropes.

Identity and Disability in Maddin's World

Celebrated Canadian director Guy Maddin occupies a strange position—both marginalized and central—in the Canadian film scene. He has
a tendency to engage obsolete (for lack of an accurate word to define an
artistic strategy that gestures toward erstwhile technology while at the
same time revels in contemporary tools to manipulate and break apart
that technology) cinematic styles that give him new (old) ways to represent
and contest mainstream narrative investments in the normative body.
David Church writes that Maddin "layers his low-budget tableaux with
the grain and grime of decades long gone" (2). And Mark Peranson says
of Maddin's films that they are "culturally toxic, and the past that he presents is one that we'd never want to live in" (in Maddin, *Selected Writings*,
11). Other critics describe his films as being in "a dream world which operates by dream logic" (Diehl 4), that "wallow in feelings of yearning and
humiliation" while still being "extremely funny" (Shaviro 70), that the
"most hackneyed of plot-twists are made to creak with the weight of divine
purpose" (Straw 61), that they visualize the postmodern, with a sense of
"bargain basement artifice" (Pevere 49), and that they exist in a "perpetual
state of crisis and hysteria" (Beard 81).

Part musical, part melodrama, part cinematic tribute to early-sound-
era films, *The Saddest Music in the World* relies on hand-held cameras,
black-and-white shots, a technique that imitates early two-color Technicolor shots, 1930s cameras and various film stocks,[2] and a soundtrack
reliant on the 1932 hit, "The Song is You," to convey a retro sense of time.
Maddin creates this retro past not crudely by embracing nostalgia for the
pre–World War II film era; rather, he employs nostalgic effects in his film
in order to project, and then, critique the commodification of time and
place, and the aesthetics of its effect. Rewriting (with George Toles) Kazuo
Ishigaro's original screenplay set in 1980s London, Maddin sets *The Saddest Music in the World* in the Canadian prairie town Winnipeg in 1933,
during the Great Depression. Indeed, the film's account of depression-era
Winnipeg (the "world's capital of sorrow") both romanticizes and fable-
izes that city, reveling in its small-town friendliness, extremely frigid tem-
peratures, excessive amounts of snow, and hockey-focused culture. By
presenting Winnipeg as a "center" of cultural capital (even if that capital
is negatively defined), *The Saddest Music* brings together a motley collection of characters, related, intertwined or co-dependent in order to
define and express their multifaceted bodies. As he introduces a critique
of national zeal (the film revolves around a music contest between com-

peting nations), artistic objectives, and the complicated layers of promotion and endorsement in a heartbreak-fascinated culture, Maddin turns to filmic nostalgia to demonstrate how codified notions of bodily exhibition, place, and time structure any performance of sadness or joy. Here, in particular, Maddin locates disability in the context of the logic of capitalism. The film ultimately insists that—paradoxically—one cannot stage disability without placing the disabled body itself onstage with all its potential to exceed or undermine the culturally designated, carefully controlled and commodified meanings assigned to it.

The Saddest Music offers the premise that beer-baroness Lady Helen Port-Huntley (Isabella Rossellini) finances a song contest to determine the saddest music in the world, open to all countries with a prize purse of twenty-five thousand "depression dollars."[3] A contest, then, invented to heal national war wounds while perpetuating emotional gratification through extreme national identity. The Eurovision style contest encourages first the commodification and staging of individually or collectively expressed suffering, then its promotion as an ideal of national unity, all within a carnivalesque box-office aesthetic. The competition will exhibit and commemorate the music of anguish, which the film aligns with disability through the performative spectacle of sorrow, as embodied through various characters, not the least Lady Helen herself who is a double amputee. Maddin's film ostensibly depicts the greed-driven side of the Great Depression as Lady Helen profiteers by organizing her international radio music contest. As host of the contest, Lady Helen anticipates a legal alcohol market that will soon emerge once the U.S. Congress calls an end to prohibition: "If you're sad, and like beer, I'm your lady," she mugs to an anachronistic television camera. Her interest in music, then, stems primarily from a business angle: she wants listeners around the world, but especially south of the Canadian border, to think of her product when they wish to indulge in (or need) a drink.

In Maddin's plot, Chester Kent (Mark McKinney), prodigal down-on-his-luck son as well as neglectful brother, returns to Winnipeg from New York, where he makes his living as a producer of musicals. As the Canadian son who embraces a USA his father detests, Chester proclaims himself the "American Ambassador of Sadness" and determines to win the contest prize money, even if he has to spend all of it (before its end) buying singers, dancers, writers, performers, and "ethnic" extras[4] to join in his excessively extravagant musical production. Alternatively, he plans to take up with Lady Helen, his former lover, and thus "win" the contest money on behalf of the USA, through back-door influence. Fyodor (David

Fox), father to Chester and also a former lover to Lady Helen, wishes to do his country proud by representing Canada in the song contest, and to reinstate himself as Lady Helen's lover by building her aesthetically perfect prosthetic legs. Meanwhile, Roderick (Ross McMillan), brother to Chester and son to Fyodor, returns to Winnipeg from Europe after his young son dies and his wife, Narcissa[5] (Maria de Medeiros), disappears in a wide-eyed haze of grief-induced amnesia.

Roderick arrives as Gavrillo the Great, entering the radio competition on behalf of Serbia. (These divisive national claims within one family are a nod to the multiple cultural backgrounds most Canadians embody, but also make clear the impossibility in North America of binding the diverse and varied body into one uncontested nation-based identity.) Roderick's skin is so sensitive that he feels pain if someone touches him, and he wears a baroque hat and veil ensemble to protect him from light. In a Maddin-style coincidence, Roderick discovers that his brother Chester's current lover is his own long-lost Narcissa. In its playful mix of disabilities and national stereotypes, the film self-consciously caters to various stock images of Canada as underplayed but proud, the USA as exaggerated and exploitative, and the troubled relations each has with other countries and their national music. Announcers claim various entries as "a cavalcade of misery" and "a frightening contest of human despair," and after each musical round (the end signaled by a hockey match buzzer) the crowd cheers, drinks wildly, and the round's winners (at times joyously and at times with trepidation) slide into a Jacuzzi-sized vat filled with Port-Huntley beer.

Lady Helen presents her contest of sorrow as a prize opportunity to focus attention away from the depression. And who better, according to her own assessment of her recent past, to judge misery? Years previously, Lady Helen, a dancer, had one leg amputated by mistake and the other amputated because of injury incurred as a result of a car accident involving two of her rival lovers: Fyodor and Chester Kent. In a flashback scene, Lady Helen rides illicitly with Chester in his car. When Fyodor steps onto the road to stop them, Chester's vision is obscured by Lady Helen, who leans over him to perform oral sex. They crash and one of her legs is pinned under the car. Having been driven to drink by Lady Helen's affair with his son, Fyodor, a doctor, is drunk when he begins an emergency amputation, and thus saws off the "wrong leg." The "right leg," irreparably crushed, was subsequently amputated as well. Years have passed since the incident, and when Chester reappears in Lady Helen's life, she launches into her tale of woe and loss to incite pity in him, as well as to remind him of the guilt he should carry for her truncated dancing career. All within minutes of the opening credits.

David Mitchell and Sharon Snyder argue that, in traditional narratives, secondary or tertiary characters act as foils for the protagonists and that when such characters are disabled, they tend to embody the protagonists' (usually tragic) flaws through "disability as a narrative device," so that disability acts as a narrative "crutch" (*Narrative Prosthisis* 49). Indeed, Mitchell and Snyder's teasing out of the central role of disabled characters as "narrative prostheses" has shaped much current disability theory. This function of disability in narrative shapes its representation such that rarely in the history of film are disabled characters represented as happy with their own bodies, let alone as having enviable bodies.[6] Instead, the disabled body is typically a trigger for, among other things, pathos of the kind that Lady Helen expects hers to elicit. Conveying and generating emotion, especially heartbreak, is such an over-coded film ambition that the number of "hankies" required by a viewer was once a marker for how much an audience would appreciate any particular film.[7] Yet Guy Maddin's film troubles this paradigm. *The Saddest Music in the World* portrays disabled characters as happy *and* fraught, full of malaise and yet decidedly upbeat. Maddin's film is one step beyond the traditional filmic usage of disability criticized by Mitchell and Snyder. Not only do *all* the major characters embody an assortment of disabilities, but it is the apparently non-disabled Chester's striking affective deficit—his utter *lack* of ability to experience the kind of melancholy that disability itself is so often used to generate—that drives the narrative of the film forward.

Staging Pity for the Disabled

When the film audience first views Lady Helen Port-Huntley, she is seated at a boardroom table, apparently non-disabled, commanding a meeting, while wearing a platinum blond wig and glittering tiara. But when Chester arrives to see her, she has arranged to be seated at a grand piano, gigolo at her side. At Chester's refusal to take her angry words seriously, Lady Helen pounds on the piano keys and pushes off the piano bench so that he and the film audience must witness her wheeling over the fur-covered floor. The shot gives Chester's viewpoint, inviting the viewer to indulge in what Rosemary Garland-Thomson critiques as the stare. "Staring offers an occasion to rethink the status quo," Garland-Thomson says, in her book analyzing the action, passivity, violence, celebration, and acceptability of staring. "Seeing startling stareable people challenges our assumptions by interrupting complacent visual business-as-usual. Who we are can shift into focus by staring at who we think we are not," she adds (*Staring* 6); namely, disabled. Rather than present the stereotypical disability trope of the "angelically pure invalid" (*Take Up*, 20), described by Lois Keith in her ground-breaking book on disability and illness in classic girls' fiction, Maddin offers a self-aggrandizing and unlikable Lady Helen who does not incite pity in audience members any more than she does in Chester. In doing so, Maddin achieves exactly the opposite reaction. Lady Helen herself, however, regards the sight of her body as (to invoke that Garland-Thomson title) "extraordinary," a body that will incite particular emotions in particular audiences. She both resents the customary reaction to her body and uses it to her advantage, abjectifying her body in order to produce the reactions she demands, specifically that Chester recognize and acknowledge her loss. Placing herself in a physically "lowly" position to invoke pity, Lady Helen wheels out to shock viewers outside the diegesis, who hadn't known until this point that she is an amputee, and to distress Chester within it, who presumably *must* already know this fact about his former lover, but who has yet to respond on camera. Lady Helen wishes him to acknowledge her utter calamity in *not* being that young performer *now*. But Chester, true to form and in contrast to what might be a predictable film viewer's reaction, responds to her mobility with a cheerful "You got a new dolly!" admiring the plank with wheels upon which she seats herself. His jauntiness and delight at seeing her again serve to reject a valuing of Lady Helen's body as categorically "less" than that it was before her accident (and letting audiences in on the punch line that he not only knows about her amputation, but already knows her method of ambulation).

In addition to a focus on her mobility (she either wheels herself in an awkward and graceless manner reminiscent of horror movie antagonists, or she has her gigolo, Teddy, lift and carry her), Lady Helen attempts to further compel Chester to acknowledge and bemoan her loss. She plays the embittered ex-"star" who has had to abandon a promising career prematurely, surrounding her office with black-and-white stills of her dancing onstage, or performing various gymnastic moves. Each of the photos prominently displays her legs. Although Lady Helen is now a rich capitalist succeeding in a traditionally male occupation, such success does not much please her. Rather, the loss of her biological legs coincides for her with the loss of her allure; she was once the admired woman of multiple lovers, including a competing father and son. These days, her "gams" don't garner her an income, but her capitalist wits do. Such achievement does provide her a measure of grim cheer, but paradoxically also undermines her sense of (feminine) self. Bitterly, as a stock has-been stage-star character made even more bitter by the ostensible disfigurement of disability, Lady Helen makes money as if to avenge her former self. She arranges to "fix" the contest for the USA and split the winnings with Chester, thereby guaranteeing that the country with the saddest citizens is also the country with the largest beer market. That she intends to rig the contest is no surprise, but even the obsequious radio announcers sound flabbergasted when, towards the end of the film, she herself appears onstage for the USA finale: "Isn't it rather odd that Lady Port-Huntley is actually in one of these numbers when she's also the judge?" The second announcer's reply—"Well, Mary, I think she looks spectacular!"—puts the emphasis yet again on Lady Helen's striking, prosthetically enhanced appearance onstage, instead of on her power as critic and arbiter. Already rich and steeped in reactive emotion, her participation in the finale comes across more as a vicious slight against all other (able-bodied) performers rather than purely as old-fashioned greed.

Unlike Lady Helen, whose attitudes and affective manipulations parody and exceed the figure of the disabled revenger, Roderick re-enacts his grief to keep it fresh and active and present in his body; being distraught perpetuates his loss as one that is fundamental to his being. Gavrillo the Great has, after all, arisen not only from Roderick's body, but also from the corpse of his marriage and, ultimately, from the tragedy of the assassination of Archduke Ferdinand of Austria in 1914 that triggered the Great War. As the actor who plays Roderick notes, although Roderick's "tactic is to theatricalize his own grief," *all* the characters' displays of grief are "comically inadequate" (McMillan). For example, Roderick carries his son's heart in a glass jar, preserved with his own tears. Maddin has made a movie not only about sadness but about the eye-catching, ear-harkening *spectacle* of sadness. The manufactured spectacle of sadness that exploits disability, nationality, ethnicity, and gender centers on identity boundaries which are cheaply (and secularly) remedied by the consumption of beer. Just as the film is about to topple into the hot tub of maudlin self-pity, it gestures toward the all-encompassing grief of the loss of a child as a quintessential, sublime sadness. For the most part, this film partakes in a double activity of poking fun at the self and national absorptions of heartache and their manipulative, commercial potential, at the same time as it praises opening oneself to tender emotion.

Ultimately, the *problem* for Lady Helen, evident in the dolly scene at the piano, is that Chester seems socially incapable of pity, and does not recognize guilt as an emotion. Indeed, viewers learn that—since the moment of his mother's death when he was a child—Chester has never cried, never admitted to personal sadness. Charlene Diehl says of Chester's perpetual buoyancy: "He is a boy suspended forever in the moment of his mother's death; having refused that moment, he has locked himself into it perpetually" (10). But Chester is more than a perpetual boy emotionally disabled by an inability to express sorrow. He is representative of a social "problem," one that enables entrepreneurial success and disables human emotion. Chester's refusal (or inability) to pity is depicted in the film as a lack, rather than the result of the potentially liberatory perspective of refusing to see amputation as loss. Because he does not identify disability as pitiful—one of the most iconic identifications film narratives ask viewers to make—Chester does not come across as a reliable character with whom the audience can relate. Rather, the social intelligibility of disability as anything but tragic works to convince viewers that just as something is "wrong" with Lady Helen physically, so, too, is there something "wrong" with Chester emotionally. That he cannot pity her may be emotional ailment on Chester's part, but if, as I am suggesting here, one avoids pathologizing his reaction, then Chester operates as a masculine devotee who refuses to objectify the feminine body; an (ostensibly) able-bodied viewer who refuses to "abjectify" the disabled body.

"Doesn't it make you sad?" Lady Helen demands of Chester.

"Well, life's full of surprises," is his chirpy reply.

Chester—charlatan, impostor, and opportunist—refuses the expected narrative of pity and awe regarding Helen's "lost" legs. He seems, in fact, unable to cling to any past, whether for his emotions for Helen, for his father, or for his emotionally distraught brother, Roderick.

Staging Capitalism

Despite being unable to emotionally move Chester by reminding him of her "plight," Lady Helen eagerly listens to his plans for the contest she will judge. "Here's an angle for you, Helen," he pronounces. "America versus Canada: a brash son comes home to duke it out musically with his war-vet pop. The old man's drowning his sorrow; the son wants no part of this. In order to win the dough, that Yank's gotta find his tearducts in a hurry." Chester outlines the plot to come, and also analyzes his own situation without pity or sentiment. Helen responds with a ready, "You've got something there," demonstrating a world view that would allow, even insist, that she strive to trade her own narrative of misery for capitalist success and fortune. Chester's plan is already working: this story of misery and distress sells tickets, sells a lot of beer, and wins the game. Heartbreak—in its most wretched state—is a marketable commodity, valuable for the pleasure it will bring to contest listeners. Says one of the contest announcers: "As far as [the crowd is] concerned, sadness isn't hurt one bit by a little razzle-dazzle showmanship." Performing sadness for Chester has the opposite effect that it does for his brother: it's a matter of staginess, rather than authenticity, showmanship rather than experiential sensation.

The film appears to position Chester's inability to feel or to express emotion with the rubric of a typically repressed masculine character or as a pathology, or both. His uplifting attitude is projected as either unfortunate (were he able to cry, he would be able to properly mourn his mother's death), crass (by exploiting other country's losses, Chester appropriates and absorbs its talents and skills), or simply dishonest (he is "faking" his cheerful outlook). But Chester also dislodges viewers from the easy emotional reactions and interpretive conclusions familiar to "hankie" films. By *not* wallowing in pity about what are basic life-related corporeal shifts, Maddin offers a Chester who models a viable alternative to a self-indulgent response to misfortune: the more Chester ignores his feelings, the film suggests, the more creative he becomes. Creativity has often been associated with struggle or distress. See, for example, Freud's essay, "Creative Writers and Daydreaming," in which he outlines the artistic impulse as a characteristic of an "unsatisfied" person (146), or Jean Tobin's argument about Freud and the post–Romantic perception of creative artists: "Poets were seen, among other things, to be impoverished, in poor health, alcohol and drug abusing, prone to early death, associated with suicide, mentally and emotionally unstable, unfortunate in love, sexually licentious, often scandalous, politically rebellious, and social outcasts" (19). In contrast, Maddin shapes a more complicated character in Chester Kent. He may not have cried since his mother's sudden death, but he has devoted his life's work to producing musical theater. The show, necessarily and cruelly, must go on.

There is yet another way to look at Chester. In his "Course in Melancholy," which he led in the fall 2011 at the University of Windsor, Alan Davies said that the 17th-century English scholar and author of the classic *The Anatomy of Melancholy* Robert Burton both "suffered from melancholy, and flourished creatively in the midst of it" (seminar discussion). Publishing in 1621, Burton designates melancholy as both a passion (of the heart) and a perturbation (of the mind). The cause, for him, could also be artistic endeavor (his writing), and the treatment (for him) was writing; melancholy, then, serves as a pharmakon, simultaneously toxin and cure. Burton vacillates over whether melancholy is "disease or symptom" (148), but distinguishes it from "ordinary passions of *Fear* and *Sorrow*," describing it as an "anguish of the mind" (149). For Burton, melancholy is deeply connected to romantic love as well as to art, and he inventively argues that the force of the imagination greatly contributes to its cause (220). In *The Saddest Music*, Chester's inability to experience sadness is tied not only to the loss of his mother in the past, but also to his inability to fully commit to romantic love in the present. Indeed, Chester cannot release romantic love from its roots in family tenderness; even as he taunts and dismisses his brother's anguish over personal loss, Chester's main love interests in the film remain his brother's wife and his father's sweetheart. So, for Chester, coupled love always connects to a triangular and familial rivalry, and thus to a blissful nostalgia he refuses to endorse.

Meanwhile, the father, Fyodor, aspires to win back his erstwhile sweetheart Lady Helen and reestablish himself as the benevolent patriarch. Motivated by grief, guilt, and love, he reveals to Roderick a pair of prosthetic legs he has made out of glass and filled with Port-Huntley Muskeg Beer. He aims to replace what he has taken from Lady Helen, and he fashions these glass legs for her because she cannot physically tolerate the wood or plastic models available. Once she tries them on, Lady Helen is ecstatic with her new legs, which she considers aesthetically superior to her original ones, flaunting them and caressing them. The fact that Lady Helen is overjoyed by the beer-filled legs suggests that the nature of her resentment has not been, in fact, the loss of physical limbs, but derives from a loss of a normalcy sustained through a male-defined and commodified image of the desirable female body. Throughout the film, Lady Helen radiates abjection and objectification; for her, the one arouses the other. She takes advantage of them in tandem to enable her to meet emotional and economic needs for profit, attention, desire, and—most of all—control.

Lady Helen's embittered character as the powerful magnate who presents herself through photography and radio voices all but disappears when she assumes the beer-filled prosthetic legs as her own, reconfiguring her—and film audience's—notion of subjectivity. She is no longer a woman-without-legs, nor has she become the original "whole" she once held onto so fiercely. Through prosthetic remedy, she transforms into Helen, a woman who dances, a woman who admires her body for the relationship she has with it, not for what she wishes it could be, or could offer. To perform in this way, Lady Helen does not need a return to her "lost" body; rather; she rejoices in her consummate, new, sleek, artificial legs. In his autobiography about his near-complete paralysis, *The Diving Bell and the Butterfly*,[8] Jean-Dominique Bauby writes: "Oddly enough, the shock of the wheelchair was helpful" (11) in that his friends could stop pretending about, and relying on, his recovery. Indeed, when Lady Helen first tries on the glass legs, she admires how they glitter (the result of light hitting the beer) and how smooth they are, exclaiming, "I'll never have to shave." Just as Bauby embraced his wheelchair for both the mobility and signage it gave him, so, too, does Lady Helen embrace her new abilities and aesthetics enabled by these extraordinary legs. Ultimately, Lady Helen is both the embodiment of capitalistic consumption and its casualty: she produces the most sought-after consumer product of prohibition—alcohol. Her prosthetic legs are full of sparkling beer while her biological legs were lost to her own consumption of semen while riding in the second most fetishized consumer product of prohibition—the automobile. But more than a botched operation, what most makes Lady Helen the casualty of capitalism is her constant ache for a past embodiment; she makes money, it would seem, out of spite. Unlike Chester, Lady Helen accepts the intense emotions that accompany physical change. Her unbridled joy at this newfound vanity contrasts with his ongoing inability to experience passion as anything but emotion for the sake of promotion.

Staging Disability as Finance Capitalism

The contest finale enacts a predictable showdown between the siblings: Chester and his huge ensemble for America and solo cellist Roderick for Serbia, each brother embracing a country "blamed" for global misery and destruction. Chester is a parody of corporate USA as much as his brother, Roderick, is a parody of nostalgia for a pre–finance-era imperialism. The two brothers fight for the love of the same woman, the attention of their father, and to win a contest that will justify their emotional choices. They love the same woman; they share the same childhood memories; they have both chosen substitute nationalities. Chester wishes to prove that sorrow is no more than a useful commodity; Roderick is determined to prove that great sorrow leads to great art. Roderick has always possessed the saddest song—a cello melody he last performed at his son's funeral—

but has resolved not to include it in the contest since he wants only to play it again upon reuniting with his wife. Once in Narcissa's physical presence, Roderick is able to launch this captivating tune in a haunting dénouement that demonstrates the power of unmitigated grief, far outweighing Helen's lament over lost limbs. His grief, though, is portrayed with such farcical overtones that it fits Linda Williams's definition of melodrama, as one of three film categories, along with horror and pornography, which relies on a "system of excess" that "stands in contrast to more 'dominant' modes of realistic, goal-oriented narrative" (25).

During the finale, Gavrillo's high cello note—the rarefied sound signifying the very saddest music—shatters Lady Port Huntley's glittering prosthetic legs. This time around, it is the reverberation of an elegiac melody, rather than a speeding consumer product (Chester's car), that functions as the destructive force that denies Lady Helen her legs, and destroys them. Amid shards of glass, she can no longer negotiate the fluid subjectivity she must display in order to live in the music-beer-tragi-comedy world she herself has created. "You can be fixed," Chester attempts to reassure her, at last demonstrating some portion of the sympathy she has longed for, saying "anything that's built can be rebuilt." But Helen is not swayed by his optimism; she stabs him to death with a piece of the glass. Glibly, Chester retorts with: "Well, now you've given me something to laugh about," refusing to grieve at even his own demise. Then both he and Helen do laugh, at the downfall of the contest, at their destructive plotting, and at the carnivalesque absurdity of their tragic love affair.

Roderick fares little better. Though his grief is genuine, it has become a talisman he carries with him everywhere. Such excess cannot sustain itself: like Lady Helen's fetishized legs, the glass jar in which he carries his son's heart also shatters. Roderick, and what he allegorically represents (the lost generation of World War I, the inciting event of that war in the heart of Europe, emotional genuineness), loses *because* he comes across as excessively and not sufficiently capitalist, and because he is unable to embrace the rapacious capitalism that demands one's own sorrows and flaws be repackaged as cultural commodity. Chester, even though he loses his own life at the end of the film, wins: he's an allegory of USA finance capitalism, which triumphed in the West in the wake of the collapse of the 19th-century monarchies that World War I swept away. Both Lady Helen and Chester Kent embraced capitalism and, through the economic appropriation of art, learned to profitably perform and exploit their own emotions.

A parody of melodrama in Linda Williams's terms, *The Saddest Music in the World* ends by bringing private and national affective excesses to the fore. A dying Chester plays the piano as a life-threatening fire rages through the theater, not helping anyone to escape, not even himself. Roderick and Narcissa leave grasping each other's arms, while Lady Helen disappears in Teddy's arms, whisked off-screen by wealth, rather than love. Given how many of the film's characters enact physical or emotional flaws, the film does not simply position Chester's "problem" as its melodramatic crux, nor does it suggest that his lack of empathy for others constitutes a character arc. By the end of the film, Chester doesn't "learn" to be more empathetic or to put others' needs before his own. There is no emotional "cure" for any of the film's depicted mental disabilities (although the tapeworm that possesses Narcissa does die). Chester's lack of demonstrable sadness underlines his arrogance and pretension. Unwilling to own such a faulty character trait, he constructs his own *lack* as a *capability* through his unwillingness to *give up* his lack. Despite finally producing a tear as his world combusts around him, Chester remains dedicated to the stage right till the end, even as all characters close to him, contestants, and audience members flee the destructive fire. He dies engulfed in magnificent flames, having completed playing and singing "The Song is You," and the film ends with his final words as a voice-over: "I ask you, is there anybody here as happy as I am?"

2

Transposing Disability

*Passing, Intellectual Disabilities,
and Accommodating Others*

In the 2000 film *Memento*, Leonard (Guy Pearce) plays a man with anterograde amnesia. Since acquiring brain damage after an attack, he cannot maintain new memories for more than about ten minutes. The most recent lasting memory in his present is the face of the attacker killing his wife. The film is an action/psychological thriller and much of the plot focuses on Leonard's chase after the killer, but the film also explores short-term memory loss in unusual and provocative ways (including presenting scenes chronologically "backwards"). By tattooing his latest discoveries onto his body (clues, hints about who might be responsible, an image of the man he remembers, etc.), Leonard transforms his skin into a memory map for his investigation. The tattoos operate as a filing system for evidence that Leonard's brain cannot store or recover, and thus render his outer body as a marker of his body's inability to record information on the inside. But his tattooed self also signifies his *process* of recording information, presented in a menacing body that those he suspects fear and respect. His body leads his investigation forward, and maintains the story he so desperately clutches at: namely, a body he repeatedly scrutinizes, reading himself over and over again as a prosthesis for mourning. Audiences read Leonard's body as the reminder he needs, while at the same time scouring his tattoos to remind themselves "when" in the narrative each scene takes place.

In the 2007 film, *Lars and the Real Girl*,[1] a young man, Lars (Ryan Gosling), introduces his family and close-knit town to his new girlfriend, Bianca, an anatomically correct sex doll. At first shocked and angered, people who love him come to accept Bianca as essential to Lars's life, and

24

even to include her in many town events. I argue that Bianca serves as a prosthetic device in the narrative: rather than providing a "solution" to Lars's mental problem (as the film is often read by reviewers), her presence in the community actually offers a means for the other characters to understand Lars. Thus she functions as a prosthetic device for the *town* to embrace Lars, rather than just a toy the protagonist needs in order to learn how to function "normally." Until he "acquires" a girlfriend, Lars comes across to members of the town as quirky and peculiar; in other words, different enough to warrant concern and care (for example, his sister-in-law constantly tries to get Lars to come to dinner, despite his obvious discomfort in even a family social setting), but not different enough for them to recognize him as *different*. When Bianca dies, the film suggests that Lars has progressed to the point where he no longer needs a "fake" girlfriend but is now ready to make more substantial connections with "real" people. More accurately, perhaps, in allowing Bianca to "die," Lars no longer feels pressure to pass. In effect, Bianca's dying indicates that the entire town has come to accept Lars as a multi-faceted person with individual needs that do not necessarily match the community's ideas about a "normal" young man.

I open this chapter with these two films to address the rubric of "passing" within a disability context. Passing itself is such an enormous concept that I cannot here give adequate and comprehensive background. The field of discussion is ever widening for the inclusiveness of the perception of passing and for what, ultimately, constitutes passing. I wish to discuss, in this chapter, the very way that disabled characters often serve as literary or filmic device so that readers or viewers might "pass"; what I mean by this is that by transposing set ideas about the normal body onto particular characters such as Leonard and Lars, those characters who present as disabled often accommodate the narrative so that viewers or audience members can identify secure identity-categories, especially when those categories appear more variable than stable, more dynamic than static. In *Lars and the Real Girl*, Bianca serves as representative of disability in that she sits in a wheelchair for most of the film. Given that most of the town initially reads her as an embarrassing joke-gone-wrong, her fixed seating in the wheelchair is actually the opposite of what she is meant to signify: namely, as a sex doll, her function is to be restricted or "fixed" to the bedroom, rather than actively moving in and around the town. Bianca's wheelchair, then, lets viewers know that she is an active participant in the town, a prosthesis for Lars's social anxiety, but also a prosthesis for the members of his community to socialize with Lars without impinging upon his social limits. In *Memento*, director Christopher Nolan cleverly depicts the protagonist's memory problems through the filmic technique of presenting scenes "backwards." Leonard, as movie hero, appears "normal." But, for most of the other characters in the film, he "passes" as normal in that the evidence and data he gathers remains, literally, only at his fingertips. Since he cannot remember what he learns or whom he suspects, Leonard is beholden to his own body as proof.[2] His passing, then, relies on audience members trusting (within plot twists) his body as "truthful," even as they accept his memory as compromised and unreliable. Tobin Siebers calls this "alternate form" of passing a "masquerade" (101).

Theories of passing in North America arose, to begin with, as a way to address the complicated and thorny issue of people racialized in one way (usually as African American), yet placing themselves (or being so placed by others) within another racial position (usually "white"). The term has bifurcated to include Jews passing as Gentile, gay men and lesbians passing as straight, woman passing as men, and so on, along Judith Butler's lineage of performing identity. In more contemporary readings characterizing identity, to claim identity itself becomes a form of passing. In *Gender Trouble*, Butler argues that "gender is a kind of persistent impersonation that passes as the real." She questions whether cisgender "naturalness" may well be constituted through "discursively constrained performative acts that produce the body through and within the category of sex," and then asks what other foundational categories of identity might be "shown as productions" (viii). Butler wishes to trouble the very idea of "natural" when reading gender, in the same way many theorists have expanded her ideas to question other "natural" states of the body (such as race or disability). In my reading of Butler on passing, much activist disability identity works to dispute what Michael Davidson calls the intractable "one-size-fits-all model of embodiment" (*Concerto*, 222). That bodies *do not* neatly fit one binary extreme or another is the crux of this chapter. I shall examine how some disabled people "pass" for the sake of convenience or expediency, but most do so as a constant accommodation *for others*; that passing itself (whether to emphasize or de-emphasize a disability) transposes disability (and the identification of corporeal and mental difference) from viewer (or reader) back onto the individual.

I shall briefly mention a few theorists who illustrate and critique literary examples of passing. This overview shall not serve to summarize the entire field, but shall serve as a foundation from which I commence my own discussion around transposing disability. More than thirty-five years ago, Claudia Tate read Nella Larsen's 1929 novel, *Passing*, by delving into the characters' "psychological ambiguity and intrigue," rather than accepting the novel as melodramatic and anachronistic (142). Gabrielle McIntire, who analyzes the same novel in her essay, "Toward a Narratology of Passing: Epistemology, Race, and Misrecognition in Nella Larsen's *Passing*," reads the notion of race as "operat[ing] as a physical, social, and psychical demarcation as well as a cultural fiction" (779). In a similar vein, Teresa Zackodnik, in her book *The Mulatta and the Politics of Race*, invokes the "highly politicized and significant figure" (187) of the mulatta, to "interrogate and challenge notions of racial difference" (xvii). Zackodnik investigates the role of the mulatta "as tabooed figure on the American racial scene" (13) who trades on her whiteness, consequently interrogating and subverting ontological identity categories (Zackodnik, x); and Allyson Hobbs opens her book with the acknowledgment that passing "enables an interrogation of race by examining the act of denying race" (8). For Hobbs, "[T]he history of passing is a composite of cultural and political history" (25), promoting racial indeterminacy as both subversive to oppressive racist ideologies and yet holding detrimental consequences for those engaged in passing tactics. "Passing was a potent weapon against racial discrimination, but it was also a potential threat to personal and community integrity" (13). Arguing that every individual has multiple identities and multiple perspectives from which to traverse those identities, Anna Camaiti Hostert says that the traditional approach to passing is "the intentional presenting of oneself to the world in a manner that conflicts with how the individual in question views himself or herself" (12), with, apparently, no consideration of how externally the categories work in connection to the individual's self-perception. Indeed, many writers have employed the term "passing" to designate a (usually fraught) transfer of identity from one category to another. For example, disability scholar Lennard Davis, in *Bending Over Backwards*, talks about "passing" in a "world of largely middle- and upper-class academics," though still bearing the "hidden injuries of class" (103). Because, says Zackodnik, passing "calls into question the epistemology of race grounded in the visibility of sign and image," it is "epistemologically disruptive" (13); in other words, there is no "authentic original" to be discerned. Zackodnik says that a continued reading of racial passing as no more "than an individual's attempt to better his or her material position" (Zackodnik, 157) limits a reading of passing as potentially subversive. Her example of the mulatta, she says, reveals "not only the failed control of 'illegitimate' racial mixing but, more important, threatens to expose the tenuous nature of whiteness" (Zackodnik, 13). It is that very ability to destabilize the powerful normative that invites disability scholars to choose passing as a generative trope for investigating the ways that disabled people often negotiate the world. In connecting these historical investigations of literary and racialized passing, I do not wish to slide from one identity category to another, without acknowledging the multiple ways in which these forces encroach upon the individual. For able-bodied white people in North America, passing is rarely a daily consideration. For white disabled people, passing becomes somewhat more familiar, though I hesitate to merely merge these matters into one smooth consortium, especially as so many people with disabilities must also negotiate issues involving race, gender, sexuality, etc. Disability frequently interacts with racialized and other marginalized identity categories, and disability "passing" functions in different ways when the passing also involves race. As Ellen Samuels notes, in "My Body, My Closet," in practice, such "analogies often both create and rely on artificial dichotomies that not only produce inequality between the terms of comparison but exclude or elide anomalous experiences that do not fit easily within their terms" (235). Indeed, in her article she wishes to "refocus our endeavors from the visible signs of these identities to their invisible manifestations" (236). I offer such context, here, to introduce a further examination of disability that hides, conceals, displays, or otherwise flaunts itself, as a valuable strategy to negotiate an ableist world.

In *Epistemology of the Closet*, Eve Kosofsky Sedgwick argues against sexuality defined through binary oppositions. She names the closet as being "the defining structure for gay oppression in this century," though she cautions against the terms "closet" and "coming out" as "verging on all-purpose phrases for the potent crossing and recrossing of almost any politically charged lines of representation" (71). Nevertheless, her ideas about "coming out" as "an authentically public speech act" (72) continue to inform and open up discussion for theorists of various disciplines. In particular, her argument that an individual's coming out implicates, in part, "the erotic identity of the person who receives the disclosure" (81) is especially generative within disability theory in that when individuals with disabilities "claim" (to use Simi Linton's vocabulary) disability (through activist struggles, or through social or textual disclosure), the declarations seem to affect the (presumably non-disabled) receivers. Samuels speaks about "coming out" in specific contexts, such as when one's "bodily appearance does not immediately signal one's own sense of identity" ("My Body, My Closet," 233). Rosemarie Garland-Thomson, in *Extraordinary Bodies*, makes a similar point when she describes the role of freak shows in 19th-century North American circus acts. In displaying themselves as freaks, the performers aim to disturb audiences, yet the boundary of the either/or velvet rope also "soothes the onlookers' self-doubt by appearing as their antithesis" (65). In his chapter, "Disability as Masquerade" (in his book, *Disability Theory*), Siebers examines the numerous restrictions placed on both passing and concealing, and argues that the pressure to conceal is "one of the constitutive markers of oppression" (97). And the editors of the only anthology on disability and passing (to date) remark that stigma "is not fixed, natural, essential, or transhistorical; rather, it changes over time and varies across regions, cultures, and other contexts" (4). Such a wide brush necessarily includes too little as well as too much. Samuels points out: "Discourses of coming out and passing are central to visibility politics, in which coming out is generally valorized while passing is seen as assimilationist" ("My Body, My Closet," 244). By expanding these expressions to encompass those with non-physical and non-visible disabilities, acts of passing *and* acts of self-identification reaffirm the unpredictability of the body as social medium.

Anecdotal examples about disability passing include Garland-Thomson, who calls her book, *Extraordinary Bodies: Figuring Physical Disability in American Culture and Literature*, the "consequence of a coming-out process" (ix). And Brenda Brueggemann, who, in her book *Lend Me Your Ears*, writes about "years of adolescent pretense" (85), during friendships and movie dates at films she couldn't hear. In attempting to do so, she says, "I found myself pressured into passing and then greatly pressured by my passing" because: some days "I could pass; some days I could *almost* pass; some other days the rug almost got yanked out from under me" (86). Nodding in agreement was an oft-invoked response she relied on to feign hearing (84). Passing, she recalls "is treacherous going" (93), especially negotiating the lack of extremes: at different times she passed herself off as hearing, deaf, hard-of-hearing, and even German (94). Her "coming out" at age thirty began a process of unmasking that she continues on the page: "[T]hrough writing, I pass," she concludes, turning the phrase to mean almost the opposite of what it has meant all her life. Now a teacher, she "passes" because writing is the "passageway" (99) that connects her to her students, to fellow theorists. And Stephen Kuusisto writes about "walking around, feigning sight" (66), and even pretending to see through binoculars when he goes birding with a friend. "I agree with everything Jim sees," he notes (visually echoing Brueggeman's nodding as agreement to her companion's auditory comments). To do otherwise, he says, turns their enjoyable outing into "an exercise in description" whereby the friend will need to tell Kuusisto what the birds look like. "By pretending to see," he explains, "I'm sparing us an ordeal." He ends the anecdote not with dissatisfaction, but in celebration of his own imagination. The friend, Jim, believes Kuusisto has seen some birds. And "maybe I have," (75) he concludes.

David Mitchell speaks about "passing" as an undergraduate student at the University of New Hampshire, where "the elevator was (apparently) not yet invented" in order to find ways of keeping other students and professors comfortable with his participation. He accomplished this accommodation by strategizing ways to navigate the best routes to his classrooms in order to avoid encounters with others, and arriving early so fellow students would find him already "seated" before class began. His actions did not deny his disability (certainly, his mobility impairment remained a visible marker that continued to signify the category of "disability"), yet such physical and material manipulations exemplify a tremendous effort to accommodate his own bodily difference in relation to others, and to accommodate others' expectations of the "norm" he could project. The goal was to ensure his disability remain a static adjective for the rest of the class, rather than a malleable state that *might* demand active accommodating (private e-mail). In "Passing in the Shadow of FDR," Daniel Wilson describes the extraordinary measures that President Franklin D. Roosevelt performed to hide the disabilities he acquired as a result of polio, and how such measures influenced other polio survivors to emulate Roosevelt "regardless of their impairments" and "in spite of considerable physical and psychological pain" (14). Similarly, for Mitchell, the extra effort and time spent to get to class early to set up, so as not to disturb fellow students, make his "passing" an act that eases their ideas and anxiety about disability.

Mitchell's energies to reduce anxiety in others mimics Leonard's efforts in *Memento* to convince others that he can "pass." Both actions misrepresent the "reality" of the body, while at the same time relying on the body to perpetuate a particular "truth" to onlookers. In *Lars and the Real Girl*, Lars purchasing Bianca works productively with ideas of passing versus "outing" in that, by openly "dating" Bianca, Lars displays his neurodiversity to the entire town. Siebers deems this strategy to be an "exaggerated self-presentation" (107).

Erving Goffman, in his pivotal book *Stigma: Notes on the Management of Spoiled Identity*, defines passing as the strategies in which individuals engage to hide, conceal, obscure, or otherwise manage their "spoiled" identities (73–75). Simi Linton, one of the first disability scholars to talk about the politics of "passing" in disability studies, writes about the popular phrase, "overcoming disability," as a way to depict people with disabilities as triumphant in some way. Since the phrase is not a literal description of a disability that has been "overcome," Linton points out that the phrase denotes a way of purportedly complimenting a person who has overcome "the social stigma of having a disability" (17). The onus remains firmly on individuals to "work harder to 'compensate' for their disabilities or to 'overcome' their condition or the barriers in their environment" (19). Linton links this burden for individuals to prove themselves (the alternative being claiming rights from the position of being members of a marginalized community) to the concept of passing. People with disabilities, she says, pass for a variety of reasons: to avoid discrimination or ostracism, to protect themselves from the "loathing" of society, or within a "herculean effort" to deny the reality of historical contexts, a form of "internalized self-loathing" (19–20).

"It is not surprising," Linton writes, "that disabled people also speak of 'coming out' in the same way that members of the lesbian and gay community do" (21). Similarly, Siebers writes about "passing" within a queer-theory rubric that develops from Sedgwick's epistemologies of coming out. As the editors of the anthology *Disability and Passing: Blurring the Lines of Identity* note. "[P]assing has been and continues to be a complex psychological and physical performance that can only be understood when situated in a particular historical and social context" ("Intro," 10). As they indicate, there is much more critical work to be done, especially in the arena of disability passing. The writers in their collection take on notions of disability and race, gender, and sexuality, yet, the editors admit, these essays "by no means exhaust the subject" (10).[3] Within all these systems, then, that extraordinary undertaking assigned as "passing" functions as a complicated and often layered interchange between multiple identities.

Siebers's essay on passing as a disability masquerade sets the tone for much critical thinking about disability, "coming out," and narratives that exchange one corporeal identity for another. In his essay, Siebers relates an anecdote about how, after being challenged by an airline employee for "claiming" disability in order to board early, the incident led him to adopt the habit of exaggerating his limp whenever boarding planes (96). For Siebers, and many other disabled people, convincing the general public that their individual bodies conform to preconceived ideas about disability criteria is an ongoing concern. Siebers designates six different "fables" of passing that give an overview of disabled people slipping into masquerade for political, social, or personal reasons (106–16). But my purpose is to discern, here, a different manner of disability "passing"; I liken it to *proportional passing*, or *transposing*. What I wish to explore in this chapter is the complicated notions in which disability itself can be the occasion for a problematic "passing" wherein individuals, in negotiating their mobility (whether anxiety disorders, physical, auditory, or intellectual disabilities) in the able-bodied world, often need prosthetic devices (and even simulated movements) as markers *for the non-disabled* to fully embrace their status of other. For Lars, Bianca serves as the prosthetic marker that allows others to recognize his cognitive differences, without need for explanation or diagnosis. When he takes Bianca to the town doctor (ostensibly for her high blood pressure), he enters a situation wherein he can freely discuss, for example, the physical pain he experiences through casual touch. Bianca not only signifies Lars's difference (it doesn't hurt him to touch her), but accommodates that difference by acting as a prosthetic device for anyone who encounters the two of them together. Indeed, she functions so successfully that humorous moments in the film occur when Lars is dismayed to discover that the town so embraces Bianca that she is invited to events and get-togethers without him. Bianca, for Lars, operates as shield as much as romantic focus. Bianca, for the town, operates as the character they need to befriend in order to understand and accept Lars. Bianca transposes these identity categories by accommodating in both directions at once.

Poet Louis Cabri who has retinitis pigmentosa (degenerative tunnel vision) occasionally uses a white cane to "pass" in new cities or institutions he has not often frequented. His cane, in these situations, acts as a prosthetic device to let *others* know he does not see the same way they do, or the way some might assume he can. When he walks without the cane, people often get irritated (or worse) that he has failed to navigate the social space "properly"; upon seeing his white cane, people are usually quick to accommodate what they recognize as straightforward blindness. For most of his mobile existence, he does not require the cane to traverse streets and hallways, but it offers a convenient shorthand for people who need visual clues about anyone whose disability does not function as a binary either/or (i.e., either totally blind or totally seeing). In effect, Cabri transposes himself into "blind," and the white cane is the signifier that allows sighted people to access his disability manifestation. A white cane fits into the ideas most people hold about blindness, which perpetuate rigid acceptance about who is allowed into the boundaries of a certain category, a rigidity that acts of passing venture to dismantle. Much like Bianca in *Lars and the Real Girl*, the white cane offers a prosthetic device so that *others* may recognize and accommodate accessibility as a potential that needs to be realized.

For a literary analogy, Francisco Stork's young adult novel *Marcelo in the Real World* presents a young man who, from a medical perspective, assesses himself in this way: "[T]he closest description of my condition is Asperger's syndrome," despite not sharing "many of the characteristics that other people with Asperger's syndrome have" (55). His father, embarrassed to present Marcelo as anything other than capable and accomplished, makes this deal with his son: Marcelo spends the summer working for his father's law firm (in the mail room), and if Marcelo can "pass" in what his father calls the "real world," then he may return to Patterson, the school he already attends and that his father thinks is too "protected" (20). If not, he must attend a "regular" school his father has chosen for his graduation year. Imbedded in their "deal" is the ironic failsafe: if Marcelo can successfully navigate a job in which he is surrounded by "real world" work colleagues, then his father will presumably interpret Marcelo's desire to return to Patterson school as spurious. Conversely, if Marcelo fails in his father's eyes, then forcing him to attend an unaccommodating school would be no more than a cruel enforcement of their summer pact. Indeed, Marcelo seems aware of this ironic transposition, when he points out to his mother that his father "is basically asking me to pretend that I am normal, according to his definition, for three months" (23). Marcelo, in effect, must "pretend" to be normal in order to secure his place at the school his father deems as non-normative. Nevertheless, he agrees; Marcelo does not read such complicated circumnavigation as paradoxical, but only as imperative.

To extend the argument further, I shall look closely at the short story "Flowers for Algernon," by Daniel Keyes.[4] In the narrative, Charlie Gordon is an intellectually disabled thirty-seven-year-old man who undergoes an experimental operation to triple his IQ (which he states as 68). The speculative fiction is told from Charlie's point of view, and he keeps a daily "progress report," through which readers discern not only the plot elements, but also the progress of his intelligence and communication skills. Charlie takes night school remedial classes and his teacher, Miss Kinnian, has recommended him for this treatment to boost intellectual abilities. The story delves into many issues that concern people with intellectual disabilities, such as "normal" people acting in ways insensitive to people deemed to be mentally "inferior." Charlie's co-workers, for example, tease him about the scar on his head: "Joe Carp said hey look where Charlie had his operashun what did they do Charlie put some brains in," and "Frank Reilly said what did you do Charlie forget your key and open your door the hard way" (507). Both comments make Charlie laugh because the jokes at his expense convince him his co-workers are true friends who like him.

Charlie is a hard-working, dedicated, and considerate man. That he always "reely wantid to lern" (503) is one of the reasons Dr. Nemur and Dr. Strause select him. Even his teacher says that Charlie has done "so much with so little" that he "deserv[es] it most of all" (504). But the story also projects a normativity upon Charlie, by differentiating him from other people with low IQs, demonstrating that his abilities to improve, intellectually, are in part based on him already being "like" someone with an average IQ (or, more to the point, like what the story projects as normal or average onto its characters). Early in the story, Charlie overhears the two doctors discussing him:

> He said Dr. Nemur I know Charlie is not what you had in mind as the first of your new brede of intelek** (couldnt get the word) superman. But most people of his low ment** are host** and uncoop** they are usually dull apath** and hard to reach. He has a good natcher hes intristed and eager to please [505].

Readers fill in the asterisks, understanding that "most" people with low IQs (here, the only measure of intelligence) are hostile, uncooperative, dull, and apathetic. Obviously, such stereotypes about personality and disposition do not hold purchase in much literature today, but in the narrative, they define Charlie by what he is *not*. By not fitting the characterizations of these adjectives, Charlie becomes the doctor's perfect test subject: he is already the person they'd like him to be, just not as good at taking tests as he will be. This excerpt succinctly demonstrates how modes of "passing" operate constantly, even when passing is not an individual's goal. Charlie, by negating the stereotypes held by the two doctors (and many contemporaneous readers), passes from one state of being (a typical retarded man) to another (a man with the potential to become "better"— demonstrated not only through his willingness to accept medical interference, but through his innate nature).

Before the medical procedure, Charlie takes a series of tests (including Rorschach ink blots and "racing" the eponymous mouse, Algernon, who is the first test subject for the experimental procedure), which he assumes he "fails," because he cannot detect pictures in the ink on the paper, and Algernon consistently completes the mazes faster than he does. Charlie's intelligence improves exponentially, he falls in love, he surpasses the intellectual acumen of his co-workers, and even discovers the flaw in the two doctors' research. And then he regresses. Shortly after his mental aptitude decreases, Algernon dies, and Charlie then notices a similar pattern in his own reasoning abilities. His spelling reverts to early progress report entries, he trips over things and finds it difficult to type, he loses the ability to read all the other languages he has learned, and—tellingly—he becomes "touchy and irritable" (523).

Despite many warnings about participating in this experiment, Charlie often feels misled and betrayed when he comes to comprehend an idea or truth that previously eluded him. For example, when Dr. Strauss admits to Charlie that he only knows elementary calculus, Charlie is annoyed because he feels as if the doctor has "hidden this part of himself in order to deceive me, pretending—as do many people I've discovered—to be what he is not" (518). Before the operation, Charlie thinks both his doctors to be at a genius level of intellectual powers. That he quickly surpasses their skills angers and saddens him, reminding readers that Charlie has never wanted to be *better than*, but only *as good as*. Thus readers feel the ever-widening gap between themselves and Charlie; he comes to represent an excellence portrayed as beyond human normality. Though Charlie has only wanted to be "like others," the story relies for its narrative power on making him a super-intellect, a man so intelligent that he can barely hold conversations with "normal" people, such as his dinner date Miss Kinnian, who spends the entire dinner staring at him "blankly" and asking him to clarify what he means (518).

Michael Gill, in his book *Already Doing It: Intellectual Disability and Sexual Agency*, speaks of a "sexual ableism" (xiv) that restricts, polices, and curbs the sexuality of people with intellectual disabilities. Gill pointedly asks in his introduction, "Is intellectual functioning a prerequisite to sexual behaviors? Should sexual citizenship depend on IQ levels?" (2). Throughout the story, Charlie has been smitten with Miss Kinnian, but only considers asking her on a date when his intelligence has reached a "high" level. When his intelligence once again "drops," he cuts himself off from Miss Kinnian: "I told her I didn't like her anymore. I told her I didn't want to be smart anymore. Thats not true. I still love her and I still want to be smart" (526). In shutting himself away from the woman he loves, Charlie preserves the invisible line between intellectually able-bodied and disabled, effectively enacting the cliché that intellectually disabled people do not—or should not—share sexuality with "normal" people. That he *can* love is important to the pathos of the story, but that he chooses to sacrifice himself shows Charlie to be different (read: morally superior) than most of the other (intellectually superior) characters.

When Charlie is again asked to take a Rorschach test, he is shocked to discover that the test is about describing what images the ink blots resemble, not trying to find pictures actually hidden inside the ink. At first he expresses anger, but then asks himself, "[C]ould I have been that feeble-minded?" (514), reflecting negative terminology for his own mental abilities, at the same time as he distances himself from his previous self. In story, book, and film, Charlie is a man made to feel that who he is needs improving, and that who he was needs reviling. His former co-workers used to torment him as an easy target, but they are even less able to cope with his new mental proficiency. "This intelligence has driven a wedge between me and all the people I once knew and loved. Before, they laughed at me and despised me for my ignorance and dullness; now, they hate me for my knowledge and understanding. What in God's name do they want of me? They've driven me out of the factory. Now I'm more alone than ever before" (517). Though chosen for being eager and cooperative, Charlie loses social connections in the process of acquiring increased intelligence. Eventually, though Charlie discloses that he once was "dull" and intellectually "inferior," he does claim community with a sixteen-year-old "retarded" dishwasher and with others when he decides to work in the field of increasing human intelligence. "These are my people. Let me use my gift to do something for them" (520).

As Charlie's mind "improves," his body experiences agony and discomfort. A month and a half after the operation, Charlie figures out that his "friends" only want him around because they enjoy making fun of him. He opens the April 20 progress report by writing, "I feel sick inside. Not sick like for a doctor, but inside my chest it feels empty like getting punched and a heartburn at the same time," and ends it by writing, "I'm ashamed" (511). The discovery signals to readers that his social cognizance improves as his IQ increases. But the scene also reveals Charlie's physical reactions to an emotional sensation. Awareness of being treated badly may indicate the "success" of the trial procedure, but aligns readers with Charlie's unhappiness as a result of this new knowledge. After the experiment begins to revert, Charlie goes back to his old job, where his co-workers now stick up for him when a new employer makes a nasty remark about Charlie being a "real whiz kid." Joe threatens the new guy, and Frank tells Charlie to call him or Joe if anyone bothers or tries to take advantage of him (526). Now that he has fallen from such heights, their pity for him allows them to protect rather than harass him. In this way, he embodies what David Mitchell and Sharon Snyder call "narrative prosthesis,"[5] whereby the disabled body serves as a "crutch upon which literary narratives lean for their representational power, disruptive potentiality, and analytical insight" (49). That he passes as a "retarded" character allows readers to recognize him as simultaneously "other" (intellectually disabled), "like us" (capable—and deserving—of miraculous cure), as well as a "fallen hero" (once of superior intelligence and now, tragically, capable of remembering what he could once achieve, but not able to remember how). But more than just offering a *narrative* crutch, wherein one character's physical disability may stand in for the character flaw of another (Siebers gives the example of *Rain Man*, in which "[Dustin]Hoffman's character Raymond may be an autistic savant," but it is his brother "who cannot relate to other people" [115]), Charlie presents a device by which *readers* may "pass" from normal to exceptional intelligence, a passing that sways them to compassion (or pity). Similar to the reaction of Charlie's co-workers, readers align themselves with Charlie not because he is like them, but because his two-way transposing underscores that he is unequivocally *not*.

Spurned and rebuffed when his IQ surges, Charlie is warmly welcomed when he once again displays a comprehension and nature consistent with his former intelligence. His co-workers may now read his passage to superior intelligence in terms of what Siebers calls "disability drag"[6] (114), and reinscribe their status from both sides of his transformation, allowing them—and readers—to continue their performance of "normal."

To conclude, I wish to note one other instance of passing that may not, at first, seem to belong in this disability-related category. The character Max Klinger (played by Jamie Farr), in the 1972–83 CBS TV show *M*A*S*H*, wore a dress for seven out of the eleven seasons. His cross-dressing objectives were not introduced to convince viewers he was transgender or that he had a queer sexuality. His motives, repeatedly stated, were to acquire a "Section 8" (a former category in the U.S. Army, in which a member is deemed to be mentally unfit, and thus discharged from service), to get out of the army, and safely home from the war. Among other "crazy" activities (such as trying to eat an entire Jeep piece by piece), Klinger, a man, dresses in women's clothing in order to pass as clinically insane to army officials. He does not want his friends and close colleagues to mistake him for a gay or an actual transgender person; rather, his employment of cross-dressing is to disguise himself as so "crazy" that the army will reject him. The character maintains a theatrical distance from the very identity he stages. For example, although he does marry in a wedding dress, the scene reinscribes heteronormativity in that Klinger participates in a conventional ceremony and marries a cisgender woman. In a military situation, if a female corporal were to consistently don casual dresses rather than her army uniform, she too would be challenging the authority of army protocol. But she would be accused of disobedience, rather than assessed as a "sexual deviant" (a discharge designation Klinger rejects at one point). In this example, Klinger plays at being "crazy" (read:

wacky, silly, outrageous, and zany) without necessitating that audiences judge his sexuality or cognitive abilities. He operates, in this narrative, as a prosthetic device not so much to infer the characterization of others around him, but to convince audience members that "war is insanity" or, in director Akira Kurosawa's words, "In a mad world, only the mad are sane" (*Ran*). Once again, the character's "drag" is about the layered actions of passing in that his performance allows audiences to feel secure in what they are not (not trapped in war, not forced to dress or behave contrary to their nature, etc.).

To return to Louis Cabri's choice to brandish his white cane as a means to inform and instruct other people how to perform around him, the white cane allows him to "pass" as blind, but the consequence is that he then feels pressured to maintain the performance. The white cane, in most North American cities, allows him access to free transportation via public transit. But once seated, he says he feels that to then pull out a book (no matter how long the bus ride) undermines his legitimacy,[7] and he fears fostering feelings of betrayal among other passengers, or even the driver, who may henceforth distrust passengers identifying as blind. In transposing his identity from sighted to blind, from blind to not-quite-so-blind, he risks pushing others into a narrative of "challenging" his visual abilities, no matter what those abilities and disabilities may be. At the end of *Memento*, the film suggests that Leonard needs the quest for his wife's killer to give him purpose. He writes a false note to himself (that he will then tattoo onto his skin), and deliberately allows a time lapse so that he will forget pertinent information. The scene, then, depicts Leonard managing his amnesia so that he may remain focused on vengeance. "We all need mirrors to remind ourselves who we are," he thinks to himself. These final words remind the viewer that the body "speaks," and that it does so as simulacra, reflecting unexpected truths in many directions. As McIntire says, passing "surprises us and asks us to double back and look again" (779). Because the body is a double entendre that we all need to reconsider. Again and again.

3

Icarus, Gods and the "Lesson" of Disability

The Fallen Mentor: Disability and Crestfallen Protégé

In a 2006 episode of the 2004–12 FOX television drama *House M.D.*, the title character, Dr. Gregory House (Hugh Laurie), quips to a colleague, "God doesn't have a limp" ("Cane and Abel"). His comment is in response to Dr. James Wilson's (Robert Sean Leonard) attempt to "save" House from Icarus's fate: namely, of thinking that he could fly with the gods. House's retort achieves its aim: to chastise his friend for ever thinking that House forgets the constant reminder of his all-too-human physical attribute (i.e., his bad leg and subsequent limp) and, of course, to allow him to continue with whatever "god-complex"–invasive-doctor-procedure he wishes to perform (while ever indifferent to hospital protocol). The character Gregory House is a stock Sherlock Holmes–like, medically gifted character: opinionated, obstinate, insensitive, antagonistic, and brilliant. Viewers know he will unravel the mystery of the patient's baffling symptoms, as long as he gets to bully his way past their need for medical nurturing, and his staff's need for him to at least pretend human characteristics. Viewers also know that House will retain his privileged and influential status as inspired medical sage, albeit a grumpy one. His comment, then, is offered less to prove how far removed he is from godly status, than to get an irritating colleague off his back. Given the nature of his character, House could just as easily have shot back: "God isn't sarcastic," or: "God isn't irritated by every other person on the planet." Such comparisons would have pointed to some of his recognizable—and sub-divine—"flaws." Instead, the show's writers chose to focus Wilson's pity on a physical *short-coming*, the *short-cut* reminder to all human beings (even doctors) that they are not gods. House, who wants all the power and authority of a god, in this scene seems to welcome the pity that comes with an acknowledgment that he has "fallen" from the heaven's graces, that his leg anchors him to the mortal world. But his comment achieves another purpose, and that is to remind viewers that God (even mixed-ethnicity Greco-Roman-Christian god), in whose image human beings have been formed, is perfection. God's body is supreme and glorious, and *flawless*. This is the lesson the Icarus myth teaches: ordinary mortals, particularly those with human flaws, cannot—and should not—attempt escape to the rarefied atmosphere allocated for the superhuman. But House is anything but ordinary; he is, in every way, extraordinary.

Rosemarie Garland-Thomson has famously said that literary and cultural representations of disabled bodies present such bodies "as extraordinary rather than abnormal" (*Extraordinary*, 137). In this chapter, I am particularly interested in looking at poetic narratives surrounding the ideal-body-now-flawed in order to read earlier 20th-century poems through contemporary disability theory. I begin with a television plotline because the metaphorical impact of the disabled body remains "useful" as a narrative device to suggest a physical "flaw" or corporeal "failing" which, in turn, re-articulates literary anxieties and social concerns surrounding the "normal" and the "ab." How, for example, do poets continue to evoke corporeal difference as the "broken" body?[1] By looking closely at the context, formal devices, and histories of two poems (one Canadian, one British), I shall critique not only the literary content of these texts, but also how these descriptive poems suture so easily to narratives whose focus is a presentation of the incurable body: the body that resists narrative cure, the difficult body, the deviant body: the extraordinary body, the excessive body, the abnormal body, that problem body.

In his oft-praised poem, "David,"[2] Earle Birney presents two characters: Bobbie and his friend David, the latter of whom is not just ablebodied, but is superbly male, superbly young, and superbly fit. In this narrative poem, set in the mountain region around Banff National Park, two friends attempt to soar above the world, mountain-climbing, leaving the ordinary mortals below "but over the sunalive week-ends / We climbed, to get from the ruck of the camp, the surly // Poker, the wrangling, the snoring under the fetid / Tents" (Birney 107). The two young men work for a land surveying company in western Canada's mountainous and unadulterated wilderness areas, and spend their free time going on exciting, extreme adventures. But it is their unsupervised exploits on dangerous terrain that Birney painstakingly details. Exciting, defamiliarized, extreme adventures, especially for the younger Bobbie, who narrates the poem.

David serves the dual role of adventurer and leader, devoted explorer and patient guide, brilliant where climbing is concerned, and holding strong opinions about what it means to *live*. Bobbie, the narrator, is more hesitant, still learning the techniques of climbing, but falling in love with landscape, and willing to trail his adventurous friend. David—who appears to be the inheritor of Greek mythic adventures—is by far the more knowledgeable, the more sure-footed of the two. Yet it is *he* who falls over a ledge and breaks his back. The unthinkable having occurred, David then begs his friend, Bobbie, to kill him rather than initiate a rescue.

Written in 1940, the poem relies on subtle homoerotic tensions. Containing forty-six stanzas of about four lines each, Birney divides the narrative into nine sections, each one advancing the progression of the two young men's friendship. The poem foregrounds their outdoor quests but, more particularly, advances the notion that Bobbie is David's protégé and admirer. David, the poem makes clear, never should climb down from Pegasus's back, does not belong in the ranks of the plebian, for "mountains for David were made to see over, / Stairs from the valleys and steps to the sun's retreats" (107). Again and again Bobbie offers phrases such as: "David showed me" (108), "David / Taught me" (109), "David spotted" (110). After his disastrous fall, the first words David "brokenly" murmurs to Bobbie (even before he absolves his friend for not testing his own foothold) are, "over ... over" (111), demanding that Bobbie push him over the ledge, push him to a fatal fall. When Bobbie argues that David will survive long enough for rescuers to reach him, David concedes, "Perhaps," then adds, "For what? A wheelchair...?" (112). The implication within this line is twofold: David does not want to live now that he comprehends that he is not a god, and he requires physical assistance to accomplish his desire to escape physical dependence. It is that very dependence that causes David to reject the implications of what rescue might mean for him: he cannot tolerate that he does not even have the strength or control to push *himself* over the ledge, over the line-break, away from the left-margin where his friend safely rests. For David, limits are for reaching over and boundaries are for trespassing; such an ideal youth is not to be contained, not harnessed, bound, hampered, or impeded. In this stanza, the lines break after "chair" and "stay," after "stretched" and "ledge" in the next stanza. Though the narrative continues—and continues regularly—the end of the line indicates completion and stasis. David believes his life, like his body, has fallen into an abyss and he clings to the one command he can exact from his friend, as the ultimate tutorial price for a summer full of lessons outlining his freedom and independence philosophy.

To characterize freedom in such a manner, both these individuals—and their readers—must rely on a notion of the unified body, the myth of the cohesive whole that suffers no flaws or defects. This character wants to *live*, and for such a character, living is corporeal perfection: the physical ideal sutures itself to the vigorous archetype. The idea of a young, robust male living any life "less" than one of great activity, Birney presents in the poem as horrific, reprehensible, and abnormal to the point of suggesting a "non-living" state.[3]

When Bobbie hesitates, David's demands become more insistent. He obstinately bullies Bobbie: "For Christ's sake push me over!" (112). The issue for Bobbie is death versus life, as his guilt over his own role in the accident haunts his thoughts and his narrative. But Birney makes clear to the reader that Bobbie is beholden to David. He has little choice but to follow where his god leads. The reader, although allowed empathy within the ballad form for Bobbie's dreadful situation, is led to root for David's desire, and is clearly expected to admire David for his belief that his body is for *use*, a tool for exploration, discovery, and dangerous escapades. His body has been commodified, in Marxian terms, so that its exchange value is dependent on its use. He does not recognize *value* in his body at any degree other than extremes. Robert McRuer and others have written about the "spectre" of disability that haunts notions of able-bodiedness. In his book *Crip Theory*, McRuer cites a much-repeated truism within disability studies, namely that "everyone will be disabled if they live long enough" as a generative insight (200). It is this very specter of disability that haunts David, as he lies paralyzed on the mountain ledge. His—until only moments before—had been a god-like body, a young and strong body, a vibrant body, a body too far from living "long enough" to even contemplate disability. For David, the issue is not death versus slow death. It is not pain or waiting that he cannot bear, it is living—even for a few hours—within a smashed and broken body. David cannot bear to live as lesser than a near-deity. The poem opens describing David as "coltish" and able to see over mountains (107), but immediately after his fall, he is "still as a broken doll" (112). This final metaphor is one of damage *and* lifelessness, but it also contrasts the image of David as sutured to nature: young and vibrant and able to conquer the unconquerable. His godliness, so much admired, now appears as mere human hubris: punishment by the gods into this small and weak figure. David's fall re-enacts Icarus's mythic plummet: from greater than human to less than human, from god to mere apparition.

Birney's poem has been cited as a significant contribution to representations of nature and human conflict in poetry,[4] but rarely (if ever) do literary critics speak to the representation of the "fallen" body in Birney's poem. The ending of the poem is especially poignant because readers learn that David's initial fall was actually caused by the novice Bobbie's mistake. In covering for his friend, David slips over an irrevocable edge; perhaps more importantly, because of his exalted position, David feels justified in pushing Bobbie over an irrevocable moral edge. Bobbie, the "lesser" man, is punished by David, who relies on Bobbie's expected pity for his accident. As a result, Bobbie descends into a kind of living Hades, while David, through death, expects to retain his status as mythic male youth, forever climbing, stretching, reaching for the heavens. What particularly interests me about this poem is the convenient metaphorical *use* it makes of the body, juxtaposed against the "normal" or ideal body. Birney reveals the availability, within normative discourse, of the problem body in order to enact a public notion of corruption. The perceived body-corrupt presents the mind- or soul- or essence-corrupt.[5]

One poem that goes out of its way to attest to how utterly miserable a disabled existence becomes for a young man who once possessed the ideal physique of Birney's David character, is Wilfred Owen's 1917 poem "Disabled." The title speaks to a nameless male character, confined—in every sense—to a static and monotonous existence. The narrative in Owen's poem *extends* Birney's bleak premonitions: the young man in this poem is what readers may imagine *would have* become of David, had Bobbie brought help back in time. Owen's character, in this poem, is forever trapped, forever restricted within his own body, forever static and fragile and vulnerable and feeble. The character, "he," has recklessly (and foolishly, for he was underage) enlisted in the army during the Great War. As a soldier, he suffered from an attack that blew off parts of both legs, permanently condemning him to what, in this lyric storyline, can only be read as a non-life.[6] Only a year ago, the poem reveals, before he "threw away his knees,"[7] he used to "swing to gay" music. "Now," the poem's speaker ominously reports, "he is old; his back will never brace," and he "will spend a few sick years in Institutes" (152). And then, presumably, he will succumb to the inevitable, early (but inglorious) death that looms alongside his chair.

Though it predates Earle Birney's "David" by twenty years, Wilfred Owen's "Disabled" suggests the same youthful, hearty, vigorous, heterosexual male as the main figure with whom audiences should identify (and subsequently pity). For what fate, each poem asks, could be worse than physical imperfection to such a magnificent being? Not even death. Both poems regard their characters as suffering too horrible a fate to warrant any future happiness, joy, desires, or even ordinary daily details. To move from strong, young male to weak, injured *feminized* male, the poem construes as a fate worse than death. This character, like Birney's David, has far to fall, of course, because his pre-injured body also represents the power and might closely be associated with the godly. The tragedy isn't disability alone, it is that such disability has befallen the healthy and the young: the healthy, young, heterosexual male. If Owen's poem were to feature a seventy-two-year-old effete male, the pathos would be mitigated by a much-shortened fall from blessed grace. If Birney's poem were titled "Davina," audiences would still feel sympathy, but a less urgent sympathy at the idea of removing the character from a pointless existence.[8]

Alive in a Wheelchair: The Spoils of War

Owen's poem begins in the past tense ("He sat in a wheeled chair"), then delves deeper in the past as the speaker reminisces about the lost strength of a young body, then shifts to an imagined future ("Now, he will spend a few sick years in Institutes"), and finally ends in the present tense ("How cold and late it is!"), as the ex-soldier waits for those now responsible for him to come care for his delinquent body. This shifting of tenses has the effect of reminding readers of the fragility of this character's *now*, and also of his perpetual state of not quite living. The word "now," in fact, begins three of the poem's lines, effectively returning "he" from his memories, and returning readers from a flashback to the character's fallen physical condition. After the third "Now," halfway through the final stanza, "he" notices how "women's eyes[9] / Passed from him to the strong men that were whole," men whose bodies, unlike his, do not carry fierce knowledge of violence and damage. His body, and his heterosexuality will not "heal,"[10] will not recover from its wheeled routine. The poem ends with a repetition that takes up half the final two lines: "How cold and late it is! Why don't they come / And put him to bed? Why don't they come?" (153). The petulant tone poses a stark contrast to the headstrong athlete from earlier stanzas, and the exact repetition and identical rhyme contribute the poetic impression that this man can no longer write his own ending, but can only pitifully appeal to his invisible caregivers to assist him into the next, dismal day. Although the subject is still alive, the poem indicates that his active life is over; he wishes only to sleep, to be put to sleep. Similarly to David in Birney's poem, he would rather be dead than alive in a wheelchair.

The poem, interestingly, does not speak to the violent events this man has lived through, but focuses on an adolescent desire to enlist, to offer up one's own body for nationalistic causes. Furthermore, the speaker does not criticize such a nationalistic motive, but informs readers that the man joined the war for frivolous reasons that even he can barely remember: "Someone had said he'd look a god in kilts," and "maybe, too, to please his Meg." His motive, then, wasn't even a naïve-yet-noble wish to serve his country, but rather a vain wish to impress his girlfriend, to appear to her—and to others—as worthy to wear the uniform of the warriors. His reminiscences include memories of soccer injuries and the glory of victories. He equates his athletic activities with enlistment: in war, too, he will return a hero, one who is "carried shoulder-high," not because he cannot walk, but because gods reside on a higher plane than mortal men. His chair, then, not only represents his utter loss of mobility, but also his diminished humanity. He is lower than men now, less capable of achieving masculine greatness. Now he will "never feel again how slim / Girls' waists are, or how warm their subtle hands." Instead, while children play outside his window, he remains stuck all day in one spot. And any girls who touch him now, do so as if touching "some queer disease" (152).

The prominent figure of the whole and healthy male in such poetry depends on the equally strong yet often invisible image of the immobile and dependent feminized male to give meaning to the construct of the so-called-normal, able-bodied world. In his book *Crip Theory: Cultural Signs of Queerness and Disability*, McRuer notes that just as "homosexuality and disability clearly share a pathologized past,"[11] so too can the link be made between "heterosexuality and able-bodied identity" (1). Invoking Adrienne Rich's notion of "compulsory heterosexuality," McRuer argues that intersections between disability and queerness challenge normative representations of the heterosexual male. The poem presents this disabled character as emerging out of "normal" young hubris, but with disastrous results. By damaging significant appendages, the character in the poem has "lost" not only his limbs, but his youth ("he is old"), his sexuality ("his Meg" does not appear in the poem's present), and his masculinity (he no longer is one of the "strong men that were whole"). As McRuer says, "[C]ompulsory heterosexuality and compulsory able-bodiedness are intertwined" (*Crip*, 3). And, as a system of normalizing bodies, to suggest a flaw in one, insists on a similar flaw in the other. To break with one's able body suggests, also, a break with normal heterosexual aspirations. By foregrounding queer and disability discourse as gesturing towards a coalition of theory and practice, McRuer makes possible a critique of literature

that tends to conflate differing problem bodies into equally homogene-
ous categories of imperfection. The poem's reproaching of its main character clearly condemns the man's foolhardy decisions that have led to his
inadequate bodily condition. By "throwing away" his legs, he has, in effect,
discarded his manliness, rejected his near-godliness, his Adonis status.
The poem, ultimately, is a morality tale, a reverse recruitment poster:
beware hasty and unwise attraction to danger and peril, for such a fate
might be yours, such a body might be what you're left with when you've
given your own away. The implied "you" in both poems being a young
man, a man physically trapped by or fleeing his own metaphorical dem-
ons. Bobbie, running madly down to the camp, must live with what he
has done for/to his friend; but readers note that he still has the body to
run. The moral of "David" is imbedded not only within a beautiful corpse
beneath the peak, but also within Bobbie's vibrant, sprinting body: the
one or the other, no in-betweens. No indeterminate morals.

At the same time as disabled bodies are being perpetuated as metaphor for moral stance, the metaphor itself excludes them as integral participants of a universalizing morality. These are not normal bodies, the
poem says, these are freakish bodies; these are not freaks, these are fallen
bodies representing fill-in-the-blank metaphor; these are not fallen bodies,
these are broken or useless bodies and the moral rupture is visible and
noticeable and distinct from an ideal corporeal aim. For such metaphor-
reliant narratives, an "ab"normal body does not—cannot and should not—
exist. "That day," says Bobbie, in Earle Birney's final line of "David," was
"the last of my youth on the last of our mountains" (113). The deed is done,
and the poem suggests that Bobbie, almost as much as David, has been
damaged by his deed. No longer the innocent disciple, he has been forced
to age prematurely; he has become—through his terrible action—the man
David trained him to be. Bobbie will live on, but scarred, haunted, *fallen*.
Birney plots his narrative ingeniously. The reader is not forced to bear
witness to the moment of Bobbie's decision, the exact moment of David's
death. The penultimate section of the poem ends with David reassuring
and ultimately bullying Bobbie through an impossible reverse contract:
"I'd do it for you, Bob" (112). His choice to use a more adult version of Bobbie's name indicates that David recognizes and initiates his friend's rite of
passage. The final section of the poem tracks a devastated Bobbie narrating
his trek back to the surveying camp: "I will not remember how nor why
I could twist / Up the wind-devilled peak, and down through the chim-
ney's empty / Horror, and over the traverse alone. I remember / Only the
pounding fear I would stumble on It" (112). Perhaps only a few minutes

have passed, perhaps several hours, but David, the mentor-friend, has already become a haunting entity, a broken body, a remnant of a truncated life, now merely a ghastly part of the landscape. Birney's poem, here, echoes Samuel Taylor Coleridge's "Rime of the Ancient Mariner," in that the ballad form shifts to represent nature as a supernatural horror that traps and tricks its narrator. Unlike the Mariner, though, Bobbie finds no momentary release in confessing his tale to others. When he gets back to the camp, he tells the other men that David "fell straight to the ice where they found him" (113). His lie safeguards his terrible secret from legal authorities, but the lie also preserves David as the perfect, flawless youth: sure-footed and dead, no half-broken, dependent body, definitely no messy in-between, lying on the ledge, which might suggest physical disability.

Earle Birney himself, who offers the character of Bobbie with sympathy and mercy, was upset when he heard that fellow poet Dorothy Livesay had written about his poem as a form of "[d]ocumentation combined with raw experience" (279). Her comment, for him, ended their friendship (reaching from 1949 until this incident in the early 1970s); as well, Birney demanded that, in subsequent editions of her publication, the offending sentence be removed. Livesay appears bewildered by his chagrin, pointing out in a letter to Birney that "personal documentary knowledge of mountain climbing had given you, as a poet, the power to depict with veracity and understanding the characters and background of your story" (May 21, 1973). Nevertheless, Birney was outraged[12] enough at being identified with a character who "commits what in Canada is an act of murder" (March 19, 1973). For the character of Bobbie to commit such an act might be attractive and noble and brave, but Birney, the creator of the tale, understands that to be literally associated with such an act is offensive. For Owen, as well, the disabled figure in his poem is there to evoke specific feelings in his reader, to invite young men (and their loved ones) to reconsider the *consequences* of going to war.[13] That figure also represents the casualty of war: a young man's youth, a human being's body, a man's masculinity. Owen does not depict his ex-soldier as heroic or noble or simply ordinary because, poetically, "he" exists in the poem for metaphorical value only.

So what does one do, then, with narrative poems that further a political agenda, while exploiting, literally, the backs of disabled people to achieve that agenda? As these two poems attest, disabled bodies within narrative, much like those bodies represented as "female" or "ethnic," have become commodified to represent the necessary Other. Such commodification sutures problem bodies to the not-quite, to the past tense, to the narrative lesson, namely: that characters should celebrate the perfect body or discard it. Don't settle for any in-between, don't expect to live well within an imperfect corporeal outfit. The *body*, in such narrative lessons, is separate from the *self*, the body becomes a choice, then, a preference, a capricious signal. For who *chooses* the *ab*normal? Even in 21st-century television, characters represented within disabled bodies are immediately suspect, immediately questionable. When creators of fiction, film, television, and even narrative poetry use disabled characters and their disability to make metaphorical points, to acquire instant sympathy, to move a lagging narrative along, they deny innovative shifts in language, in representation, in paradigmatic thinking. In conventional scenarios, disabled characters always mean something, and what they tend to mean is a metaphorical impact within narratives that reconstruct and suture their bodies as a tangible contrast to conventional bodies. Both these poems, for example, adhere to strict poetic form, indicating an unwillingness to "break" away from normative poetry models. The disability represented in both poems appears especially exceptional and distorted within these regularly metered and measured tales. Both main characters are quite literally trapped within a confining form, one that doesn't change, even as their bodies shift and change and develop and resist. The static formula of these texts contains both its characters and their stories; neither can escape the doom imposed within its fixed narrative legend. In such "legends," disabled characters don't get to speak from a disability activism standpoint, but maintain their representational status as specters of the able-bodied. In other words, they are characters speaking about disability *from and for* an able-bodied point of view, but propped up (on metaphorical ability-crutches) for show as disability authority. Readers and viewers, then, can learn that how disabled characters interpret their own bodies is in exact (and perfect) alignment with how the hierarchy of ability persistently construes problem bodies.

Ramping It Up: The Body's Poetic Disjunctures

In the final third of this chapter, I wish to switch gears from analyzing the subject matter of narrative, ballad poems, to the form of contemporary disjunctive poetry. Poets and critics regularly invoke the language of accessibility to either chastise or challenge a particular poetics. Often a poem is derided for being either too obvious, or not accessible enough; a poem is difficult or opaque versus one that achieves accessibility or readability.

Joshua Marie Wilkinson, in his article entitled "On Poetry & Accessibility," describes the appeal of accessible poetry as featuring "familiarity, recognizability, even avuncular friendliness in tone, form, and diction" (online); conversely, critics accuse poets as being "elitist" if "the poem's language resists immediate familiarity" (online). The argument is ongoing. Rather than land on one side or another, I want to take a moment to discuss the language of the argument itself. What does "access" mean when one speaks of poetry? Wilkinson attempts to get at the implications lurking within the linguistics of such descriptions:

> When we reduce the discussion to the terms of "access" and "accessibility," what is implied through these words is that entry has been barred, that we are prevented from experiencing the meanings of these difficult poems, despite the fact that many of us are literate adults [online].

Yet, despite challenging the "meaning" behind such discourse, Wilkinson still grasps at the language of accessibility as purely metaphorical, at least when it comes to poetry. The word access, he says, when applied to poetry, rhetorically stages the poem "as the esoteric structure of a willful obscurantist" (online). Indeed, even when he writes of "literal access," Wilkinson can only project a metaphorical notion of poetry, in that "literal access, as in *entry*, *admittance*, and *permission to use*," he writes, establish poetry "*as* accessible."

But in the world of disability activism and disability rights, the struggle for *literal* access is vital. Wheelchair users who cannot access ramps into buildings are disabled by an architecture sustained by ableism. If an office building has only steps leading to its entrance, an employee may not have access to the building (and thus to the job); the same building with ramp access means the employee can enter the building and get to work. Access is a human rights issue. So, to hone in on the language of access as an indicator of poetry that is "user-friendly," what do critics specifically mean when they claim certain poems to be *in*accessible? I'll start with an obvious example of poetry that "excludes" specific readers: a poem composed in American Sign Language cannot be comprehended by anyone who does not understand ASL. Introducing a translator into either of these examples changes the scenario from one of inaccessibility to accessibility, although the lengthy discussions on translation (and the "poetics of trans") continue. Obviously, critics who ask for a more accessible poetry do not refer to poems written in languages they do not speak when opening the conversation about accessibility; indeed, they often do not mean access at all, so much as *ease* of access. This distinction, I suspect, leads to the heart of the matter.

For many, disability rights are not, actually, about rights, but about benefits and even what some see as preferential treatment. Why *should* "we" have disability-access bathrooms when only a select few really need them? The trick in that question is who belongs in the category of first-person plural pronoun. To those people who have not considered the disabling aspects of what Rosemarie Garland-Thomson describes as those in the minority navigating a world built for the majority ("A Case for Conserving Disability," 346), the discussion is only one in which "we" (able-bodied people) need to make things easier for "them" (disabled people). In terms of poetry, then, the *problem* with so-called inaccessible poetry is that it is not *easy* for some readers to access (and by easy access, I mean more than that certain poems might be available for free online). But in this scenario that I'm proposing, it is "they" (those obscure, elitist poets) who need to make the poem easier for "us" (readers who wish literary accommodation). In this reversed binary, the first-person plural pronoun favors the equation that demands the access ramp, that needs the translation. Ironically, a social byproduct of the ramp is that it has many advantages for non-disabled people who also wish to enter this building: bike couriers can zip up or down without dismounting, parents with strollers can gain easy access without having to lift stroller and baby, etc.

Access, then, provides admission, entrance, inclusion. Access is *not* about the patronizing benevolence of the helping hand of state; access does not "minister to special needs" so much as it liberates specific groups from particular barriers. Access, in this scenario, is about evening out the playing field. The working field. My question, here, is: Could this particular idea of access enter the *writing field*? This idea of access, drawn from disability studies, is quite different from the literary scenario I presented earlier, of the critic who disparages a work for not being accessible to a reader. Further questions arise as a consequence of my first. Do we want *any* idea of accessibility to infuse the poetic field, even the open field of Charles Olson and Robert Duncan? Christopher Beach, in *The ABC of Influence*, traces the idea of a compositional field from Pound through Williams to Olson and Duncan, and he notes that within this compositional field a poem "should be conceived and formed within a larger field of objects and energies that the poem can communicate but never completely contain" (146). And if this particular idea of access, drawn from disability studies, *could* enter the writing field, do we want it to? The answer depends on how different this idea of access really is from the one we're used to. A critic's job is not to judge whether a book of poetry is accessible; a critic's job is to read the book of poetry.

How, then, might accessibility—or, more to the point, *in*accessibility—figure into a disjunctive poetics? Wilkinson ends his article with these words:

> One of the definitions of *accessible* is "open to the influence of—as in, a mind *accessible* to reason." To be *open to the influence* of the unknowns of a poem, that is the kind of accessibility I hope to encourage here. Not for poetry to accommodate our expectations, but for *us* to accommodate the strangeness of what a poem might present its reader with [online].

Accessibility, then, invites not only varied readings, but insists on difficulty and impediment as thought-provoking, poetic stimulus. My interest in destabilizing poetic expectations conjoins with my curiosity for physical, mental, and emotional destabilizing, for upending an assumed single-mindedness, of a presumed physical control. So my next question: How might disjunctive poetry generate innovation? Rosemarie Garland-Thomson makes an argument for "conserving" disability, indeed, for encouraging disabilities to flourish, because to do so shifts the discourse from understanding disabilities as deficits to admitting the possibilities of disabilities as benefits ("Case for Conserving," 341).

For Olson and Duncan, the "open field" was about process, rather than conclusion. Reading a poem, as everyone already knows, relies on the work of *reading* the poem. Yes, poetry can be difficult,[14] yes, some poems are extremely challenging and may require many readings, as do some fiction writings.[15] The poetry I'm interested in, the poetry that *disjuncts* the body and the page, is a poetry that urges readers to re-re-re-re-read—to bump up against stairs, to decry the lack of lengthy and complicated ramps, to agitate for multifaceted and the difficult. Not because of poetry's inherent density, but because rhizomatic lines/enjambments/tropes/images/puns/etc., compel readers to go back into the poem, to revisit each page, to journey again and again over that ever-widening ramp path, that slope between pavement and entrance that expands, even as it becomes ever more enticing.

Nikki Reimer's first book of poetry, *[sic]*, begins with a section entitled "illness narratives." Living up to its title, the poem *does* offer a narrative of sorts, one of women trapped by their bodies in patriarchal discourse that also traps the feminine within narratives of pathology. In this piece, Reimer meshes the language of disease and treatment with the language of advertising and pop culture. In a way, Reimer is not only making use of these disparate discourses, but revealing the extent to which the language of advertising co-opts and absorbs the seemingly defunct language of politics and activism: "Women of the world, raise your right hand!"

shouts an ad from the Diamond Trading Company, a subsidiary of DeBeers, aimed at single women, who should apparently buy themselves diamond rings for their right-hand ring fingers. Reimer's poem responds with these lines:

<pre>
                                      women
          open their eyes
                    blink once for yes raise your candle
                    blink twice for no
          yes

          no
                         yes   hand right [13].
</pre>

Reimer critiques a global economy that relies on both feminism and patriarchal oppression. The poem demands that consumers recognize and resist seductive advertising. At the same time, the poem identifies the difficult position of women who struggle against enforced readings of their bodies, and how even political crusades such as feminism can be co-opted into a larger capitalist agenda. Reimer moves into wider and wider critiques of the exploitation and compartmentalization of the female body. Her poem "a medical discourse" opens with the lines:

<pre>
     centre a poetics on irritable bowel syndrome
     symptoms oscillate
                    cramp congest ice fish pickaxe bloat
                    fruit fly goddamn frottage diesel diarrhea
                    cloven-hoofed constipated golden calf
     who's too skinny and/or just ate a sandwich [28]
</pre>

Aligning poetics with an unpleasant bodily ailment, Reimer's poem insists on poetry that not only foregrounds the body but on those very bodies that do not appeal to any generic ideal. Indeed, a body with irritable bowel syndrome demands a particular kind of attention, one often encased within a medical construction of health and ability. In addition to the bowel issues, this poem mentions cramps, bloating, diarrhea, constipation, and an eating disorder.[16] But given the irregular syntax, these very pointed bodily "problems" melt into a poem that does not overtly frame them as medical issues in the language of health and ability. Not only do various "symptoms oscillate," but the words and lines within a normative sentence waver at the end-break, undulate from the left-margin, fluctuate wildly from one image to the next. Reimer reminds readers that kosher idols such as the golden calf tread on cloven-hoofs, hoofs that clomp down inside poetry that includes well-being and doctors and biblical allegory and an abject born from denying food in order to worship fashion.

In this poem, then, what is the access ramp that best moves the reader from the "centre" that the first word offers, to the diabetes and conjoined dorsals (28) of the last stanza? Gaining a ramp does not automatically make entering a building *easy* (using a ramp often means the ambler must travel nine times the distance of steps or elevators; as well, many ramps are still placed at awkward angles or end at a very distant place from where they began), but ramps do provide access that may otherwise be unavailable. For some, "esoteric" poems such as these require footnotes: hints and directions from an invisible authority. But I would like to argue for ramps not so much as a prosthetics that makes gaining entry into the poems' "aboutness" *easy*, so much as mobility devices that move readers through the bumpy, wild, unfamiliar, and uneven turf of the poetic field. The ramp I'm arguing for doesn't explain the poem, but allows readers to keep moving—even when experiencing some dis/comfort—across/past/within the poem, to keep reading through and beyond those damn difficult poetics.

I find a disability concept of access in poetry to be tremendously useful. My final question: What happens when a poem conceives—as do most disabled people and disability activists—disabling as an affirmative experience or as a generative practice? I wish to argue for a poetry and poetics that leans on the notion of *dis*ability, hinges on a poetics that evokes the varied embodied forms of body and poem. In this chapter, I investigate poetry not so much "about" those lived experiences that usually function outside the projected "norm," but rather tackle the poetic problems of difficulty and innovative writing alongside the world of physical and cognitive disability. My aim is to invite readers to access diverse, distinctive, and atypical representations of the body, without reproducing normative syntax.

Icarus's fate comes from the hubris of thinking he could achieve that which the gods achieve: flight, eternal life, reaching Valhalla. But bodily perfection is *not* part of the mythic lesson. Had the *House M.D.* writers known their Greek mythology a bit better (or were they willing to have any one of the lesser characters win the quip wars for which House is famous), they could well have had Dr. Wilson cleverly retort: "God doesn't limp? Hephaestus limped. Hephaestus limped all over the Volcano he inhabited; and he forged a magnificent walking staff to accompany his heroic, limping stanzas."

4

Freaks, Misfits
and Other Citizens

When I imagine the archive on "freaks," I imagine a medical museum that organizes bodies according to whether they should be "studied" under the category of unbelonging. In my imaginary scenario, I disparage the freak museum at the same time as I hover in its doorway, savoring this passage of in-between. As poet, I want to get lost in its arcade, steal the skeletons of the conjoined twins Chang and Eng, write poems that contradict my senses, write narratives that undo common sense, and let loose the wretched orphans onto the vast and expanding risk of the page's extremities. But as critic, I want to show that the museum upholds an imaginary science of categorization, and needs to change the way it organizes bodies. The circus freak show, says Robert Bogdan in his book *Freak Show: Presenting Human Oddities for Amusement and Profit*, featured exhibitions designated as "monsters," which Bogdan points out was "the medical term for people born with a demonstrable difference" (6). In this chapter, I look at four narratives that challenge the double-bind that sideshow performers faced of needing to fit into the category of either metaphorical marginality or medical marvel.

Throughout its 2015 season, *American Horror Story: Freak Show* pays tribute to Tod Browning's 1932 film, *Freaks*. Set in Jupiter, Florida, in 1952, the series features a troupe of actors belonging to the last of the freak shows. In the penultimate episode of the season, "Show Stoppers," the characters, victimized and exploited by con artist Stanley (and in homage to the famous revenge scene in *Freaks*) attack and carve him up, effectively turning Stanley into "one of us." The 2013 "Treehouse of Horror XXIV: Freaks, No Geeks" episode of *The Simpsons* parodies and plays tribute to Browning's *Freaks*. In the episode, Homer (Dan Castellaneta) plays the strongman, determined to poison Moe (Hank Azaria), who has just married Marge (Julie Kavner). Moe, "[T]he most hideous creature of all," appears as he does in all *The Simpsons* shows. When the strongman disparages the "freaks," Marge stands up for them, admitting that one of her eyes is blue and one pale brown. Homer convinces Marge to marry Moe because he's dying, telling her, "From you I have learned to feel compassion for these disgustos." Homer subsequently tries to poison Moe's drink, and when she discovers this, Marge kicks him out of her trailer. He goes out into the rain, where a group from the freak show have gathered and creepily advance on him, chanting: "One of us, google-goo. One of us, google-goo." The episode ends with Homer on the couch, relating to the kids how he met Marge; he has no arms or legs and is covered in feathers.

Other allusions to Browning's film range from album covers (Frank Zappa on *Tinseltown Rebellion*) to other film classics (in *The Player*, Detective DeLongpre [Lyle Lovett] repeats the line "one of us, one of us" to unsettle his suspect during an interrogation). In part, such tributes acknowledge *Freaks* as the classic cult film of all time. Christopher Golden has said of the film that it "stands alone in a subgenre of one" (297). But I suspect the appeal is also the subject matter: despite rumors of audience members running screaming from theaters during its initial run in 1932, there is a certain attraction in the sideshow "freak." Browning's film deals with characters who—within the confines of the circus freak show—are represented as "freaks" of nature, as freaks of the "normal" human form, as people who occupy societal fringes. I use the term "freaks" to speak both as representation and referent, to include those bodies that represent sideshow actors and to those people who did work in circus sideshows. The term accurately couples opposing extremes: on the one hand, the term evokes a history that has deeply troubled disabled or differently abled bodies; on the other hand, the term celebrates those who have had to perforce display their bodies out of economic necessity or even for the pleasure of the show. The term "freak" covers those cultural processes that have both emphasized and dismissed so-called "atypical" bodies. "Freak" is both a magical term and a derogatory term that Browning's film questions and (partially) reclaims.

Freaks is about a circus troupe whose membership includes nondisabled and disabled performers who make up the sideshow. Despite dating Frieda (Daisy Earles), Hans (Harry Earles), a dwarf (though billed as the circus freak show midget), falls in love with Cleopatra (prolific silent screen actress Olga Baclanova), one of the trapeze performers. Though she is in a love relationship with Hercules (Henry Victor), the strongman, the two plot to steal Hans's fortune. She agrees to marry Hans, and then will poison him slowly. But the other sideshow actors discover her plan and take revenge: together, they kill Hercules and alter Cleopatra into such a grotesque creature that she ends up as an especially terrifying freak show exhibit. With the exception of this "duck woman" at the film's closing, Browning decided that the film's sideshow characters were all to be "real human freaks, not mere creations of the makeup department" (Jensen, 198); Browning insisted there would be "no pretend monsters in *Freaks*" (201). According to Tom Milne, writing about *Freaks* in 1963, "Browning manages to evoke the closed world of the freaks, the intensely human emotions contained in inhuman exteriors, in such a way that fascinated revulsion turns into tender comprehension" (151). And in a (relatively) recent review, Mark Smith writes, "*Freaks* is a wild ride, but it's not the monster-trip some say it is. It is macabre and disturbing, but Browning chose to humanize the deformed characters at the movie's shadowy center, not to demonize them" (Smith). Such praise is often in response to early reviewers who commented on the film's disturbing elements (see *New York Times* review, below). But such commentary also reveals a growing sense, in the 20th century, of audience connection with marginalized characters.

As objects of the gaze, says Eugenie Brinkema, in "Browning. Freak. Woman. Stain.": the sideshow performers "see too much," thus "their marginal bodies produce their surveilling powers" (166). She suggests that, for audiences, this shift in power (who looks at whom) is the real horror of Browning's film. Writing about the film through a psychoanalytic lens, Brinkema expresses sympathy for the audience: "As surely as the freaks spy on Cleopatra and Hercules, we feel for certain that they see us too, that our punishment is next" (166). This "us and them" dichotomy feeds the strong reactions to Browning's unusual tableaux. A pivotal scene is the wedding banquet where the bride and groom sit with sideshow actors who chant, "One of us! One of us!" welcoming Cleopatra into their fold. As the sideshow actors continue to chant, "Gooble-gobble, gooble-gobble; we accept her, we accept her," Hercules shouts at Cleopatra: "They are going to make you one of them, my peacock!" She is so horrified by the idea that she could "belong" to the sideshow crowd that instead of drinking from the communal goblet she shouts, "You, dirty, slimy, freaks! Freaks, freaks!" and throws the wine at Angeleno (Angelo Rossitto) who, offering sips to the guests one by one, has danced over on the table to offer her the goblet. In his preface, Bogdan notes that freak shows are "not about isolated individuals, either on platforms or in an audience." Rather, he claims, they are about "organizations and patterned relationships between them and us" (x–xi). And it is this very relationship between "us" and "them" that Freaks develops and manipulates.

The film's representations of dwarfism, actors with microcephaly, conjoined twins, and other diverse physical forms reveal not only how Hollywood views "abnormal" bodies but also a great deal about the contemporaneous audiences who were shocked and repelled by the film that has become a cult horror classic. In the film, the circus members who enact revenge upon the murderous intentions of the trapeze star and her strongman lover, are depicted as a homogenous and identifiable community, as an "us" chanting in unison during the wedding banquet scene. At the same time, the filmic gaze is complicated in that audiences are asked to relate to an "us" that is usually portrayed very much as "Other." During that infamous wedding banquet scene, not only do the sideshow performers chant and drink from the communal goblet, they eat (often without arms or hands), sing, and chat with one another; in other words, they celebrate a typical wedding. Much of Browning's film is made up of scenes depicting "regular" life, such as the Bearded Lady (Olga Roderick) having a baby with the Human Skeleton (Peter Robinson), or the Human Torso (Prince Randian) rolling and lighting a cigarette. Such scenes remove the actors from behind the velvet rope and apprise audiences of how each actor's daily routine is commonplace, rather than titillating.[1] Lennard Davis, in his book on the normal body, says that just as "coded terms signifying skin color ... are largely produced by a society that fails to characterize 'white' as a hue, so too the categories 'disabled,' 'handicapped,' and 'impaired' are products of a society invested in denying the variability of the body" (*Enforcing Normalcy*, xv). This denial of even a small deviance from the accepted body type is what Leslie Fiedler calls the "tyranny of the normal." And whatever their actual bodies, audience members fulfill a cinematic desire to align themselves and their viewing with "normal" viewers indulging in "normal" curiosity and beholding.

The cinematic gaze in *Freaks* affirms and approves of deviations from the physical norm and allows the audience identification with those deviations. Audience sympathy, says Angela M. Smith, in her book *Hideous Progeny: Disability, Eugenics, and Classic Horror Cinema*, lies "increasingly with the freaks, the targets of the prejudice, greed, and criminal actions of the physically attractive but morally monstrous Cleo and Hercules" (87). Some of the identification comes from film audiences being let into the tricks and gaffs set forth to fool circus audiences. For example, Smith notes, "Several scenes feature sideshow personnel rehearsing their acts, repeatedly revealing circus tricks and bodily surfaces as a matter of props and prosthetics, their effectiveness dependent on the audience's will-ingness to be fooled" (106). "In revealing the mechanics of illusion," Smith continues, Tod Browning in effect "enacts a critique of voyeurism" (106), or as Will Dodson puts it in his article on Browning's expressionist modes in film, in *Freaks* "the revelation of the trick is that there is no trick" (235). Certainly, his film critiques audience demands that sideshow acts wholly and exclusively include the bodies they put onto display. Speaking of the voyeuristic gaze of the cinema in contrast to the two-way looking that goes on in the carnival sideshow, Dodson says: "In the carnival, the spec-tators and performers share the same space; they can look at each other. In the cinema, the spectator is a voyeur in the shadows." The cinema, then, provides a venue more susceptible to the voyeuristic gaze. Browning's mise-en-scène, according to Dodson, mimics "the wandering trajectory of spectators moving through the carnivals. *Freaks* is a film, and cannot therefore eliminate the voyeuristic relationship with its spectators, but it can shine a light on it, and emphasize viewers' subjective emotional expe-riences, which the camera instigates through its positioning and tight focus on the freaks' positioning and movement" (235). Scenes in which audiences watch non-disabled characters observe and react to the side-show performers transpose filmic viewers and question their identity posi-tioning.

Ask film theorists Gamman and Marshment: "Can we really assume that audiences identify on the basis of gender (or even sexual orientation) rather than on the basis of other categories that contribute to the con-struction of our identities?" (7). That audiences *do* "identify" on the basis of "other categories" underpins the necessity for disabled actors and per-formers to maintain a daily struggle against the exploitation of their bodies as freakish, extraordinary, and ceaselessly on display. In contemporary performance artists Shawna Dempsey and Lorri Millan's video, *The Head-less Woman*, the voice-over proclaims that the headless woman originally severed her head to impress a boy, then stayed in the circus because there were not many places for a "woman, all body, approaching forty," and because "she was a genuine freak, no mirrors or masks or sleight of hand." This statement of "genuineness" convinces the audience of the irony in the speaker's words. An irony that presents headlessness, no matter that it is described as a "party trick," as the ultimate freak show—the female body as the body most viewed and gawked at.

Dempsey and Millan capture that desperation of a woman out of place in her body, fit only to display her obvious[2] (headless) "lack" through the antics of a circus act or trick. Her character is not a metaphor of a woman who must survive, somehow, without basic and necessary intelligence, nor is she simply a metaphor of a woman trapped by patriarchal expectations that a woman be all body and no brains. Rather, she is a character who believes she must damage and distort her body in order to fit into an image already established for her. The Headless Woman has figured out that it is better to be a woman without the obvious signifier of thinking, than to actually stop thinking; her shrewd act itself, though self-destructive, displays an act of self-preservation as well. As the film progresses, the Headless Woman must deal with the infidelity of her sword-swallowing husband,[3] as well as her growing awareness that, more and more, she lives entirely in her body, which, for her, is a frightening place to be. What was once caprice and "pure showmanship" has become who she is perceived as being and who she can *only* be, not more. As the audiences apparently move from their initial fainting fits at the extremity of the show to a jaded desire for more and more perilous antics, the Headless Woman begins to realize that "the love between illusion and reality, revulsion and awe was over, leaving just a tumble of guts; no mystery and no answers. How bleak for a freak: a female body." While to herself, the Headless Woman has been reduced to a sexed body of organs without cultural identity, she remains an idealized feminine form to the male gaze. Here, then, is both the idealized female body (entirely "body" and no "brains") made into a freak show, and the freakish spectacle revealed as a mere physical enactment of an ideal societal standard. The Headless Woman, then, is less freakish because she lives without a head than she is because she lives within a female body. Dempsey and Millan's video captures the bizarre image that is constructed from the only-human. The normal-made-abnormal is exactly what circuses have traditionally represented.

On the one hand, *Freaks* proposes that physical freakishness is only a superficial defect of the normal human body, curable by medicine and modern science. On the other hand, the "code of the freaks" and the subsequent murderous uprising in obedience of that code, suggest a deeper and significant difference between "normal" people and circus freaks. Joan Hawkins, in her article on Browning's film, points out the layers of audience identification, both with the victimized sideshow performers and against the femme fatale antagonist. Hawkins writes that it is "precisely when the freaks turn monstrous—when they seem to step outside the bounds of normal social constraints—that they become enforcers of patriarchal convention" (274). By not only attacking the two conniving lovers, but also mutilating Cleopatra (destroying her beauty and turning her into a sideshow novelty herself), the avengers reinscribe patriarchal rule and punish the woman who has used her sex appeal to conquer her male companion. "It is when they become monstrous that they most clearly function," says Hawkins, "as one of us" (274). In speaking of short stories that deal with horror, Claire Larriere, in her essay "The Future of the Short Story," says that "our horror, even more than our taste, will be shocked by exaggerated mawkishness" (197). *Freaks*—as do many genre horror films—often invites audiences to approach the subject matter as maudlin *and* horrific. The shock, in a scene such as sideshow actors murderously crawling through mud to enact vengeance, comes in the pairing of the hyperbolic with the gruesome.

Shawna Dempsey, in a 1993 essay on homophobia in the film *Basic Instinct*, writes that the scenario of lesbians killing asshole-ish men somehow "appeals" to her. "Maybe we shouldn't boycott *Basic Instinct*, maybe we should refer to it as a primer" (5), she says. "Maybe" there is a similar adage to be discovered in Browning's film. Rather than object to the "insult" of exploiting human differences that such a film as *Freaks* presents, Dempsey's article suggests that the viewer embrace the designation "one of us." I think this is a strong reading that the film itself allows for, because its gaze permits sympathy for, and identification with, human differences. Certainly since its cult revival in the 1960s, audience members root for the so-called freaks. The film also presents a female character using her body to entice and seduce men. She uses sex as a tool to get her way, to manipulate the male characters into surrendering to her (destructively female) desire. Mary Ann Doane points out: "The very fact that we can speak of a woman 'using' her sex or 'using' her body for particular gains is highly significant—it is not that a man cannot use his body in this way but that he doesn't have to" (82). Traditionally, in the movies, men kill for "bad" reasons—usually revenge, lust, or money. In those movies where women kill (such as *Basic Instinct, Double Indemnity, Fatal Attraction, The Lady from Shanghai, Single White Female*) these "killer-femmes" attack not so much because of external evil motives, but because women, simply and unambiguously, are essentially evil. In Dempsey and Millan's *The Headless Woman* performance, the agency that women gain is not so much control as it is recognition of a thwarted ambition: male agency may be strong and may be violent, whereas female agency—as portrayed in traditional roles—is contradictory. In their film, they extend the metaphorical limits of the female freak, shifting the binary from either "essentially evil" or passively subservient into an active, albeit sometimes misguided, role.

Robert Budde also sets his novel, *Misshapen*, in the circus world, the turn-of-the-century freak show. In his novel, the character named "slip" (no capital first letter) literally falls into the circus, a lost child, adopted by all the circus performers. Although slip does not appear to have a gender, the narrative does, rarely, attach the "he" pronoun to slip's name. Like many circus sideshow acts of the time (such as Prince Randian, who also billed himself as The Human Torso or The Caterpillar Man), the novel's characters have more than one name, and their identities shift throughout the book. Framing the narrative is the story of Rice (slip as an adult), who returns to the Ghost Lady (also known as Rebecca the Human Pin Cushion) to hear slip's own life story, because slip lacks the capacity for memory. Budde's novel weaves physical and mental differences into one narrative that encompasses all outcasts, and makes family of those who don't seem to belong anywhere. Budde's text constantly reminds readers that the freak show is "off to the side" (Budde 85), not part of the main circus show. The big tent, in fact, is where normals *perform*, whereas the sideshow, traditionally, is where freaks are on display, where customers visit to re-establish their (normal) status by staring at what is so obviously "not." In Browning's portrayal of circus freaks as being at the center of a narrative, audience members found it difficult to "read" the circus body metaphorically. In a review attributed to "L.N.," the *New York Times* suggested that *Freaks* should have been shown at the New York Medical Centre, rather than the Rialto (web). Nevertheless, the "freakishness" of the film's characters is not only belied by the many ordinary domestic scenes, pre- and post-circus show,[4] but also, as Angela Smith points out, by being enacted "in front of able-bodied characters who do not view the moment as extraordinary" (104). Such behind-the-scenes scenes, she says, "elicit a kind of voyeurism," but lack the "staging and spiel of the sideshow act" (104), thus normalizing them further.

So, too, in *Misshapen*, do the circus "freak" characters display their "abnormalities" and at the same time reflect for the audience the "normalcy" of those doing the viewing. The novel introduces its readers to the characters and to the context physically different bodies will have in this world with the familiar circus barker's voice shouting: "Behind this thin canvas awaits the greatest assemblage of oddities ever exhibited, monstrosities that defy words, curiosities of all descriptions" (Budde, n.p.). The "greatest" show on earth includes, apparently, "oddities" and "monstrosities" that defy description, yet are entirely constructed of the circus barker's promises, and the viewer's curiosity.

The exotic difference that the audience expects to see is, in fact, an expectation of the mirror's reflection—distorted and made strange by the funhouse effect of paying to look, viewing without being viewed, voyeurism made easy and legitimate and safe. Over there, "Off to the side, the freak show" (85) is where one goes to re-establish what is normal, by staring at and judging what is "not," especially, what the *viewer* is not. Inside the definition of "not," live the characters in Budde's extraordinary novel. Made up of the Fat Lady, Jojo the Dog-faced Boy, the Strong Man, Chris-Christina, and an invisible and climactic Tattooed Man, Budde's circus is a many-ringed one wherein those characters usually seen as secondary or off to the side become the main attraction for the reader. Like audience members for *Freaks*, readers enter the world of the sideshow, not the main tent. The novel only tangentially mentions the big tent circus performers such as the Tightrope Walkers or Lion Tamers, the circus owner shows himself only momentarily, and the audience appears only for the moment of looking. In fact, the sideshow freaks come mainly from that part of the United States that 19th-century "America" was not willing to admit existed: the poor and the homeless, the abandoned and the damaged, the indigent and the immigrants. The Ghost Lady and King Sirrah "shared the same Mama, just at different times" (17) growing up in Alabama, yet are touted as exotic beings from the heart of Africa. The Caterpillar Man and his wife are from French-speaking New Orleans. So, in order for an audience to find these "freaks" freaky enough, the evidence of their personal history and humanity (of their *ordinary* lives) must be ignored and suppressed.[5] For those deemed a "freak" of nature, the disability or disfigurement or extra limb or missing pigments become who they are and how they are perceived. The "Fat Lady" cannot afford to lose weight, the "Midget" cannot afford to grow an inch, and the "Human Pincushion" cannot display discomfort or pain or infection, or they risk being seen (and ironically then *not* seen anymore) as mere mortal beings.

And it is being exactly what one looks like that is at the heart of *Misshapen*: *why* does an audience member feel both tantalization and horror at viewing what, within the pages of this book, are ordinary people? And for the sideshow characters, whose livelihood depends entirely on that performance of themselves as exotic and bizarre "freaks," the disgust they perpetuate when they display their bodies is necessarily invited and required. The narrator of this novel, the Ghost Lady, tells readers again and again of the tricks and maneuvers these characters must pull off in order to convince the audiences of their supposedly "real" selves: "You hooked them with the 'real' holes and then the gaffs are a sure thing. Easy" (47). Of course the gaffs are "easy" when the audiences are begging to be deceived and to believe the tricks. They want, ultimately, to believe that a woman is born with holes all over her body, gaps in her skin where needles belong. The more holes they see in her, the more they can trust the solidity of their own bodies, the more complete and real they become to themselves.

Thus, in Budde's turn-of-the-century circus, the players have a double identity crisis: not only must they exist as abnormal "freaks" to the "normal" viewers, but they must also maintain and even amplify that existence as freak. For Rebecca, being a black albino is not enough of an "act" to make it into the show, she needs the added gimmick of being punched full of holes. She is one of the many whose bodies fit into the unspoken definition of "not" normal, and the circus is the only place she can both live and work in her body. "Potential freaks would come in for an interview" and the circus manager makes the call of "freak or not freak" (Budde, 111). Being labeled *not* a freak relegates these rejected performers to the double misfortune of displaying a freakish body, without the advantages of charging for the display. The circus, then, voyeuristic and exploitative a home as it is, becomes the only safe haven for many disenfranchised disabled people. For the freaks who "make it," the audience relegates to them the status of both immortality and sub-humanity. In the first instance, they are denied the right to suffer or cry or smile or act bored; in the second instance, they are reviled for their successful display of the grotesque, for the "normal" body they so obviously lack. Their bodies are at one and the same time desired and reviled; they are sought out as special and unusual, yet roped off and pushed away because of their specialty.

The main character, slip, a "normal," enters into circus life with a dramatic falling as showy and miraculous as the circus itself. Rebecca the Ghost Lady determines that slip is from Canada. And the reader has no reason to doubt her conclusion. In a very concrete and practical way, slip just does not belong, although slip loves and is beloved of the circus individuals. Nevertheless, the novel reveals over and over that slip cannot hang onto a single fact about this world for longer than a day or two. As slip literally slips from page to page, gathering stories by listening and writing down other's memories, he is convinced *this* story or *that* detail will place the history of slip properly into the circus, will make slip the child, and slip the adult, finally at home there. As the child slip slips into the adult Rice, Rice has no memory of being slip, and he needs to be continually told stories in order to hold onto them.

But home is an emotion the other circus members have either willingly yielded or hidden too deep inside their memories for others to find. Home is not what the circus freaks seek; they long for the opposite of home: "faceless" anonymity. They desire the freedom to be strangers without being considered strange, to wander through random places in the world where they can pass people and *not* be stared at, *not* be pointed to, and not be regarded as so mutilated or so bizarre or so different that they *must* be from the circus. Every normal, whether a paying customer or not,[6] regards them with the same glance: these people *must* be freaks, must come from the circus that is in town; the freaks are regarded with a steady gaze that continually places them inside a history so distorted that only the circus will provide them with a semblance of what they, for lack of a better word, call home.

Given these conditions, slip is in the circus partially out of desperate need to join this caravan. But in the economic world of circus freaks, slip has no value whatsoever, and the characters immediately set about attempting to create a "use" for what would otherwise become simply an extra mouth to feed. So, in an attempt to make magic from disproportion, they place slip in the palm of the Giant's hand. By offering a "use," slip fits in with the nomads who occupy this transient and intangible world of entertainment, and slips into the rhythm and grind of daily life. *Misshapen* demonstrates that slip has no need of memory in order to perform in the circus as a freak. By joining the circus, slip is born. By leaving Canada, slip discards the necessity for either memory or home, identity or nation. Needing no home, for slip, becomes the same as needing no memory.

By placing his narrative at the pivot of two centuries, Budde offers his reader a doubled glance at the displaced body. Where circus freaks fit is a question the characters themselves take up. As they petition for their "rights," the owner takes up their plea and sells it to the press as a claim that the "freaks" wish to be "more than human" (165), and the petition loses momentum through the ridicule that follows its announcement. What began as a manifesto of rights and equality magically transforms into yet another "gawk-fest." Relying as they do on both the circus and its owner, the characters unhappily resign themselves to their unglamorous employment. "The show became just a show," Rebecca the Ghost Lady relates. "The love between illusion and reality," to recall Dempsey and Millan, "was over." More than ever, the sideshow performers merely do their job. In Budde's novel, performers must make a choice between the metaphorical or the social: between their bodies as a paying job, or their bodies as deserving of rights and distinctions.

The later release of Browning's *Freaks* included an exceedingly long textual introduction. This "prologue" discusses not the film's content but the medical nature of circus sideshow displays. It was inserted by the film's distributor (Metro-Goldwyn-Mayer) long after the film's release, in the late 1940s, and all VHS copies of *Freaks* included it as the opening of the film. The DVD also includes this text, but relegates the words within a special section one accesses through the DVD menu. The prologue appears to apologize for its controversial spectacle of the circus freak, at the same time as it reassures audiences that the "horrific" bodies they are about to view will soon be extinct as science works to "perfect" the human physique. Such a reassurance is only for the naïve and the ignorant. Given that it was offered shortly after World War II and revelations of Nazi extermination camps and killing hospitals, I read this prologue as carrying historically nuanced horror. The prologue declares that the "ABNORMAL and the UNWANTED" are mere "accidents of abnormal birth" and, in doing so, serves a number of purposes, including to reinscribe the very differences that it purports to annul. The prologue states: "The majority of freaks are endowed with normal thoughts." Such a sentence underlines the vast difference laid out between "freak" and "normal"; in effect, the prologue dramatically shifts the bodies of disabled circus performers from the world of monsters to the world of medicine. At the same time that these words diminish the sideshow performers' figural capabilities, it usurps their performative power. Another purpose of such a textual introduction to this film is to reassure audiences that the bodies they are about to view are not, in fact, freakish, so much as they are injured or damaged or *naturally* disabled. The message, then, is one of recovery: with the proper doctors, and the right medical intervention, these bodies can be cured. In writing a philosophical account of monsters, Patricia MacCormack suggests that "two inclinations" resonate with two effects encountered with "monsters": "Irrefutable and irresistible wonder and terror have led, in the life sciences, to a compulsion to cure or redeem" (293). The "quest and cure for monstrosity," she says, "is not truly about monstrosity, but about "preserving the myth and integrity" of the "normal human" (293). The impulse to "cure," then, is really an impulse to make "them" more like "us."

For the characters in Adele Wiseman's novel *Crackpot*, the love between illusion and reality is intricately connected, often in ways they themselves do not recognize. For the main character, Hoda, the crack between illusion and reality is filled with her father's stories, which tell her family's history, but in elaborate and metaphorical ways. Stories of how Hoda came to be, how her parents fled from "the old country" to Canada, and how, as a child, her father looked "too boldly" at the sun, and became blinded as a punishment for such blatant curiosity (10). Hoda, her father says, has been blessed with "a hump-backed" mother (Rahel) and a "blind, useless" father

(Danile); she herself suffers from "obesity." Yet Hoda, the child, does not recognize her body—or the bodies of her parents—as problematic or disfigured. She understands, quite literally, that her parents have been able to establish their life in the new world because of the bodily image they carry forth for the community, but that these body images are not final or limiting or exclusive. Wiseman, in opening her novel with disquieting descriptions of disparate bodies, shows her readers that the "normal" body does not, in fact, exist. Although crucial to how their lives develop, the bodies of her characters are never merely the sum total of who they are. Rather, their bodies are a part of the story Danile tells Hoda, the blessings that have brought them all here, together.

As Danile tells it, Rahel and Danile were, in the old country, thrown together because of misfortune. Not so much their own as the town's: because one is blind and one "a little crooked" (10), these two people are offered, by the town, as a marriage sacrifice to save the town. Because of a plague that swept through the nation, the "beautiful ones" decide to "take the two poorest, most unfortunate, witless creatures, man and woman, who exist under the tables of the community ... and they bring them together to the field" to marry each other (Wiseman, 17). In this way, by marrying off the two most unfortunate people in the community (by celebrating "life" in the midst of a "field of death"), the entire village can be saved. The members of the community, however, must also do their part. They provide a dowry, they furnish a hut, the couple is provided "a proper wedding" (17), which they could not have afforded under "normal" circumstances. Such a marriage will lift the curse of the plague. Rahel and Danile each fits such a call for "unfortunates," not so much because of her crooked shoulder and his blindness, but because there was "a shortage of idiots," and because of the plague, attacked both Gentiles and Jews, and because the anti–Semitism surrounding them blamed the Jewish town for suffering fewer deaths from the plague than did the Gentiles.[7]

Although Hoda's mother, Rahel, disapproves of Danile describing (what she thinks of as their bad-luck) stories to their daughter, she also understands that Hoda thrives on the stories.[8] Hoda, in fact, demands Danile repeat the same stories over and over in much the same way that slip demands repeated stories from Rebecca. The difference, of course, is that Hoda remembers and revels in the repetition, whereas slip remembers only that something has been lost, something that needs to be held onto. The words of how the three of them belong together in the world are as much food for Hoda as the snacks Rahel constantly feeds her.

Concerned for her daughter's health, Rahel feeds her daughter constantly, even at the expense of her own hunger. Such dedication to her daughter's well-being demonstrates not only Rahel's devotion to her child but also her unshakable conviction that this child of the New World is, indeed, in bodily danger. For Rahel, the body is both weak and absolute at the same time. Rahel's body has betrayed her by refusing to heal from the persistent pain she feels but refuses to acknowledge to any physician. Her husband's eyesight has proven itself to be a sign of the harm that can befall anyone. That Hoda grows more and more enormous, however, is of no concern to her parents. Indeed, rather than viewing Hoda's size as freakish, her parents consider this the one physical sign they have that she is healthy and robust; that, unlike their first child, Hoda will live long and well. Yet Hoda's appetite also marks her body as a site of ridicule and torment. Like her parents, Hoda is seen by many adults and children as "disabled." The women for whom Rahel cleans houses often scold her "for letting her daughter get so fat" (8), or worse, they deprive Rahel of the meal that they are obligated to provide since she obviously brought her own food along. And the children in the neighborhood chant after her: "Run, Hoda, run!" and "Hoda weighs a ton!" (34). No matter how the conversations or the children's teasing begins, Hoda ends up the butt of the other children's jokes. And usually, the punch line is her size and shape. Hoda, like her parents, has come to represent the oddity that proves the other children "normal." Her parents were virtually exiled in the old country, and, in Canada, Hoda is persecuted.

As Paul Longmore points out in most film and literary representations of disabled people, "[T]he deformity of the body symbolizes a deformity of the soul" (133). The freakish or grotesque body is characteristically portrayed or read as metaphor for emotional or spiritual deficiency. Metaphorical thinking, then, replaces an actual body with an idea behind that body, suggesting what that body *means*. So, when the freak is in the periphery, s/he is a necessary metaphorical prosthesis to the main plot; and when the freak is central to the narrative, s/he is taken literally as a medical oddity requiring cure. Longmore points out that what we fear "we often stigmatize and shun and sometimes seek to destroy" (132). In *Freaks*, Cleopatra and Hercules loathe and dismiss the sideshow stars with whom they work. Destroying Hans, therefore, is defensible and justified. They fear and are disgusted by the freaks, they have no qualms about killing Hans or stealing him away from his fiancée, Frieda. As Robert Bogdan's son says to a friend who cannot keep straight the difference between the good guys and the bad guys in an adventure film, "If they *look* bad, then they *are* bad" (Bogdan 6). This child's directive reveals what every moviegoer instinctively knows: namely, that people who *look* "different" *are* different, and that is why "we," the viewing audience, are and should be afraid of them. In Wiseman's novel, both the villagers in the old country and their new neighbors in Canada rely on Hoda's family to convince themselves they are healthy and normal and well. The neighbors rely on the "freak" characters to reinforce their own "normality"; and in this way, they conflate looking and being, solidifying the power of the gaze.

Hoda's parents, as "cripples," have come to represent the well-being of those around them, simply through demonstrating what their neighbors consider the opposite of well-being. But they continue to do so, especially once they immigrate to Canada, by displaying a poverty and a lack of physical and economic ease that their neighbors can view and compare. Thus, the community of immigrants define themselves by hiring Rahel mostly out of spite,[9] though occasionally out of pity. Hoda's family also reassures them that the fate of poverty is deserved (or has been deliberately invited). Longmore describes a recurring theme in narratives involving disabled characters: "God or nature or life compensates handicapped people for their loss, and the compensation is spiritual, moral, mental, and emotional" (138). So, the surrounding characters can dismiss Hoda's family as stigmatized for a Godly reason, or at least compensated in some unearthly way for their hardships. These compensations may not perhaps be readily apparent, but *must* exist in order for the other characters to maintain their distance.

Although Danile does, indeed, demonstrate the desire to feel "compensated" for his blindness, Rahel feels hampered and restrained by her body. Bothered by the lump on her shoulder all her life, Rahel knows this "deformity" is not life-threatening.[10] The real danger she faces—a life-threatening disease—is easier for her to dismiss and ignore, as it has no outward physical appearance. Though Rahel recognizes a problem coming from inside her body, she considers it mere physical pain that she ignores and contains for as long as possible.

At the beginning of the novel, Hoda is content. She has two parents who love her and whose main concern is her well-being. That her parents' bodies are viewed as damaged or "incomplete" is only a part of the story that ends up with Hoda at its center. But eventually Rahel, who has always attempted to deny and surpass her body, finds herself with the insurmountable problem of needing surgery. Rahel moves from the realm of having a disability into the realm of being seriously incapacitated. When her doctor tells her she desperately needs an operation, she responds: "What about a corset, doctor?" (28), hoping to find a way to pack the pain in, rather than have it carved out. Rahel wishes to reduce not only her pain, but the necessity of paying attention to her body's growing inability to perform cleaning tasks or look after her family. She grows weary, not only of caring *for* them, but of caring *about* them. She is tired of being put in the position of the noble sufferer, the mother who must care for her family's bodies more than for her own deteriorating one. The attraction of the malignant tumor to her is that, through her death, it will release her from her familial duties, and from the images of her body—perpetuated by others—that repeatedly constrict her. Danile's uncle calls her "the sack," whereas Danile himself refuses to acknowledge that his so-obviously-competent wife is in any way disabled.

"There is a difference between having your deformity minimized and having it belittled" (11), Rahel states. In the first instance "you" yourself may choose to ignore or reduce a physical difficulty in the world; in the second, someone else decides to ignore or disregard "your" disabling physical condition or the socially restricting constructions of "your" body. Rahel and Danile suffer the very real hardship of being treated unkindly and unfairly by the normals, the "beautiful ones" surrounding them. But it is not entirely their physical differences that separate them from the rest of their community; it is also their status as poor (and subsequently as immigrant) that binds them into a daily struggle to accommodate representations of their bodies as freakish, extraordinary, and "not" normal. As they are poor, they must be grateful for what they have, and work harder to overcome what has been proscribed to them as their fate. Hoda, too, is a character who accepts her fate, though she constantly rewrites what that fate is and why it has been imposed on her.

Paul Longmore criticizes "the common notion that with the proper attitude one can cope with and conquer any situation or condition" (139). Budde's slip and Wiseman's Hoda move through their stories towards a "normal" life; not one that only embraces conventional standards, but one that shifts the status quo so that whatever is normal for them becomes part of an overall standard. In contrast, Dempsey and Millan's Headless Woman is left with "just a tumble of guts; no mystery and no answers." But like many of the characters in Browning's film, the Headless Woman is and is not ensnared in her role as barker. As Sally Chivers puts it in her incisive article about *Freaks*, "The Horror of Becoming 'One of Us,'" in enacting retaliation, the sideshow performers "refuse to remain trapped in the narrative roles by their nonconformity with an acceptable body image" (60). With that argument in mind, the "uprising" against the "normal" becomes more about an oppressed minority struggling against oppression than simple revenge. Says Chivers: "For the majority of the film, the elements of horror are muted and exist only in foreshadows and challenges to ableist assumptions" (58). While Dempsey and Millan's Headless Woman *is* the freak story, Budde's slip and Wiseman's Hoda feed on freak stories, and gain strength from them. In this way, as characters, they perpetuate the "LAAAAADIES AND GENTLEMEN, BOOOOOYS AND GIRLS OF AAAAALLLLLLLL AGES" (Budde, 85) circus barker. Hoda and slip empower themselves through the stories they desperately need to hear; the Headless woman, a "genuine freak," rejects the stories in order to live, ultimately, in the most frightening place of all: the female body. Browning, while invoking this stock view of women through the character of Cleopatra, ultimately shows the same essential evil to be ascribed to the disabled bodies in his film. "Collectivity comes from the unlike," says MacCormack; thus "we are all monsters in our singularity" (307).

5

20th-Century Fables

Fiction, Disease, and—
oh, yeah—Disability

[L]iving is just a series of unexplained, uncomfortable medical
conditions.—Porter Jones, narrator, "Studies Show/Experts Say"

When Diane Price Herndl writes in a special issue of the PMLA on Disability in the Humanities that "most people in the disability community do not want to be considered ill, and most people who are ill don't want to be considered disabled" (593), she exposes a truism that seems so blatant it need not be highlighted: how *obvious*, of *course, oh, yeah, but* why do these two categories disavow each other even when they overlap? And why do medical practitioners and most lay people (at least when identifying as "healthy") align the two? And that disability activists, theorists, and most patients wish to separate the two, remains a vexing concern for all. She attempts, in her article, to outline a disability/illness "matrix," scrutinizing ways in which disability and illness intersect, and analyzing resistance to those intersections. Much resistance comes from a disability studies antagonism to the medical model, a term she says tends to operate as "the definitive antithesis of our position" (596). Herndl also takes the Medical Humanities to task for not studying disability in theoretical (especially post-structural) domain, showing that the "practitioners" of these two fields of study are convinced of their disconnections (or, as she also points out, that the one belongs as a subset to the other).

Like Herndl, I iterate a characterization of disability that usually asserts itself against a backdrop to disability studies: namely, that disability is a social construction, a way in which one's body relates to the world, to others, the way bodies advance through the days, encountering problems, difficulties, pleasures, and (often limited) choices. Disability, most scholars and activists will argue, is not something you have, but the way you negotiate the world through physical, cognitive, and social accessibility. What place, then, does illness and disease have in studying the representations of disability? Herndl uses the examples of post-polio syndrome and AIDS to argue for diseases that lead to or include situations of social disability, as well as medical consequences. I could add such overlaps as chronic illnesses, wheelchair users who must guard against pressure ulcers, and that even a psychological state of depression can lead to debilitating physical symptoms. That some people, as Herndl points out, who locate themselves in one category of either sick or disabled, do not wish to define themselves as in the other category, draws attention to how medical, social, or economic systems construct, address, and catalogue certain bodies. Every subject—reliant on the body as identity-marker—relies, also, on those markers as fluctuating and mutable (even as—at points—some people cling to certain categories because of the advantages such categories may appear to offer).

Much of the way that people process such concepts as aging, disability, childhood, race, ethnic identity, sexuality, gender, etc. (etc., etc., etc.) is shaped via the narratives we tell ourselves, the multiple ways that oral stories, dramatic (including filmic) narratives, and literary works reflect and represent bodies. In this chapter, I look closely at the ideas of modern medicine that, as Michel Foucault argues, stem from the relationship between power and knowledge, and how such power dynamics play out in three fiction narratives. Foucault's *The Birth of the Clinic* outlines the origins of modern medicine, how it is that the "science" of medicine moved from a biological study of species to a social study of anatomy. Foucault describes an Enlightenment thinking that has influenced how contemporary Westerners regard the role of medicine and, subsequently, illness. Medical practice, through its microscopic stare into isolated body parts and cellular membranes, has managed to associate and conflate progressive diseases with healthy disabled bodies. It is this process that I wish to focus on here; as well, I shall discuss how a Foucauldian reading of institutionalized medicine and care allows for an analysis of the institutionalized body—constructed and contained by the hegemony of the institution—even when such a figure may not, ultimately, be hospitalized.

By focusing on a novel by Alan Lightman, one short story by Flannery O'Connor, and one by M.A.C. Farrant, I look critically at the presentation and juxtaposition of ill and disabled characters, especially within Foucault's theories of how social construction lends itself to literary analysis that shows such characters may be classified, constrained, isolated, and excluded. Foucault's writings about power as pervasive suggest a reading of everyday practices (such as, in my three literary cases, interaction with family and strangers) in the way such practices structure human subjects. His investigations into the history of medical practices and his analysis of the experiences and perceptions of mental and physical health lend themselves to a fruitful analysis of the disabled body, and also to a crucial analysis of the intersections between the physical and the cultural. I explore, in this chapter, how some contemporary narratives dictate that the technological world is often read as "bad" for individuals to the point of causing debilitating illness and bodily ruptures. Such cultural assumptions not only interfere with medical attention to actual disease by assuming illness as merely metaphorical for a greater social "ill," but also blame "progress" for increasing numbers of difficult-to-prove illnesses.[1] Disease and disability, in such a reading, are not simply bodily realities, but transform into moral allusions about the technology that surrounds the *able* body. Paradoxically, these moral allusions pertaining to able or "healthy" bodies are represented on the image of the disabled or diseased body. In this way, a character presented as "less" than able is not only a moral marker of social ill but is also a physical embodiment of cultural blunders.

Focusing on the "rational discourse" that permeated 18th-century France, Foucault examines the semantic turn or "mutation" in medical language, wherein seeing and saying ceased to be considered an activity for the patient and became the act of seeing (objective observation) and naming (medical judgment). Rather than the patient *telling* a doctor what was wrong (the assumption previously being that patients have thorough knowledge of their own bodies, and access to what they can easily notice and discern), the doctor simply asks what hurts (where, in the body, the problem can be located) and then observes with an objective eye the pathology that is the patient's scrutinized body. The rise of this model of sight parallels the way in which contemporaneous medicine has reorganized disease according to patterns of syntax. The eye has become the word. As Foucault says:

> At the beginning of the nineteenth century, doctors described what for centuries had remained below the threshold of the visible and the expressible, but this did not mean that, after over-indulging in speculation, they had begun to perceive once again, or that they listened to reason rather than to imagination; it meant that the relation between the visible and invisible—which is necessary to all concrete knowledge—changed its structure, revealing through gaze and language what had previously been below and beyond their domain. A new alliance was forged between words and things, enabling one *to see* and *to say* [xii].

With the beginning of the Enlightenment, says Foucault, the "gaze is no longer reductive, it is, rather, that which establishes the individual in his irreducible quality. And thus it becomes possible to organize a rational language around it. The *object* of discourse may equally well be a *subject*, without the figures of objectivity being in any way altered" (xiv). Foucault's discussions of the medical gaze (and his subsequent examinations of other power-gazing structures) in *The Birth of the Clinic* in 1963, as well as Jacques Lacan's notion of the gaze he develops in his "mirror stage" in 1966, evolve into varying discursive terms such as the male gaze (Mulvey), the female gaze (Gamman and Marshment), the postcolonial gaze, the gay gaze, etc.[2] In 1998, Sherene Razack speaks out about ways of undoing an ableist gaze (131); Kurt Lindemann neatly defines it as: "The ableist gaze is one that marks disabled bodies as different and, therefore 'normal.' For example, this gaze is enacted in medical diagnoses of disability as an impaired body in need of 'fixing'" (Lindemann, 110).

In *The Birth of the Clinic*, Foucault evaluates the system of medical care during the late 1700s and early 1800s. He introduces into historical research the ways in which medical discourse organizes itself in relation to other power structures (social, cultural, economic). Enlightenment physicians, in looking for symptoms in the body of the patient, shifted their medical practice to one of an observant eye gazing *at* the ill body, to a dissecting eye gazing *into* the body, what Foucault calls the "privileges of a pure gaze" (107), one which "refrains from intervening: it is silent and gestureless" (107). Skin, tissues, organs, and blood have become the locational sites of illness, the repository for disease that travels along the map of the body. In this model, anatomy becomes the science of cartography, with the physician as both cartographer and medico, and microscopes the technology that invites doctors to gaze into the unexplored regions of the patient's body. This silent seeing invites the physician to know his patient's body as he observes it: "The clinical gaze has the paradoxical ability to *hear a language* as soon as it *perceives a spectacle*" (108). As in unexplored territory, what is observed is invisible and what is invisible becomes, through the medical gaze (a gaze aided by the technology of stethoscopes and microscopes), comprehensively—and systematically—visible.

By subjecting Enlightenment medicine to its own interpretative gaze, Foucault questions the language that constructs power relations between patient and doctor. Operating on "the principle that the patient both conceals and reveals the specificity of his disease" (105), doctors gazed on and at the body with an appraising eye "that knows and decides," an eye "that governs" (89). At the same time, Foucault perpetuates a patronage of perception by invoking this doctor's gaze as symptomatic of the new clinical field. Newly developing medicine observed and evaluated the body as in the process of dying. Each "symptom" of affliction was a sign of pathological progress: the body decomposing from its original whole and natural state. The process, then, was one where the original body—free of sin—moved away from its pristine state towards ultimate death and decay. The contaminated body became a marker for moral decay, exteriorizing the process of death. In this way, illness and disability both indicated a disreputable body, one that asserted its individuality through ultimate demise. In Foucault's analysis, death shifted from its role as moral equalizer, in the centuries preceding the 18th century, to becoming another marker of individuality. And the diseases and disorders that led to death became symptoms of that mappable decay: "Disease breaks away from the metaphysic of evil, to which it had been related for centuries; and it finds in the visibility of death the full form in which its content appears in positive terms" (198). Disease, ultimately, manifests itself as the "positive" presence of death. As each death is individual, so too is each malady a story of singular decay.

The many disabled people who have been scrutinized by a medical establishment that focuses on remedy is an obvious example of the conflation of disease and disability. Deaf people, for example, who pre–18th century would likely present themselves as healthy, under this new model become silenced, symptomatic maps into which the physicians gaze (and subsequently judge).[3] As Rosemarie Garland-Thomson says, "The medical model that governs today's interpretation of disability assumes that any somatic trait that falls short of the idealized norm must be corrected or eliminated" (*Extraordinary*, 79).[4]

Such a narrative of "cure above all" generates from the stories, the folklore, and the narratives that continue to perpetuate a sense of bodies that deviate from what Fiedler labels "tyranny of the normal." Such narratives arise from the rational idea of the body as an instrument in constant need of care and adjustment. This recent approach to a degenerating body in need of constant maintenance instigated a view of individual "health" as a social responsibility integral to the larger society, and led to what Foucault calls, in *Power/Knowledge*, a "Politics of Health" (166), announcing a strategy of "cure" rather than assistance. There are many, many texts that take on the medical establishment's focus on cure and treatment. For this chapter, I attend to narratives that arise from incapacitating illness, even when those instances are haphazardly understood to be modes of disability.

In Alan Lightman's *The Diagnosis* (finalist for the 2000 National Book Award in fiction), the body of a middle-aged, middle-class white businessman is gradually overtaken by paralysis. Bill Chalmers becomes the object of a medical gaze designed to objectively evaluate the body, at the same time as the process of this gaze dismisses the individual subject. The plot of this 369-page book is even simpler than the O'Connor 27-page short story (though perhaps on par with the Farrant). A junior executive, Chalmers—overworked and far too dependent on the technological— goes from an episode of short memory loss to numbness, to almost complete paralysis by the novel's end. The story consists mainly of his (and a multitude of doctors') attempt to diagnose his "illness." The book closes, as it began, with a character disconnected from his job, his family and social life, disconnected from his own raison d'être. Like many horrific and gothic parables, such as Kafka's *The Trial*, this book is a modern allegory, replete with warnings about power, science, technology, and money.

Describing the shift from nosological medicine (biological classification) to anatomical study, Foucault reveals common 18th-century doctrines. Extracting evidence from a medical book by Dr. S.A. Tissot, published in 1770 at the time of the discursive shift, Foucault states:

> Before the advent of civilization, people had only the simplest, most necessary diseases. Peasants and workers still remain close to the basic nosological table; the simplicity of their lives allows it to show through in its reasonable order: they have none of those variable, complex, intermingled nervous ills, but down-to-earth apoplexies, or uncomplicated attacks of mania [*Birth*, 16].

Remarkably, this analysis of the 18th-century approach to disease typifies many contemporary attitudes to the (often undiagnosable) causes of disease. Continuing to draw from the Tissot text, Foucault says: "As one improves one's conditions of life, and as the social network tightens its grip around individuals, 'health seems to diminish by degrees'; diseases become diversified, and combine with one another; 'their number is already great in the superior order of the bourgeois; ... it is as great as possible in people of quality'" (16–17). Here appears the exact "theme" of the Lightman novel: as "our" lives get more and more complicated, so, too, do our diseases; ultimately becoming untreatable (and even unrecognizable in the Foucauldian sense of the word). In a recent book discussion on Canadian national radio, reviewers agreed that Lightman's novel symbolizes a growing dependence on, and fear of, technology. *The Diagnosis* is "about a guy who has a big fat breakdown because he's overwhelmed by our high-tech, high-speed world," about "an American executive who breaks under the strain of modern living" (Brown, et al.). Yet the body is (supposed to be) an efficient machine. The implication in Foucault's research and Lightman's novel is that pampered upper-class bodies suffer greater (and more complicated) diseases because of their affected lives and "artificial" social environs. Contained within structures of power, discipline, and domination, the "working man" in this book is an overextended businessman. Although nobody directly controls staff working hours, each businessman monitors his own hours and productivity[5] in their corporative panopticon. The company motto, "Maximum information in minimum time," demands speed, money, efficiency, and *information*.

The Diagnosis, ironically named after the medical information Chalmers so desperately (and unsuccessfully) seeks, is predominantly a narrative of *loss*: Chalmers loses his memory, motor control, and perhaps even his mind. Each of these characteristics cannot physically disappear, but I believe this idea of relinquishing that which one once so capably held firm, to be a significant metaphor within disability studies. Loss implies the shift from "normal" to "abnormal": a woman who "loses" her sight, or a man who suffers the "loss" of his hearing suggest that their bodies no longer function to the same degree they once did. When a student questions performance poet Aaron Williamson about when he lost his hearing, Williamson's response is: "I choose not to say when I *lost* my hearing but rather when I *gained* my deafness" (*Concerto*, 33).[6] But the discourse of loss also offers a subtle reproach of the person who has undergone this bodily shift. People tend to lose important papers or money or—*oh, yeah*—shopping lists when they don't pay enough attention, when—instead of gripping tighter—they loosen their hold on a precious item.[7] A particular bodily ability is perceived as "lost," and then that loss is marked/imposed upon the previously "normal" body. Such language indicates that the "normal" bodily function was once in existence, and it has been accidentally lost or deliberately discarded. At the same time as ableist narratives propose the able body as the original wholeness which gets "lost" by degrees, so too is normalcy the default standard to which any *ab*normalcy comes as a—usually unwelcome—addition. This metaphor shows the complicated ways in which a body "loses" *ability*, but "gains" *abnormality*. The fault, ultimately, lies with the los*er*, and the disease—rather than the acquisition of an unequivocal diagnosis—represents the "loss" of a fit and sound body. Ironically, after his first (and most drastic) memory-loss incident, Chalmers remembers "the most minute detail" (66) of his nightmare encounter with doctors in charge of experimental laboratory machinery.

During the night of a series of painful tests and humiliating examinations, Chalmers cannot recall his name, his family, his workplace, or any detail about his life besides a vague recognition that he is a businessman devoted to meetings and faxes and cell phones. Brought to Boston City Hospital by police, Chalmers experiences a surreal night of CAT scans and microbiology, and the ominous "CGA" which the doctors assure themselves is "state of the art" (29) and "beautiful" (31). Two doctors anesthetize him, strap his head to their precious contraption, and grind a giant needle into his skull—only to discover something is wrong with the machine. "He's okay," says one doctor to the other. "I'll examine him later. But something's wrong with the machine" (32). Once he flees from the Kafka-esque hospital, however, he recalls each excruciating minute with no respite from memory. His body—and the mind once safely ensconced there—has already begun to betray him, deleting vital information, and restoring intact what he desperately wishes would collapse into oblivion. Chalmers, contained and isolated by his Emergency Ward institutionalization, becomes the surveyed body into which scientific technology literally probes.

Bizarrely, this story of a progressive and debilitating paralysis begins with a breakdown of the function of the mind, leading readers to wonder/conclude that Chalmers's ultimate and total "loss" of body movement is the result of his mental breakdown in the first chapter. It is important to note that many physical diseases intertwine with mental health, and that the intersection between mental and physical illness is often interdependent and complicated. But this novel suggests that, for Chalmers, the loss of both memory and bodily command indicate a loss of spiritual control in his life, a control that—no matter how many doctors and therapists he visits—will continue to elude his grasp. Chalmers's body, through its incremental paralysis, exhibits Foucault's notion of the body as a functioning machine that records upon its surface the everyday practices of power and discourse. In this case, Chalmers—a man at the hub of big business activity—notices his body shift from one which, daily, has the power to command authority and power (his working world is almost entirely male; most of the female characters appear as "wives"), to one which belongs less to him than it does to the medical narratives that wish to wrest knowledge from its malfunction. In the novel, Chalmers's son becomes more and more agitated at his father's paralysis, ostensibly over concern for a bewildering and progressive disease. But the book also suggests that Alex is "embarrassed" by his father's loss of masculinity. When offered a part-time job, Alex, at one and the same time, asks his father's permission and offers an apology, for receiving "such an endorsement of his abilities at the same time that his father lay useless and paralyzed. Bill Chalmers reads his son's hesitation as "embarrassment at displacing" and "usurping" his father (340).

In Lightman's novel, the narrator implies that Chalmers's "problem" is one of artificiality; in other words, his life has become dominated by a technological push-and-pull, professionally and personally (his son spends his free time reading about Socrates on the Internet and his wife engages in a non-corporeal e-mail affair). Chalmers sees even the progress of his disease as that of a machine collapsing—still attached to its power source, but no longer an uncontrived physical entity. The narrative suggests that Chalmers has disrupted his "natural" bodily functions and being, that his body is no longer a body, because it does not function as it *should*: "The bony legs, the stomach, the white buttocks in the bathroom mirror were not body but merely numb things attached to his brain stem" (320). This scene demonstrates that Chalmers, even this late in the book, separates his body from his mind, his ineffectual body from the image of body parts he surveys.

Chalmers's son suddenly becomes interested in taking an online college course on Plato, and the readings depict Athens during the time of Socrates's execution. Alex reads some of the chapters aloud to his father, and these scenes reflect an allegorical echo to events in the 20th century. A slave sent to spy on Socrates in his final moments reports: "He said that death is only the separation of the soul from the body. After that the soul is pure and free. He said that men who fear death love the body, and probably power and money as well" (337). Death is freedom and an escape from the corrupting power of money and ambition governed by corporate avarice. Loving the body is as fatal a flaw as loving money. The novel draws a clear line between Socrates cooperatively drinking poison, rejecting the corporeal, and Bill Chalmers's physical disorders. Just as Foucault analyzed attitudes in the Enlightenment about the original body supposedly free of sin and moving towards ultimate death and decay, in this novel Chalmers's body echoes that outlook. The essence of North American "lifestyles" has caused his disease, and, morally, unless "we all" retreat from modern technology, then and only then will someone like Chalmers (the new-age canary in the technology mine) stop becoming ungovernably ill. The novel invites readers to align with the protagonist's terrifying plight.

Lightman's novel is about the "knowledge" doctors have about what they cannot see—a disease that permeates Chalmers's body to such an extent that it is both invisible and debilitating. Foucault says: "We are doomed historically to history, to the patient construction of discourses about discourses, and to the task of hearing what has already been said" (xvi). So that, to "see and to say" (xii) has become the modern language of diagnosis, the judgment upon the failing and overdetermined body. Despite Chalmers's paralysis, which develops at a shocking rate, most readers interpret this novel as pure allegory. The *New York Times* book reviewer says that Lightman's novel "forcefully captures the great confluence of our times: information overload, unimaginable prosperity and spiritual bankruptcy" (Verghese). In a Canadian national radio discussion, one commenter says that "once the doctors fail to diagnose his problem ... there is progress ... with the beginning of paralysis, he starts trying to stop and smell the roses" (Brown, et al.). The book invites such a glib reading of illness as "lesson" by persistently presenting Chalmers as a character sinning through technology, a man fallen from original grace. His paralysis, then, is a gift: a lesson that teaches him to rebuff technology in favor of basic nature. According to Foucault, in the years

> preceding and immediately following the [French] Revolution saw the birth of two great myths with opposing themes and polarities: the myth of a nationalized medical profession, organized like the clergy, and invested, at the level of man's bodily health, with powers similar to those exercised by the clergy over men's souls; and the myth of a total disappearance of disease in an untroubled, dispassionate society restored to its original state of health [31–32].

In *The Diagnosis*, there are more and more layers of medical personnel observing and offering diagnoses, but they only repeat what information the character and reader already grasp, and offer no *new* knowledge to help the patient. Bill Chalmers goes from one specialist to another, each one thinks his problem is biological, neurological, psychological, etc., yet no doctor will declare categorically from which specific affliction the main character suffers. In fact, the only diagnosis Chalmers gets in the entire novel is from another patient sitting in the waiting room:

> "My fingers are numb," Bill said. He slapped his hands viciously against the center table.
> "Anything else numb?"
> "Both hands and arms."
> "I see," said Bineas, shaking his head gravely. "You are quite right to see a doctor."
> "What do you think I have?" asked Bill.
> "You could have a pinched nerve. Or possibly some kind of tumor or disease. But we laymen can only guess at these things" [114].

Unlike the fictional doctors who do not even offer so much as a guess, the other patient has taken on the Cartesian medical language of asking the patient to point to the problem areas; he then offers "objective" interpretation. Chalmers, desperate for terminology to explain his physical changes, refuses his own knowledge of his body, and grasps at the simple (and unspecific) observations of an opinionated other.

Arthur Frank, in *The Wounded Storyteller: Body, Illness, and Ethics*, writes about the powerful drive of the chronically ill to tell stories as "moral witness" to their bodies' affairs. In attempting to discern a model to suit real people and ideal body types, Frank opens the discussion about illness narratives to uncover the "crisis of control" (30) some ill people experience. In responding to these crises, bodies negotiate between what Frank distinguishes as four "types" (the "disciplined body," the "mirroring body," the "dominating body," and the "communicative body" [29]), shifting along a monadic or dyadic continuum. Rather than focus on a cure, Frank builds on Talcott Parsons's theory of the "sick-role."[8] Leaving aside Frank's notions of the autobiographical in "wounded" accounts, I wish to investigate the prevalent societal urge either to "cure" physical disability through medical intervention or, more importantly, to represent societal moods or failings through increasingly debilitating disease. The fictions I discuss in this chapter represent disability or illness as a means for giving the reader a message, a clue, a *symbol* that guides a reading for the subtext: namely, that bodies betray what minds cannot fathom. Too often, in fictional narratives, bodies *mean*, as allegory, as portent, or even as evidence/clue to the ongoing investigation that is medical practice. Just as frequently, bodies mean even more when there is a *lack* of evidence. When Bill Chalmers cannot wrest a diagnosis from his myriad of doctors, his body strikes readers as even more meaningful in its story deficit.

Whereas readers might sympathize with Chalmers's condition, they will relish the extreme hypochondria of Porter Jones, the narrator and protagonist of M.A.C. Farrant's short story, "Studies Show/Experts Say." At one point, he dramatically whines to his girlfriend/nurse Georgina, that "you're not supposed to die in the prime of your life." He further complains: "Not when you're a 42-year-old, white-collar Welfare Worker, three-bedroom home-owner secure in the middle-income profile bracket" (148). His words seem to lament a terminal diagnosis; in fact, the story portrays Porter Jones as someone who will go to any lengths to convince others of his continual suffering. The story begins when Isobel walks out on him during a dinner discussion on the effects of "butylated hydroxalade," screaming: "I'm leaving you. Sicko. Pea brain. Bag of shit. You've got gas up the ass" (147). Georgina lasts only three weeks (though she returns at the end), accusing the protagonist-narrator of having "premenstrual syndrome" (148). He then meets "businesswoman-hippie" (152) Wanda at a health food store, and recognizes her as his perfect match when she tells him, "I can always tell a victim of 20th Century Disease" (149). Wanda prepares herbal remedies, plants and gathers herbs, and administers to his every somatic grievance. Furthermore, she removes all synthetic material from the house and paints his walls white. "I spend my days wandering through the bare room in an orgy of illness. I've never felt better in my life" (150), he declares.

Porter Jones wants the backing and assistance of the medical establishment, wives/girlfriends, and his employers, but wants such support without enduring actual affliction or agony or drastic change in his body; rather, his ailments produce pleasure. Indeed, his convalescence requires constant bedtime, and the implications are semi-sexual. When Georgina unzips his pants so he can show her where it hurts, the scene ends with her "hiking up her skirt and getting comfy" (148). When Wanda offers her 20th Century Disease diagnosis, the narrator immediately takes to bed (149). And when Georgina returns to his life, he cannot remember having intercourse with her, the suggestion being that she and her lover drug him to the point where he keels over in mid-sentence, falling asleep like he's "dropping dead," yet believes that they have conceived a child (154). He is semi-aroused, a semi-father and—*oh, yeah*—he's semi-famous.

Frank delineates the disciplined body and the mirroring body as monadic, and the dominating body and the communicative body as dyadic. Definitely not disciplined (he never takes control of his supposed diseases, but relies on others to analyze and treat him), Porter Jones also shows no interest in mirroring the outside world. Rather, he wishes to show off his body as a unique medical phenomenon, and bullies others (mostly women) in the process, exhibiting what Frank would call the ideal dominating body. To initially lure Georgina after Isobel has left him, he calls her up and cites capricious facts: "About forty percent of women who separated while still in their thirties will never re-marry. Now's your chance" (147). Later, as Georgina and her children are leaving, he calls after them: "There's a strong possibility I may be bleeding internally" (148), chastising them for ignoring his health problems. His words attempt to bully others into feeling pity and responsibility for his body's inability to display physical debility. Porter Jones relies on what Frank calls the contingent nature of the body (its ability to shift from one state of body-self to another), but he relies on such contingency too heavily. Frank's "ethical ideal" body is the dyadic, communicative body, which accepts contingency as a normative ebb and flow. Frank defines dyadic as the "recognition that even though the other is a body outside of mine, 'over against me,' this other *has to do with me, as I with it*" (35). Farrant's protagonist completely embraces the notion that others must have something to do with him, but his is a selfish connection, one where all other characters (even his fictional son) center around his body, his diseases, his syndromes, and he himself bears no responsibility to the lives or corporeal experiences of others.

Announcing that Porter Jones is "allergic to everything," and then naming him "Bubble-Man" (150), Wanda charges admission, allowing "sightseers" to peer through his window. He ecstatically revels in the attention, yet persists in asking Wanda to "tell me why I am dying. I have this pain" (151). He accepts her brush-off (that pain has "corporate significance") but insists that she "get me some ginger ale and some Vick's cough drops, cherry-flavored. And fix my pillow and rub my back and bring me some magazines and bring me the thermometer" (151). Ultimately, he wants someone to take his malady seriously, but predominantly he desires *care* more than analysis (or even the much-craved medical verdict that doctors deny Bill Chalmers). Looking closely at his self-descriptor as a "42-year-old, white-collar" "three-bedroom home-owner" in the "middle-income bracket," I read Porter Jones as seeking justification for being male, financially comfortable, and relatively competent at his job (though he does meet Georgina as a client in the Welfare Office), yet still desirous of a fantasy helpmeet to attend to his indolent longings.

Overtly flouting the responsibility Talcott Parsons outlines as part of the sick-role contract, Porter Jones does *not* make every (or any) attempt to get well, instead rejoicing in his ongoing "treatment" and nurturing. Eventually, Wanda "sells" him to a private medical practice: "Buy low, sell high" (152), she says as she leaves, duplicating the final act of his previous girlfriend/nurses. When he's ousted from his medical enclave by nuns and priests who wish to tap into "whispers from heaven" via donating themselves to medical science for "[r]esearch," "[s]oul transplants" and "[t]hat sort of thing" (153), Porter once again calls Georgina, asserting that he suffers from scabies, deposits on his tibia, migraines, plague, virus, and narcolepsy. The story ends with Porter Jones anticipating showing off his medical scrapbook, newspaper clippings, and disease souvenirs to his future son (though the story suggests that an ambulance attendant who was "always hanging around" is the likely father), musing that his son will "have his own diseases to discover" (155).

"Storytelling," says Frank, is a "medium through which the dyadic body both offers its own pain and receives the reassurance that others recognize what afflicts it" (36). But for Porter Jones, telling his story (to readers, but also collecting paraphernalia from his days of fame for the future generation), becomes another form of disassociation. What's happening to him consumes him, but only as long as he's hooked on scrutinizing his body's problem(s). The medical team—and, presumably, his paying audience—that "buys" his symptoms from Wanda agree: their interest holds only so long as his problem is corporeal. When the doctors "find nothing wrong" (153), they discharge him and renovate his pristine room to accommodate the incoming residents. The story mocks a character so desperate for attention that he neurotically imagines multiple medical conditions. Yet Porter Jones is loath to include emotional or mental illness in his list of complaints. In the opening scene, Isobel calls him "Sicko," suggesting a fault in his mind, not a physical ailment. And when Georgina leaves, her son, Ronald, declares that Porter Jones is a "basket case" and the narrator counters this attack with one of his own; namely, that Ronald "has psychological problems" (148). Desperate for sick leave, Porter Jones accepts three-quarters of his regular pay by claiming a "stress leave" from work, even as he concedes, "I hate to admit to failing emotions but it's the only way I can get off work to minister to my swollen liver" (149). According to one Centre for Addiction and Mental Health (CAMH) study,[9] 38 percent of the people surveyed said they wouldn't tell their managers that they had a mental health problem. When asked if they'd be concerned if they knew a co-worker had a mental illness, 64 percent said "yes" (CAMH, "Would you tell…"). As well, 50 percent of the people surveyed would tell friends or co-workers that they have a family member with a mental illness, compared to 72 percent who would discuss a family member with a diagnosis of cancer (CAMH, "Mental Illness…"). Mental illness is a leading cause of disability in Canada. "The terms 'mental illness' and 'addiction' refer to a wide range of disorders that affect mood, thinking, and behavior. Examples include depression, anxiety disorders, schizophrenia, as well as substance use disorders and problem gambling" (CAMH, "Mental Illness…").

To summarily declare that the protagonist has "psychological problems" of his own reduces the story to a mere punch line, but also perpetuates the impression readers will have that there is "nothing wrong" with Porter Jones. Ironically, his endlessly pursuit for medical scrutiny seems to demonstrate at one and the same time that he is not in the least bit sick but that he may be *sick*. It's all in his head, *oh-yeah-but* in a medical system that has corporate interests at its nucleus, doctors (and other viewers) need to *see* to believe. Porter Jones desires Foucault's "clinical gaze" to allow doctors and caregivers to fashion his illness as visible and concrete, to allow him to occupy an identity that straddles the object and subject locus, and to present his spectacle-self to an appreciative audience. Porter Jones willingly embraces the communal/community aspects of his body that Frank decrees necessary for a dyadic body. He shies away from hints of mental illness for the very reason that it separates him from others. "Sicko," Isobel yells at him, denying his quest to uncover disease. His workplace cannot deny him stress leave, but it does not provide the shock and awe he might receive with a diagnosis of scurvy. "Bodies are realized—not just represented but created—in the stories they tell" (52), Frank asserts. Porter Jones wishes to create himself as laid up, invalid, incapacitated; as long as his mind is sound enough to enjoy it all.

Except for its protagonist's first name, Flannery O'Connor's short story, "Good, Country People" depicts no pleasure or enjoyment in the body, at least not for the ironically named Joy, an overeducated and unhappy woman who has one wooden leg. The story focuses on Mrs. Hopewell and her daughter Joy (who later changes her name to Hulga). Mrs. Hopewell despairs that her daughter will be disabled not only by her artificial leg, but by her outward appearance and manner; Joy refuses to embody a traditionally feminine demeanor. Indeed, Joy invokes an entirely different narrative structure by relating to a classical male figure, ugly yet powerful: "She had a vision of the name [Hulga] working like the ugly sweating Vulcan who stayed in the furnace and to whom, presumably, the goddess had to come when called" (174). That is, Joy mistakenly believes that, like Vulcan, she has a lame leg, but has the power to call forth great beauty, dedication, and love in another.

The narrator repeatedly describes Joy/Hulga, each time drastically differently from the last, scathingly detailed description. The narrator says of Joy/Hulga that she is "a large blond girl who had an artificial leg" (170), that she is "thirty-two years old and highly educated" (170), and that she is a "poor stout girl in her thirties who had never danced a step or had any *normal* good times" (173). Most tellingly, at one point the narrator says Joy/Hulga is "someone who has achieved blindness by an act of will and means to keep it" (171), suggesting that her disabilities (she is not actually blind, but does have a severe heart condition) are both controllable and deliberate; as well, such language perpetuates the idea of Joy/Hulga as having in some way a disabled personality: she relates to a mythic lame character and she *strives* for blindness.

The title of the story, "Good, Country People," comes from Mrs. Hopewell's snobbish description of people she considers beneath her, yet whom she is willing to designate as good, simple, and honest. Mrs. Hopewell feels sorry for a traveling Bible salesman because he has a heart condition in a way she does *not* feel sorry for her daughter who also has a bad heart. Unlike Mrs. Hopewell's attitude to her daughter's *artificial* leg (which marks both Joy's physical disability and technological solution), her attitude toward her daughter's *weak* body part is of the Enlightenment model which suggests that "nobility" and "gentlefolk" have a moral duty to remain healthy (15–19). When Talcott Parsons describes sick people as not being "responsible" for their illness, he also argues that they are responsible for seeking a "cure" (96).

The title also ironically describes Joy's own views of her mother and friends; people she disdains in part because she has a Ph.D., yet desperately—for her own sense of superiority—needs to believe are both simple and good (i.e., simple and easily manipulated). When the door-to-door Bible salesman, Manley Pointer, befriends her, Joy/Hulga thinks that she will seduce and shock him, but that he is *too* innocent for her to corrupt. In fact, it is country folks' unquestioning decency to which she needs to feel superior: only one as wise in the world as she would recognize its corrupt nature. Her new friend, using Joy's own gullibility against her, tricks her into climbing into the barn loft and removing her wooden leg for show-and-tell, then strands her so that he will be long gone by the time someone finds her. The Bible salesman/con man leaves Joy/Hulga in a place that literally occupies higher ground, and also humiliates her. Rosemarie Garland-Thomson argues that the fact that "anyone can become disabled at any time makes disability more fluid, and perhaps more threatening" to those who identify themselves as possessing normative bodies than do "seemingly more stable marginal identities as femaleness, blackness, or nondominant ethnic identities" (*Extraordinary*, 14). Since the category of disability is one into which any able-bodied person can shift, those invested in hierarchies based on the dominant body (white and male, for example), create fictions to explain the Other's inferiority. Not only has a "simple" man deceived Joy/Hulga, but he has left her in a compromising position: rolling in the hay, waiting for a man who has stolen a piece of her body. Joy/Hulga's "predicament" becomes one which the "average reader" must *not* identify with, in order to find amusement at the story's conclusion.

O'Connor has herself admitted that summaries such as the one I present here make her story sound like a "low joke" (in Geddes, 370). In an essay on short story writing, she says of her own story: "The average reader is pleased to observe anybody's wooden leg being stolen" (370). This statement perhaps says more about what O'Connor thinks of the "average" reader than it does about her knowledge of disability, but it certainly admits to a perverse sense of humor and satisfaction that emerges from reading about someone else's disability that—apparently—could never happen to "you," the "average reader." O'Connor's short story, however, does far more than simply present a joke in bad taste. O'Connor states the strong point of "Good, Country People" is that of

> letting the wooden leg accumulate meaning. Early in the story, we're presented with the fact that the Ph.D. is spiritually as well as physically crippled. She believes in nothing but her own belief in nothing, and we perceive that there is a wooden part of her soul that corresponds to her wooden leg [Geddes, 370].

Although the narrator never refers to Joy/Hulga as "crippled," O'Connor nevertheless decides that a metaphorical presentation of moral character is best served through the complicated ways in which the "average reader" relates to, or identifies with, disability. The story contains Joy/Hulga through the *idea* of herself as crippled or damaged (the leg had been "literally blasted off" [174]), despite the absence of this label. Joy/Hulga—like the groups Linton describes as "reviving" the terms "cripple" and "crip" in order to label themselves through an identity that (quoting J.P. Shapiro) "scares the outside world the most" (in *Claiming Disability*, 17)—gives herself an "ugly" name to exteriorize her understanding of and identification with her own body.[10]

In this way, Joy's body symbolizes an undesirable aspect of her "inner" character. O'Connor sets up the story so that the "average reader" will find amusement in Hulga's distress, partly because she herself has been conned by belief, partly because the narrator presents her as a "damaged" human being, warped and disfigured by her own "misshapen" cynicism as much as by the man who steals body parts for his "oddities" collection. His parting words suggest that he never was the innocent country bumpkin both Joy and her mother snobbishly assumed him to be but, rather, a devious con man with his own agenda. "'I've gotten a lot of interesting things,' he said. 'One time I got a woman's glass eye this way. And you needn't to think you'll catch me because Pointer ain't really my name'" (195). Just like Hulga, he has changed his name to suit his purposes: she to reject a name that implies standard feminine beauty, and he to escape retribution for his previous thefts.

The construction of the overaged daughter as both awkwardly out of place and clumsily dependent secures her position as an unlikable and unsympathetic character. Garland-Thomson says that "gender, ethnicity, sexuality, and disability are related products of the same social processes and practices that shape bodies according to ideological structures" (*Extraordinary*, 136). In this way, the text represents the disabled main character in the story as physically "weak" through both ability and gender, yet "superior" in economics and education. Her physical "inferiority" and her class snobbery combine to form a character who—the "average reader" will conclude—gets what she deserves and deserves what she gets. Readers cheer for the rogue salesman because he has overturned the status quo— at least the economic one. In all other categories, this character remains what Foucault designates as the modern ideal of the "norm" to Joy/Hulga's marginalized body. Readers thus celebrate a character who bests the upper classes yet who still embodies a "normal" body.

The Bible salesman, Manley Pointer, first gets Mrs. Hopewell's attention by lamenting: "People like you don't like to fool with country people like me!" (179). His calculated statement makes her immediately want to distance herself from any perception (though accurate) of snobbery. He confesses that, unlike others, he does not sell these Bibles in order to get into college; in fact, he's only interested in devoting his life to "Chrustian" service. He further confesses: "I got this heart condition. I may not live long. When you know it's something wrong with you and you may not live long, well then, lady…" (180). Mrs. Hopewell's snobbish attitudes prevent her from regarding this man as a suitable "match" for her daughter, but she aligns the two of them because of their afflictions, and hopes Joy might learn a more positive outlook from the salesman. Hulga, though she thinks this man is entirely inferior to her (186), *does* see a connection between them; indeed, she trusts him with her wooden leg and with her own naïveté. Culture intersects with physical reality in the intersection of Joy/Hulga's disability with her gender. "Disabled girls and women," say Rubin Jeffrey Rubin in his foreword to *Women with Disabilities*, are "the denizens of this apparently worst-of-both-worlds combination of being female and being quintessentially unattractive through disability" (ix). Joy/Hulga may embrace a condescending attitude toward the seemingly innocent Bible salesman, but she too readily succumbs to his "simple" charms and finds herself the vulnerable (and jilted) lover. In fact, it is her belief in his "simplemindedness" that allows Joy/Hulga to be so easily duped. She places her physical disability on a higher plane than his intelligence, believing she has the independence of her mind and pitying others who do not. Ultimately, she conflates limited education with lesser intelligence, and lesser intelligence with lack of acumen. His deceit wounds her because she cannot fathom someone who presents an uncomplicated *and* devious mind.

David Mitchell and Sharon Snyder argue in their introduction to *The Body and Physical Difference* that the "bridge constructed by the ideology of the physical seeks to lure the reader/viewer into the mystery of whether discernible defects reveal the presence of an equally defective moral and civil character" (13). O'Connor herself glibly suggests that a physical "flaw" or "defection" necessarily announces a corresponding moral "defect." The "average" reader laughs *at* Joy/Hulga and *with* the devious Bible salesman because—despite his obvious disregard for the religion he peddles—*she* is the morally bankrupt character, she is the damaged soul, as signified by her wooden leg and her physical deficiency without it. Despite the patronizing pity O'Connor's "average reader" may feel for someone physically hampered at the conclusion of the narrative, the story indicates a certain triumph—of the uneducated over the learned and of the country bumpkin over the snob. Perversely, the story also maintains the status quo by offering the "average reader" a triumph of the able-bodied over the disabled, and of male over female. I suspect that much readerly satisfaction with the ending of this story may derive from the "underdog" male character swindling an overly confident and rude female character. The story depicts his conquest as "exceedingly hilarious" because a low-class man has put an uppity woman back in her place, and a "normal"-bodied character has revealed the disabled character for the "abnormality" she "truly" (deeply, fundamentally, and essentially) must be. Razack argues, in her attempt to identify and confront strategies of oppression, that the way to maintain the focus on avenues of domination is to do so "in a context-specific way that recognizes the interdependency of systems of oppression." As an example, she repeats a friend's question: "Could we have racism without sexism, heterosexism, ableism, and capitalism?" (Razack 22).

In the final scene of the story, Mrs. Hopewell, watching Manley Pointer head for the highway, remarks: "Why, that looks like that nice dull young man that tried to sell me a Bible yesterday.... He was so simple ... but I guess the world would be better off if we were all that simple" (195–196). The wooden leg that—for entirely practically purposes—once belonged to Joy/Hulga, has been triumphantly looted by a swindler who appropriates it for his own purposes, namely as a curiosity and souvenir, representative of his cunning nature. The Robber has won, the Lady has been humiliated, and the Fact of the disability has been abandoned up there in the hayloft, along with any semblance of a character who might, with the proper prosthesis, make her dignified way home. The story does not present to readers a woman disabled by a rogue preacher when he steals her leg. The meaning of the story, then, resides in its language as much as its plot. As Jay Dolmage writes in his book *Disability Rhetoric*, the idea of thesis "emphasizes the obliqueness of thought and suggests that the disabled body is the engine for the creation of meaning" (108). Ironically, Joy is punished and humiliated by the very symbol of her ruin—her prosthetic leg—which ultimately "means" more than the rest of her body. O'Connor's disabled character presents as subtext of an ableist gaze that seeks to disempower her mental capacities by reducing her character to one that is entirely located in her physical attributes.

Farrant's, O'Connor's and Lightman's narratives allow the reader to "blame" characters who are increasingly distressed by the modern world (Chalmers tries to "keep up" in a losing rat race, and Joy/Hulga disdains anyone who has not achieved her level of education) and Porter Jones wants to be ill. Disturbingly, though Lightman's novel may lead a reader to sympathize more with Chalmers than O'Connor's story does with Joy/Hulga or Farrant's does with Porter Jones, the texts depict all three characters as recognizably deserving of their fate; indeed, they invite it. The danger of this "narrative of cure" for any bodily circumstance outside the domain of healing is that such a narrative places blame onto the body of the disabled or ill subject. Conflating disability and illness makes them into one and the same experience. With the same gesture, mental illness and physical illness (or even high-tech stress and long-term infirmity) can combine into one, simplified package, coercing disability to mask as illness, and disease to represent itself as a "loss" of wellness and ability. Readers, then, have the easy task of consuming narratives that offer a complex representation of chronic illness, as narratives in which disability operates metaphorically or even allegorically.

These narratives "surprise" the reader, not so much with a twist ending, but with a textual uncovering that indicates a path towards the "real" or "true" defect in character that has caused each particular physical representation. The reader, like a clinical doctor, has become literary and medical "detective," who observes and gazes upon the "patient"/disabled character in order to decree a solution/cure. Each of these three fictions offer more power to the reader/viewer than to the character/patient who has become not only object in this investigative narrative, but embodied *clue*; and, in the form of clue, that body has been caught in the process of the medical gaze that insists (through medical judgment) upon curing the extra-normative bodily function that, ironically, has been "lost" from the normal body. Joy/Hulga is an immoral (or at the very least amoral) character whose missing limb signifies her lack of moral "health." Porter Jones reveals in the process of diagnosis. And Bill Chalmers is the progressively regressing invalid, incapacitated by his own inability to "figure out" his declining moral fiber.

Though these texts are written decades apart, they convey distrust for technology and for a reliance on the intellectual. The evils of the body reflect the evils of progress, of the mind that believes itself independent of its physical container, of consciousness divorced from the everyday social networks that play themselves out on the body (i.e., the physical and sensual roles each character has of daughter and lover, of husband and father, of nerdy lover). The ableist gaze in each becomes a verb that embodies a process of "seeing into" the soul, the essence, the moral core of characters who lack such an integral center. Mitchell and Snyder, in *Cultural Locations of Disability*, "associate ableism with ideological formulas that equate devalued bodily conditions with decreased social value" (18). Medical investigations, then, include the discovery of no invisible secret hidden in the recesses of the body's tissues. Instead, the secret clue to each character's "flaw" displays itself overtly in the character's physical and psychological "defectiveness." These texts—both through disability, and across illness—elucidate how "Othered" bodies invite "average readers" to interpret their differences as their entire identity. The body may appear to "betray" the protagonist, allowing societal pressure to infect from the inside-out, but to expand on Mitchell and Snyder's discussion of Melville, the body also maintains itself as a wedge able to distance itself from its own "seemingly stable social meanings" (51).

6

The Body in Pieces

*Lacan and the Crisis
of the Unified Fragmentary*

Hystericized Fragments

What is wrong with a body in parts, with the fragment?

In this chapter I argue, via an assortment of examples, that disability theory asks readers and viewers to rethink the fragmented body in the way the latter is represented culturally (in film, poetry, novels, the media), and within Lacanian theory. I will elaborate further on, but Lacan's reasoning in the mirror stage is that we are all fragmented—but we misrecognize ourselves as whole through the imaginary, through an imaginary notion of wholeness. A few years ago, I accompanied my then-three-year-old nephew to his pre-school classroom. The class consisted of twelve children. Each school day, the teacher "featured" a different child by inviting a parent or guardian to the classroom (as observer, but also as helper). The teacher would ask the day's featured child to do various things: sit in front during the picture book reading part of the day, lead the other children outside for play activity, and count—always by gender—the number of students in attendance that day (how many girls sit in the circle this morning? How many boys?). As my brother and his spouse had rarely made a point of remarking upon differences between the genders of their children, my nephew initially had difficulty recognizing a visible difference between boys and girls, in order to make an accurate count. As fall progressed, he began to display an anxiety about gender-restricted roles, becoming distraught if anyone in his family, for example, called the designated "father" character in a book "the mother," or vice versa.[1] My nephew began to cling to the normative ideals of gender difference displayed in picture books, even as those ideals in no way matched his own immediate family situation. "That's the GIRL," he'd tell me, because "he has long hair"[2]—holding his statement to be true even after I'd pointed out that both of his beloved teenage (male) cousins had long hair.

In this example, my three-year-old nephew has moved from being unable to distinguish genders among his classmates, to insisting on his being able to recognize absolute distinction between genders based on the way gender is portrayed, for example, in picture books. What I find so interesting about my nephew's anxiety is the gap he underscores between reality and representation. His anxiety is not directly over the realities of genital variation; rather, as he acquires the skills to distinguish between his classmates on the basis of gender, he transfers that confidence to the symbolic level of pictorial depictions of gender norms, depictions that resolve his anxiety through firm category divisions. Visual representations encourage a process of assimilation or rejection based on the subject's recognition (and interpellation of that recognition) of he/r own place within a gender matrix. Recognizing the power structure of gender difference, my nephew was struggling to pose the question "Am I a boy or a girl?" in order to acquiesce to that structure's demands, acquiring an anxiety about the positioning of sexual roles and appearances.

The dominant—which for Lacan "does not imply dominance"—for the hysteric appears in the form of a symptom. And it is around this symptom "that the hysteric's discourse is situated and ordered" (*Seminar XVII*, 43). Such language appears to pathologize the role of both analyst and hysteric, though the symptom in Lacanian theory is the subject's response to normative language. In the anecdote about my nephew, whether or not a person has an actual penis was not the issue (though the idea of the phallus may have been imaginatively present in his mind, his expressed anxiety appeared to arise from the need to "correctly" categorize gender based on gender *roles*; thus, the notion of an intersexed individual, or one with ambiguous genitalia, does not even make it into such a conversation). What was at stake for him was *how* a gendered character was represented, and then gender-appropriately labeled. Freud explains: "Sooner or later the [male] child, who is so proud of his possession of a penis, has a view of the genital region of a little girl, and cannot help being convinced of the absence of a penis in a creature who is so like himself. With this, the loss of his own penis becomes imaginable, and the threat of castration takes its deferred effect" ("Dissolution," 314). For Lacan, it is not so much the literal fear of castration that designates gender roles and adult sexuality but, rather, the foregrounding of the function of the phallus.

My nephew was struggling to answer the question, "Who is a boy and who is a girl?" just as Lacan cites as a primary question for the hysteric: "What is a woman?" (*Seminar III*, 161) because hysteria originates within the very idea of a subject's sexual location, and the perpetual anxiety concerning that sexual positioning. The clinical hysteric is a fragmented subject whose body exhibits an "imaginary anatomy" relying more on phantasy than on physiology. For Lacan, hysteria is not simply a diagnosis based on symptoms, but a discursive structure, from which the hysteric often desires to recreate a heterosexual norm. I turn, now, to disability studies to argue that a similar desire—for wholeness, completeness—also creates (and is often posed as re-creating) an able-bodied norm. This able-bodied norm inevitably denies all but the existent anatomy of two separate and distinct genders, and assumes disability as a state-of-being that has hysterically fragmented from an originary whole. In Lacan's Four Discourses, social bond overtakes the clinical structure. The hysteric, then, is no longer simply patient, but a schema for understanding how a subject is socially bound. And within that social bond, says Lacan, the analyst's role is "to 'hystericise' the discourse"; it is the "structural introduction, under artificial conditions, of the hysteric's discourse" (*Seminar XVII*, 33); the analyst's role is not simply to provide answers (i.e., cure), but to perpetuate the "*objet petit a*" of excessive questioning.

The Mirror Stage and Disability

In a talk in Brussels in 1977, "Remarks on Hysteria," Lacan comments:

> Where have they gone, the hysterics of yesteryear, those marvellous women, the Anna O.'s, the Emmy von N's…? Not only did they play a certain social role, but when Freud took to listening to them, it was they who permitted the birth of psychoanalysis. It was from listening to them that Freud inaugurated an entirely new mode of human relation. What replaces those hysteric symptoms of old? Is hysteria not displaced in the social field? [*Quarto*, 1].

For Lacan, as perhaps less blatantly for Freud, the hysteric directs the discourse of psychoanalysis as much as the analyst. The hysteric is not only a figure within discourse, but a (female) gendered being, even when that female gender may come to him in a male body: "([A]nd the male hysteric? one doesn't find one who is not a female)" (*Quarto*, 2). By describing a heterosexual construction of sex and sexuality, Lacan appears to remain fixed within a patriarchal model, though he does point out that there are "several types of castration": "[W]e know that for us jouissance is castration. Everyone knows it, because it is quite obvious: after what we call without considering it the sexual act (as if there were an act there!), after the sexual act, one loses one's hard-on" (*Quarto*, 4). Thus phallic jouissance is also a form of lack, but after the sexual act men cannot hide their lack by way of an imaginary phallus. As Nancy Gillespie says, "[J]ust because men may have a penis does not mean that they are *not* lacking because their relationship with their penis as an erect object is not fixed" (private correspondence).

For numerous feminists, the notion of the woman as assuming the role of "lack" has been, to say the least, problematic. As Freud has famously written: "A female child, however, does not understand her lack of a penis as being a sex character; she explains it by assuming that at some earlier date she had possessed an equally large organ and had then lost it by castration" ("Dissolution," 315). Just as one absorbs and thus performs gender through an identification with, and contrast to, the Other, so too does one (for Lacan, during the crucial mirror stage) absorb and perform notions of morphological wholeness and normativity. Lacan's proposed mirror stage takes place in the infant at around six to eighteen months; he suggests that a subject's sense of the body as whole and unified is cultivated even before that subject recognizes and absorbs gender as a major signifier of he/r identity. I focus on this well-investigated theory of Lacan's because I find it significant that, according to Lacan, a child's sense of wholeness happens before any sense of sexual differentiation. Thus it is the desire for an ideal body (configured through the child's interpretation of the mother's body as whole and complete) that precedes any sexual desire for the Other. It is his realization that the mother has a desire beyond the child that leads to Lacan saying that man's desire is the desire of the Other. And when Lacan uses the metaphor of the fragmented body in his argument, he assumes that the bodily experience of fragmentation is traumatic to the child. Lacan insists that experiencing such fragmentation is an important part of analysis. Part of the process of analysis is an acceptance of fragmentation, to overcome the imaginary illusion of wholeness. Margrit Shildrick, in her book on disability and sexuality, points out that Lacan's imagining of the fragmented body in the mirror stage reminds readers not so much of actual disabled bodies, but "certainly of the sociocultural fantasies that have always surrounded disability" (91). The trope of disability as negative, abject, and tragic is nothing if not a resilient one.

Like many feminist theorists, I question psychoanalytic readings of the female body. Such a "lack" might be because of the troublesome relationship in Lacan between the signified and the Symbolic. In her important feminist scrutiny of Lacan, Elizabeth Grosz notes, "[W]hile providing arguably the most sophisticated and convincing account of subjectivity, psychoanalysis itself is nevertheless phallocentric in its perspectives, methods, and assumptions" (3). Grosz acknowledges that Freud in many ways articulated the beginnings of women's social and psychical experiences within patriarchal cultures. "Yet," she cautions, psychoanalysis "has also contributed to women's increasing hystericization and their subsumption under male norms" (7). Grosz concludes that psychoanalysis may be subject to "far-reaching feminist questioning" (7). Further, as with disability theorists, I remain wary of Lacanian readings of the "imaginary anatomy" proscribed to the hysteric. Tobin Siebers, in *Disability Theory*, talks about the able body being "the true image of the Other" (60). For me, thinking through poetry, subjectivity, and agency requires thinking through disability in terms of the "problem body," my term that refers to multiple representations of the disabled body. There is a scarcity of Lacanian discourse in most disability discussions (with the significant exception of Margrit Shildrick[3]) and, although many theorists turn to psychoanalysis—especially when analyzing film—for an evaluation and critique of normalized subjectivity, Lacan and Freud make only cameo appearances. However, there are some key exceptions which I will address here.

Michael Davidson iterates some of these feminist concerns. In speaking of what he terms the "phantom limb" within 1940s Hollywood film noir, he flags "psychoanalytic models that generalize the connection of bodies and sexualities around narratives of loss and lack" (*Concerto* 64). One example he cites is Claire Johnston, who interprets the title sequence of Billy Wilder's *Double Indemnity* (1944)—which depicts a man advancing on crutches toward the viewer—as "plac[ing] the movie 'under the sign of castration.'" Says Davidson: "By equating visibility and acts of looking with castration, by equating feminine 'lack' with physical difference, this theoretical approach always renders the missing limb as a missing phallus" (64). There is a convention in film noir criticism, he argues, of suturing the "incomplete" physically disabled male character onto the psychologically "incomplete" woman (64). Such a wounded masculinity, sutured onto the femme fatale, alters her femininity. She is not just psychologically incomplete, but her lack of conventional femininity projects her as usually murderous. Davidson allows one to read the "phantom limb" of film noir as instead "residual sensation of narratives that the film cannot represent" (60), a reading that is not possible to do if one conceives of this limb as the missing phallus alone. Davidson cautions critics not to use a psychoanalytic model in such a way that it overlooks the complexities entailed in the representation and reception of disability. But I also want to extend his argument to say that by *arguing against* Freudian and Lacanian theories (i.e., vehemently objecting to definitions of women as castrated, for instance), some feminist theorists—including Mulvey, Williams, and de Lauretis—perpetuate a horror-stricken response to disability as belonging to the realm of the Other, an abject position which their own theories thus reject.

A disability approach to castration problematizes the Freudian reduction (and the feminist rejection) of women to lack of penis. Pivotal for film theory is Laura Mulvey's "Visual Pleasure and Narrative Cinema" essay, in which she argues that in film, "Woman's desire is subjected to her image as bearer of the bleeding wound. She can exist only in relation to castration and cannot transcend it" (7). Mulvey inadvertently equates disability with the objectified feminine position, and in doing so perpetuates an ableist stance. In describing her role in analysis and in human sexual relations, Lacan says of the hysteric: "[S]he is the fall, the fallen object, fallen as an effect of discourse, which in turn is always broken at some point"; the discourse is broken by the hysteric (*Seminar XVII*, 34). Though operating at a metaphorical level, his description nevertheless moves through the equation: woman→ fallen object→ broken/fragmented, which arguably enables a Mulveyian reading, but I read this fragmentation as not necessarily deleterious. Davidson complicates Mulvey's argument by pointing out the role of disability in Mulvey's film examples, specifically, Hitchcock's *Rear Window* (1954): "In [the Lacanian] terms made familiar by Mulvey, [the protagonist] overcomes his physical limitation—his impotent position in a wheelchair—by focusing his gaze on solving a crime and by his controlling [his girlfriend's] actions in his line of sight" (66). At the same time, Davidson's larger point is that there are many ways "that disability in a compulsorily heterosexual and ableist world is figured as feminine" (68). As such, it would be far more useful, I think, for feminist critics to reassess the potential of aligning arguments, sensibilities, and critiques to discourses that investigate "problem" bodies rather than to discourses that present psychoanalysis simply as failing women by subjugating them into the apparently offensive category of "lack." By thinking of the female body as existing within the greater notion of a problem body, one can begin to realign marginalized bodies as fitting within a corporeal spectrum. The argument, then, isn't simply to rethink the feminine against the automatically disqualifying masculinist discourse. Rather, my aim is to align the hysteric's discourse within a disability-centered critical discourse.

Staging the Body as the "Unified Fragmentary"

In conventional storytelling, a disabled character predominantly takes on the role of what David Mitchell and Sharon Snyder deem "narrative prosthesis."[4] Extending their ideas, Davidson says: "If narrative closure depends on restoration of the able-bodied individual (to health, society, normalcy), the disabled character represents a form of physical deviance necessary for marking the body's unruliness" (45) and, I would add, for marking the so-called normative body as that much more "whole."[5]

A conventional fantasy of disability that still circulates in most cultures is that there was once a cohesive, able body that is now disabled and but a fragment of a former unified self.[6] This fantasy includes popular television shows such as *Monk* and *House M.D.*, Hollywood blockbusters such as *Million Dollar Baby* (2004) and *Avatar* (2009), novels from the canonical *Jane Eyre* to *The Day of the Triffids*, and also literary theorists who continue to invoke the disabled body as ubiquitous metaphor for all manners of a "fallen" human being. Anthony Easthope, in summarizing Lacan's mirror stage, suggests that "[d]ry-mouthed terror at the possibility of your body coming to bits" is "fundamental to human experience" (60). Easthope quotes Lacan himself as imagining this experience as "the worst thing in the world" (60), and enthuses to readers about such an evaluation of fragmentation as a "dazzling insight" (60). Indeed, when Lacan discusses the images that represent aggressive mental phenomena in the mirror stage, he writes that these are "images of castration, mutilation, dismemberment, dislocation, evisceration, devouring, bursting open of the body, in short, the *imagos* that I have grouped together, under the apparently structural term of *imagos of the fragmented body* (*Écrits*, 9).[7] Lacan himself speaks of such fear as defensive against fragmented subjectivity, which offers some explanation of why ableist responses to a disabled body persist in most popular culture. Like the master's discourse, ableist discourse hides its own lack. One can't always dismiss these representations as genre conventions, for they implicate political and social realities in complicated but undeniable ways. In spring 2010, Ozzy Osbourne released *Scream*, songs composed on the theme of death. The tenth track, "Mercy," is Osbourne's response to the Canadian case of Saskatchewan farmer Robert Latimer's filicide of his daughter, Tracy. Said Osbourne in a recent interview with journalist Sandra McCulloch, "It must be a very difficult thing when you give birth to a child that is so messed up, she doesn't have any quality of life" (McCulloch). Not having met either Tracy or Robert, Osbourne assumes that—because Tracy had cerebral palsy—Robert Latimer conceived of his action (the attempt to end his daughter's life) as an act of mercy.

When issues of disability confront parental rights over their children's lives, parents who kill their disabled children are often portrayed in the media as neutral, or even as merciful, rather than as murderous—as they would be were their children considered "normal." Underlying the power of this neutrality is a historical narrative that plays a formative role in constructing disability as an unwanted or pitiful Other, a tragedy perceived as so profound that eliminating it is considered a preferable option to supporting the ways and means of living with disability. The seeming neutrality practiced by the media in fact keeps citizens in ignorance about how the media's portrayal of stories such as the Latimer case revive unseemly histories from the cultural past, histories of eugenics and euthanasia. The legacy of eugenics is that certain stories mask murder as euthanasia, while never straying far from the discourse of "mercy" killing. In 1993, Robert Latimer killed Tracy Latimer by putting her in his truck and inserting a hose from the truck's exhaust pipe into the truck's cab. In the controversy that followed his arrest, repeated media reports announced that Robert Latimer so loved his daughter he could not bear to watch her suffer. He was depicted as a caring father who loved his child "too much,"[8] who wanted only the best for his child, and believed death was better than the life of pain she faced. For Robert Latimer, his daughter's body signified a failure of the normal.

When Robert Latimer's case was (finally) tried for the last time by the Supreme Court of Canada in 2001, the jury gave a unanimous ruling (7–0) of guilty, convicting him of second-degree murder. *Globe and Mail* columnist Jan Wong wrote that she "would have done what Robert Latimer did" (A4). She goes on to describe a time when she was pregnant, when for one hour she thought she might have a "Down's Syndrome baby." Going through that hour, she says, gave her a "hint of what Mr. Latimer must have gone through" (A4). Ironically, Wong's words are more telling than she perhaps intended, revealing her own inability to parent any child but a physically and mentally "normal" one. Her musings, then, disclose the ways in which she not only expects a "normal" child, but the radical "solutions" she might embrace were her child not to fit in a societal spectrum of the norm. In a chapter on the ethics of surgically shaping children, "Thoughts on the Desire for Normality," Eva Kittay writes: "The price of normalcy and the cost of avoiding what is not normal are high, especially when surgical procedures, often repeated, are intrusive, painful, time-consuming, emotionally wrenching, minimally helpful in improving the body's functionality (and sometimes, as in the case of genital surgery, impede function), and expensive" (90). In seeking to achieve physical normalcy for their children, parents who opt for risky surgery reveal that—as much as normality is often paired with banality—avoiding physical abnormality is worth corporeal risk. Kittay argues that the relationship between what is normal and what is desired is filled with ambivalence (92), in that "the descriptive and objective senses of the term [normal] are in fact infused with prescriptive and subjective elements" (94).

In thinking about having her child, how close to the norm does the fetus have to be, for the potential parents to want it? In Wong's *Globe and Mail* article, disappointment, anxiety, and fear derive not from empathy for a disabled child and for the role of parenting such a child, but for herself as an idealized mother—judged as a "failure" who cannot produce a "normal" child[9] and as a parent who may face extra "duties" in order to offer caring treatment to a disabled child. In addition, that Wong likens the killing of a twelve-year-old girl to an abortion, is troubling to say the least. Wong shifts attention from the murdered female victim (Tracy Latimer) to the choice a woman—not yet a parent—might make about her ongoing pregnancy.[10]

In Terry Trueman's young adult novel, *Stuck in Neutral*, the narrator, Shawn, has "severe" cerebral palsy. So "severe"[11] that he has absolutely no control over any of his muscles. His mother and siblings entirely care for his physical self and, though he loves them in return, he has no way of conveying that information, nor do they perceive his desire to communicate at all. To the reader, Shawn tells his story humorously and with narrative panache. Despite experts' repeated "diagnoses" of Shawn as having a cognitive disability, Shawn tells the reader that he is in fact closer to a genius than he is to the sub-average intellectual functioning that psychologists bestow upon him (4–5). He is an extremely bright character but, according to his own analysis, one whose intelligence is "trapped" (12) in a body that won't behave in any way he wants it to. Shawn *is* "trapped" in that he himself has a story to tell, but no one in his social world can access that story, or even knows he has a story to tell; most of Shawn's family and social workers treat him as if he is, indeed, what he calls an "idiot" (11). Shawn is a cheerful optimist who enjoys his life, his social milieu, and his family. Yet despite Shawn's pleasure and satisfaction with his life, his father has decided to kill Shawn "out of love." Shawn critiques his father's justification for murder by making clear what will be *Shawn's* consequences in such a narrative: "[W]hatever the wonderfulness of his motives, I'll be dead" (12). The narrative turns, then, on Shawn's self-evaluation and on his father's investment in delivering Shawn through what he purports is an act of mercy. Although the book feeds into a plethora of narratives about the "right" of disabled characters to die,[12] it departs from most such narratives by making the disabled character the protagonist.

What I call the "unified fragmentary" is the disabled body that ostensibly represents the notion of missing or lack, but at the same time is presumed to maintain a unity in the midst of such deficiency. In other words, people with disabilities are expected to embody corporeal consistency: their lives should be completely given over to representing one fragment of existence as if that fragment itself unifies their representation. I'm thinking, for example, of the shocked reactions from the non-disabled who witness someone in a wheelchair momentarily getting up, or who notice that someone who walks with a cane or a seeing-eye dog may stop to read street signs. Given the binary construction of a disabled body versus an able-body, narratives rarely—if ever—leave room for what Fred Wah refers to as "inbetweenness" (103).[13] You are paralyzed or you are not. You can stand or you cannot stand. A perfect example of such expectation for either/or is the situation of Miss Wheelchair Wisconsin 2005. "Caught" standing, when a local newspaper published a picture of her teaching her class, Janeal Lee was stripped of her crown and asked to return the scooter she used for mobility. According to one Associated Press website, Lee is "a muscular dystrophy sufferer who uses a scooter as her main way to get around but says she can walk up to 50 feet on a good day and stand while teaching." But organizers dismissed her as eligible for their contest because of public reaction to a photo of her *not* in her scooter. As long as the idea of the fragmentary remains contained within the construction of a stable, able-bodied world, it does not carry power to unsettle the boundary of the normal.

The unified fragmentary, then, is not so much a demand for one kind of body or another, *this* [adj.] body or *that* [adj.] body, so much as a societal response to the crisis of meaning that exists in that gap (similar to the gap between representation and reality) between a body that signifies a particular subjectivity (for example, a white cane signifies blindness) and an action that contradicts the binary extreme of such signification (for example, a blind person who can make out street signs). Fragmented subjectivity doesn't seem to have the same appeal on critics' imaginations when referring to illness or disability. When it comes (especially) to disability, one is either wholly disabled or not (fragmented or whole), with very little discussion about the fluidity of body ranges, types, and abilities.

Poetry and Disability

While the fragment as metaphor for the body remains predominantly a negative one in the larger culture, I now turn to how poets write about the fragmented subject[14] and about fluid sexuality that cannot easily be encased in an either/or binary. I turn to disability theory as a method of reading contemporary poetry. Lisa Robertson, in *The Weather*, writes:

> The rain has loosened; we engage our imagination. The sentence opens inexpensively; we imagine its silence. The shrubs and fences begin to darken; we are deformed by everything. Therefore we're mystic. The sky is closing in; we mediate an affect. The sky is curved downward; we desituate memory. The sky is dominant; we lop off the image. We come upon our thought. The sky is lusty; so are we [38].

Here, "deformity," along with the negatively metaphorical "darken," signify the poet situating herself against an all-encompassing normative. In situating such language up against its putative neutral as well as negative context, Robertson invokes—albeit ironically—the age-old cliché of disability as marking one's psyche as much as it does one's body: "[W]e are deformed by everything. Therefore we're mystic." At the same time, she plays, tongue-in-cheek, with literary notions of pathetic fallacy. By embodying "us" as lusty-like-the-location, the poem allows for a disability-centered desire to prevail: "we" are deformed and "we" are lusty. Yet who gets included in this "we"? Shildrick notes that it is a "very common complaint," that representations of disability "veer between the asexual and the hypersexual" (86). If we are deformed, we must, then, be excessively sexual. Or at least hearty. So much of the poetry that interests me rejects notions of a complete subject, and thus fits neatly into Lacan's model of the hysteric's discourse. The "we" shifts from ubiquitous everybody, to a displaced I/you discourse. As Žižek pointedly says in *How to Read Lacan*, "Hysteria emerges when a subject starts to question or to feel discomfort in his or her symbolic identity" (35).

And in what ways might Meredith Quartermain's *Vancouver Walking* be reframed by imaging a persona who wheels, rather than walks, through the city?[15] In her book, Quartermain fuses history onto the contemporary vista of an urban city that stubbornly ignores its own chronicles of the past as she challenges readers to gaze backwards at the bodies the city's progress has discarded and disregarded (the trope of *seeing* is also vital to this book). The poem invokes a critique of commerce and a poetic interruption to an imaginary "step-by-step" municipal narrative of progress, which allows only for an ableist pedestrian. In "Walk to commercial drive," for example, the poem advises the persona or readers (or possibly the historical Chinese workers, who immigrated to Canada to construct that country's "dream" of a national railroad, and were killed in the Fraser Canyon) to, "Run quick. The train's back" (11). Its form still presents the ever-changing vistas as easily accessible, as a place where mobility is never a problem, where walking, absolutely, is a viable political alternative to blithely "driving by" people and actions that don't fit the capitalist market agenda.

As a final example, I turn to Nikki Reimer's overly fragmented and hystericized female body in her chapbook, *fist things first*. I here quote from her poem "uterus":

> to reproduce nineteen hundred catholic embryos. containment vessel sometimes harbours fugitive organs. my uterus sits sideways but not a revolutionary angle. if he hung three days bloodless defer the lining. adjust midway angle, don't assume oval. womb not recommended for dinner by three out of four.
>
> to finish the term take cortisone and tylenol. Joanne endures lupus antibodies, assume squatter's womb, then murder. undulate nine months and two months and three months and. squeeze the membrane. wait six years to bear the christ child over the river. tilt sideways. collect the umbilical cord. leave [7].

Her poem takes on the various roles assigned to women in religion, medicine, and contemporary culture. "In Lacanian theory," says Paul Verhaeghe, "there is no such thing as a truth which can be completely put into words" (5). Reimer's poem tries not to encompass its "truth" through absolute statements, but instead presents excessive iterations of what Lacan calls the "half-speaking truth" (Verheghe, 5), half-speaking, because knowledge functions as the impossible goal of the Real. Verhaeghe says that "hysteria as a social bond puts the impossibility of desire to the forefront" (10), making a master out of the Other. I read the "hysterical" in this poem as confronting and challenging the role of medical and religious evaluations of the subject's body, not as mastering these evaluations. When the medicalized female patient—undulating nine months, then two months, then three months—seeks treatment, she is treated within and by this system as demanding a master. Meanwhile, her representative power to bear the christ child is dependent on her role as both virgin and maternal Other. Lacan's solution—the analyst discourse as paradoxical knowing—is for the analysand to endlessly construct and reconstruct herself. Meanwhile, suggests Reimer, the uterus tilts, the revolution waits. Verhaeghe describes the four discourses via Freud's "formula of three impossible professions: '*Edukieren, Regieren und Analysieren*'" (13). Says Verhaeghe, "[T]o educate, that's the university discourse, to govern, the master discourse, and to analyze, the analytic discourse, each giving rise to a particular brotherhood" (13), and he points out that Freud forgot "the most obvious one, the one which holds us together on a mass scale, namely to desire" (13). But what we desire, within Lacan's model, is imposed upon us as much when we speak as when we are spoken to. Reimer's helpful advice to "leave" at the end of her poem is presented ironically, as we are all trapped inside ideology. Yet her words do still allow for a feminist critique within wide-reaching medical discourse. Immediately after mentioning "his" bloodless lining, the poem advises that the "womb [is] not recommended for dinner by three out of four." But that fourth—whether impossibly functioning analyst or ever-frenzied hysteric—ah, that fourth recommendation digs in and consumes the womb for supper with gusto! By insisting on binary epistemology, the unified fragmentary does not allow for diverse forms and functions of the body.

A Bathroom Story

Let me offer, as a sort of bookend, another kid anecdote in which a child internalizes and projects gendered societal regulations: A few years ago, one of my students told me about her sister, who had just started elementary school. After a week of first grade, this young sister started insisting that the family observe separately sexed bathrooms at home. She drew a picture of a man and a woman, and asked her sister to tape one drawing on each of their home's two bathrooms. She did not require that one bathroom specifically represent one gender (i.e., that the smaller be for one gender, or that the upstairs bathroom be used by one gender), but only that absolute gender division was to be maintained. If anyone in the family used the "wrong" bathroom, she would become very upset and explain to her sibling or parent that men need to use the Boys' and women need to use the Girls'.

Lacan observes that one's "public life is subject to the laws of urinary segregation" (*Écrits* 115). "By contrast with public spaces," argues Mary Anne Case, "few private homes in the western world rigidly segregate toilet facilities by sex: Even when invited to a home with multiple bathrooms, for example, dinner party guests are rarely directed to different ones depending on their sex" (Case 224, fn8). Case invokes Lacan to argue about the liminal passage that bathroom users imagine but cannot enter. Siebers notes: "Had Lacan visualized an accessible restroom at the train station, he would have had to tell a different story. More often than not accessible toilets are unisex. There are no Ladies and Gentlemen among the disabled because the ideology of ability conceives of people with disabilities ungendered and asexual" (168). Siebers argues that the practice of using "unisex accessible toilets exposes the fact that able-bodiedness overdetermines the assignment of gender" (168), as well as reflecting a common belief that gender (and by association, sexuality) is not important for disabled people. Says Siebers: "In the game of signifying practices, the difference between ability and disability trumps the difference between Ladies and Gentlemen every time" (168). But that trump is exactly the crux of agitating for "separate" bathrooms. Case describes how John Howard Griffin "repeatedly describes the colored restroom both as a place of sociability with others "black like me" and as a refuge from the insults of the white world" (10). But, she argues, that "colored" bathrooms could operate as a haven from racism cannot be an argument for such segregation.

In his short story, "UPDIKE," Neil Wood satirizes John Updike's story "A&P."[16] Wood writes of a teenage employee, Lenny, who becomes fascinated with three transvestite customers at the donut shop where he works: the "Catholic school girl queen," the "hooker queen," and the "king queen of the queens" (51) When they get up to go to the bathroom, Lenny cannot see which of the three (the pisser, the ladies, or the supply closet) doors they choose. The narrator's boss pointedly tells him to go clean the bathrooms, presumably to ensure the customers have chosen the "correct" door. But Lenny only cleans the men's, and so does not have to confront the customers. When the three re-emerge, the manager chastises them for using the "wrong" bathroom, explaining that "the ladies washroom is for ladies only. The men's is for men" (57). Ignoring their flamboyant outfits, the manager continues, "You're obviously men. If you come back in here again, use the men's bathroom. It's simple. This is just one more thing your parents should've taught you. Boys washrooms are for boys. Girls are for girls. I don't care what you do in your private life, okay? Your private life is private but when you're here, you're going to have to act certain ways and that means using the proper facilities" (58). Regardless of their gender choice, the manager decrees that they have no choice when it comes to entering the "right" bathroom. Their "real" tits be damned, the assumption of their dicks dictates where they may pee, even if "using the proper facilities" is for make-up purposes only.

Sick at his own complicity in this scene, Lenny makes his way to the bathrooms, and runs for the utility closet where he vomits into a bucket. His "choice" effectively reflects how often the binary gender bathroom choice is inadequate for a spectrum of the body's purposes, desires, and needs. The narrator, turned on by "my queens," ultimately lets his manager humiliate them because they have the audacity to prefer the ladies' washroom to the men's. Having participated in degrading them, Lenny himself opts for the third door.

This idea of a "third" door in public washrooms is complicated and tantalizing. For me, what it serves as is an infinitely constructive option—especially for Case, who makes a claim for de-gender-segregated bathrooms—is Case's proposal of the "handicapped stall" as "solution" to the persistent anxiety in choosing between this excremental either/or gap. Case asks readers to consider the establishment of "relatively spacious, single stall, fully enclosed public toilets" that operate as "Family/Handicapped/Unisex." Such toilets, she argues, allow family members as well as caregivers of one sex to assist children or disabled adults of the opposite sex (Case cites as examples that reveal the problems of two-gendered public bathrooms: a mother sending her young son into the Men's Room alone, an adult son who must wait outside the Women's Room for his mother who has Alzheimer's). Such toilet arrangements, Case argues, also relieve the anxious dilemmas of devout Muslims who observe ritual ablutions, and transgendered or otherwise gender-fluid subjects. "After all," she writes, "walking into a toilet segregated by sex requires that each of us in effect self-segregate by hanging a gendered sign on ourselves" (7–8).[17] What fascinates me in Case's article advocating de-gendered public bathrooms is the way in which disability opens up a third option. The disability stall provides a solution to those subjects for whom the either/or option of male/female is insufficient. Male/female/disabled/whole. Disability, then, provides a "solution" to gender binaries. Perhaps a hysterical response to overly coded engendering. Perhaps the hysteric's only access to privacy from the overly coded discourse of "cure." Perhaps.

7

The Narrator Witness

Dis/connections Between Disability and Death

Dying to Tell

In the Spanish film *Mar Adentro* (*The Sea Inside*, dir. Amenábar, 2004), protagonist Ramón Sampedro (Javier Bardem) petitions his nation's courts for the right to die. He argues that, because he is paralyzed from the neck down, he does not enjoy the "choice" of death available to able-bodied citizens. The film's depiction of Ramón as a noble hero fighting against church-infused bureaucracy calls out for sustained critique, especially as Ramón constantly reminds visitors that he does not wish to judge other quadriplegics, but that he only wishes to achieve his own death, yet the film's focus is only on this one character's desire to die. The shot of Ramón arriving at the court steps is a complexly telling one. Contrasting the scene inside the building—where Ramón's lawyer eloquently argues for the right of someone like Ramón Sampedro, who "deems his condition as degrading," to take his own life—the scene outside serves as a tribute to euthanasia. As Ramón approaches the building, reporters surround him and the camera pans to the crush of demonstrators, which consists entirely of able-bodied people, many holding signs that demand: "Decriminalize Euthanasia Now." As the reporters lionize Ramón by giving him a public forum, the backdrop re-establishes what Ramón's petition is actually about: not, as the film (and Ramón) constantly reiterate, the right of an individual to kill himself—for not once does Ramón challenge Spain's actual suicide laws—but, rather, for the right to *assisted* suicide. The challenge, then, is for the courts *not* to prosecute friends and family members who assist in the death of a disabled individual.

In Amenábar's film—Oscar and Golden Globe winner for Best Foreign Language Film in 2004—the protagonist is "heroically" determined to kill himself. This highly crafted biopic manages to embody the ideal self that real-life Ramón purportedly strived to achieve. Every character in the film who celebrates and admires Ramón is able-bodied. Besides members of his family, the single character who contradicts his standpoint is a wheelchair-bound priest, a caricatured figure who leaves audiences convinced that the official stance of the church on such matters has become obsolete, and that the *only* contradictory standpoint on assisted suicide is a religious one. Interestingly, the film portrays Ramón's attorney, Julia, as suffering from the degenerative disease CADASIL. At one point, she decides to join Ramón in suicide, but later changes her mind. Unlike Ramón, who is not sick, Julia has a disease that is progressive; she will continue to experience a series of strokes and, eventually, succumb to dementia. Her role in the film is to act as Ramón's love interest and to represent a fearful foil to his unwavering determination. The film ends not with Ramón's suicide (that occurs in the penultimate scene) but, rather, with Ramón's friends visiting Julia at her lovely seaside home. They bring a final letter to her from Ramón. Julia turns a blank face to her visitors and tragically asks, "Ramón who?" Her words reinforce the by-now obvious point that she has made the *wrong* choice in refusing death. By conflating these two extremes as disabled characters' only choices and starkly contrasting their ultimate ramifications, the film conflates illness and disability, suggesting that all able-bodied people should react to any variety of physical conditions in exactly the same way. Julia is an able-bodied character living through ongoing strokes, while Ramón is a disabled character who does not suffer physical pain or a cognitive disability.[1] By the end of Amenábar's film, however, Julia has become the visual representation of Ramón's unchosen fate. She literally embodies the tragic result of his failed "heroic" crusade.

The Sea Inside can be productively juxtaposed with Julian Schnabel's *Le Scaphandre et le papillon* (*The Diving Bell and the Butterfly*, 2007). The protagonist, Jean-Dominique Bauby (Mathieu Amalric), is a character who has become disabled because of a life-threatening stroke. Based on Bauby's memoir of the same name, *The Diving Bell and the Butterfly* received much critical attention, winning Best Foreign Language Film and Best Motion Picture Director at the Golden Globes in 2007. Each text establishes internally diverse, contradictory viewpoints on the contentious issue of the "right to die" and, for that matter, on the very definition of what constitutes a livable life. Such complicated narrative layerings suggest that how one tells the story of "self" determines the "value" of that story and that life. *The Sea Inside* ostensibly presents the story of a Spanish man who decides that his life is so unlivable that he would, to use media-driven parlance, be "better off dead."[2] Conversely, *The Diving Bell and the Butterfly* presents its French protagonist as a noble "super-crip" who faces a trying life with no control over any of the muscles in his body, with the exception of his left eye. The film moves between scenes that emphasize Bauby as "trapped" in a body that cannot move and flashbacks that celebrate Bauby's former self as a charismatic rogue. I find it illuminating, in turn, to bring these two film narratives into dialogue with a prose memoir that is politically, culturally, and ethically engaged with the everydayness of living with the disabling effects of terminal illness. Canadian poet Frank Davey's *How Linda Died* (2002) recounts one woman's dying year through the narration of her husband's notes and recordings of her ideas, ideals, and wishes, all celebrating Linda's body, however diminished, due to an invasive and inoperable brain tumor. Here, the protagonist's story—if, indeed, Linda and not Frank Davey is the protagonist—is told by her male spouse.[3] In contrast to Ramón and Jean-Dominique, Linda does not rage predominantly against the lack of sexual activity her new body enables; rather, she rages against dying, most particularly against the feared future loss of sensual delight.

The Norm in Dis/ease

Jean-Do, in *The Diving Bell and the Butterfly*, laments the sensual loss Linda fears she will experience, and in so doing, re-establishes his heteronormativity, his masculine delight in consuming food, wine, sex. Throughout *The Sea Inside*, Ramón equates his paralysis with emasculation. He says to the lawyer who has come to help him with his case (and with whom he's falling in love) that he was unwilling to love—to be in love, or to let his girlfriend from before his accident to continue to love him—"in this condition." In addition to the "castrated" male disabled body constructed as "not quite" masculine enough, disabled bodies have also been devalued in the media as, in many ways, "not quite" human enough. Paul Longmore, in *Why I Burned My Book*, writes that the North American pro-suicide movement is "a generally unquestioning adoption and reinforcement of social prejudices against people with disabilities, the elderly, and even sick people" (150).

Nearly four decades ago, Susan Sontag incisively made the now-

obvious argument that cancer has been used as a metaphor for social problems. She cites, for example, politicians invoking "cancer" as the radical
evil that governments must rail against (82). The use of illness as metaphor,
Sontag argues, encourages "fatalism and justifies 'severe' measures" (81).
Similarly, Lennard Davis points out that derogatory disability metaphors,
even as writers reject their use when writing about disability, continue to
be invoked to display and critique social ills.[4] The preservation of such
discourse in metaphors reinscribes the disabled character as somehow
embodying the evils that the metaphors invoke. Linking the metaphorical
weight of disability and illness encourages each to be dependent on the
other in order to construct meaning in narrative. Thus, disability and illness have been conflated in such a way that each not only perpetuates the
idea of the other, but each also serves as (unquestioned) metaphor for the
other. *The Sea Inside* proves that such prejudicial conflations persist while,
in contrast, Davey's *How Linda Died* rejects any comparison of her illness
with disabling metaphors, even as her cancer impairs more and more of
Linda's physical and mental abilities.

In *How Linda Died*, Linda initially reads her cancer diagnosis as a
vehicle guiding her toward disability; yet, as the memoir progresses, readers see her eliciting more and more pleasurable sensations from her body
and rejecting her own earlier interpretation of illness as somehow dishon-
orable. Both *The Sea Inside* and *The Diving Bell and the Butterfly* depict
paralyzed middle-aged men, devoid of physical sexual activity but, at the
same time, sexually attracted to the beautiful women who visit them. To
establish these two characters as sexually appealing, the films construct
them as *potentially* virile, ironically convincing audiences of the protagonists' normative heterosexuality even as the films depict their bodies as
having "lost" an essential masculinity.

Disability critic Robert McRuer points out that queer characters are
often understood as somehow disabled, in a medicalization of identity
while healthy disabled characters are typically understood as ill or sick
("Compulsory," 93–94). In a comparable identity process,[5] healthy disabled
characters are typically "understood" as ill or sick, in the same process of
"ongoing medicalization." Just as Laura Mulvey (1975) argues that the par-
adox of phallocentrism is that the symbolically castrated woman gives
order and meaning to its world (6), McRuer, in his book *Crip Theory*,
argues that the prominent figure of the whole and healthy male depends
on the equally strong yet often invisible image of the immobile, dependent,
and "castrated" male. Invoking Adrienne Rich's vocabulary, McRuer proposes the term "compulsory able-bodiedness" (1–32)[6] to argue that disability

and queerness are similarly invoked to both challenge and reaffirm the white heterosexual male. Not surprisingly, this "compulsory" identity revolves around the notion of "normal" and its insidious twin, "abnormal." McRuer draws on Michael Warner's *The Trouble with Normal* (1999): "Nearly everyone," Warner writes, "wants to be normal. And who can blame them, if the alternative is being abnormal, or deviant, or not being one of the rest of us? Put in those terms, there doesn't seem to be a choice at all. Especially not in America, where normal probably outranks all other social aspirations" (53). Warner's argument focuses primarily on what he calls "America's longest-running sex scandal" (45), the politics of the gay and lesbian rights movement. For McRuer, the *compulsion* towards normality comes not only from its appeal as the perfect and desirable opposite to abnormality, but also from the positioning of both as "choices" within a system of bodily extremes. Such an appearance of choice, McRuer says, is really about reconfiguring homogeneity: "A system of compulsory able-bodiedness repeatedly demands that people with disabilities embody for others an affirmative answer to the unspoken question, Yes, but in the end, wouldn't you rather be more like me?" (*Crip*, 9).

In *The Sea Inside*, Ramón would rather be "more like" himself, as long as that self is the one from nearly thirty years ago. In an attempt to get to know the man behind the legal case, Julia looks through photographs of Ramón before his accident. He is young, strong, handsome, and usually depicted with a girlfriend. He is the Ramón who stopped existing when he dove into too-shallow waters. McRuer says that "people with disabilities are often understood as somehow queer" (as paradoxical stereotypes of the asexual or oversexed person with disabilities would suggest), while queers are often understood as somehow disabled (as an ongoing medicalization of identity, similar to what people with disabilities more generally encounter, would suggest)" ("Compulsory," 94). Drawing on McRuer, I argue that Ramón presents himself as a *somewhat* or *sort-of* queer man. That is, he performatively takes on the stigma of queer, though with neither the culture nor the politics of a reworked notion of queerness. In his book, *No Future* (2004), Lee Edelman uses Freud's notion of the "death drive" to read queer theory (and its role within a structure of "reproductive futurism"), and to make the radical argument for embracing stigma as a form of queer resistance.[7] What Ramón's story shows, however, is that the economy of queerness is not simply about sexuality per se, but that it potentially intersects with multiple forms of embodiment and social positioning—intersections that complicate and reconfigure the boundaries of social, political, or ethical arenas. Ramón is heterosexual; he longs for a romantic relationship with his lawyer, Julia, but he eliminates even romantic fantasy from his life because he is physically unable to perform what he considers to be the normative male sexual act of penetration. If he cannot achieve heterosexual manhood, he decides, then he must be nothing at all.

Telling, and Telling About

Generic and formal features distinctive to autobiographical documentaries shape how the two films imagine disability, illness, and the right to die. Although both films are "based" on actual historical persons, neither *The Sea Inside* nor *Diving Bell* is a documentary; indeed, both subjects died before the directors began filming. Yet, in order to heighten their fictional authenticity, both films rely on audiences to accept their subjects as people from "real life." Structuralist Philippe Lejeune famously posited an "autobiographical pact" between author, narrator, and protagonist, a pact that relies heavily on the author's name being the same as the tale's speaker. In film, that use of a "real" name—often combined with an opening declaration that the film is "based on" a real historical event or actual person—in many ways establishes a "biographical pact" between director and narrator/protagonist. Such a pact determines the structure through which audience members accept that the film depicts real events in a real person's life, and that it represents the authentic person's thoughts and reflections as much, if not more, than those of the director. When Lejeune says that a real person creates "his own existence when he emphasizes individual life, particularly the history of his personality" (14), he opens the cinematic doors to films that, by emphasizing a protagonist's personality, tacitly promise audiences an "actual" life from which the film draws creative inspiration.

Referring to Lejeune's pact, Susanna Egan writes that its "very claim on an audience already splits the internal and external manifestations of the writing self" (2). Egan's notion of such a "split" widens Lejeune's definition of autobiography to encompass texts—such as the films and novel under consideration here—that map a different order of investment in both the autobiographical and biographical versions of disability representation. Just as biographers such as Frank Davey narrate the story of their lives, the lives of their loved ones, and the intricate and necessary narrative bond between the two, so too do filmmakers Amenábar and Schnabel narrate the biographies of Ramón Sampedro and Jean-Dominique Bauby.

Further, when Egan quotes Miller—"Every autobiography, we might say, is also an autothanatography" (246, fn3)—she brings the story of death into the story of self. Though I bristle at Egan's chapter on thanatology, wherein she glibly states that death is "entirely universal" (195) and critiques Western medical practitioners for "hiding behind life-extending technologies" (196), her research is useful in that she asks how to make sense of a life depicted entirely as anticipating dying, as well as arguing that an autothanatography merely encompasses one voice among several (198). By Egan's definition, Davey's *How Linda Died* is a thanatography. It is also a biography, as the author states that the book encompasses diary entries he makes regarding his wife's last year. Finally, it is, by definition, an autobiography as well, as the book is a day-by-day collection of Davey's own thoughts, emotions, reactions to, and interpretations of, his wife's dying. I do not wish, here, to rehash the many discussions about the biography/autobiography split (indeed, Egan notes, the discourse surrounding autobiography has refined to such a degree that critics have expanded and played with their definitions of autobiography[8]). Rather, I use the rich tapestry of such discussions to argue, not so much for a new term to identify the cinematic-biographical-fictionalized-biopic, as for a way of reading such films through the cleaves that structure them: between fiction and fact, between biography and the imagined life.

When Sherrill Grace, too, invokes Lejeune's "autobiographical pact," she expands his tripartite notion of speaker into the realm of performance (67–69). Taking that pact from page to stage (and so, too, to the dynamic screen) opens up useful discussions of the performative aspects of autobiography. Onstage—and as, I would argue, onscreen—the pact includes at least five players rather than three: author, playwright (screenwriter), actor, audience, and director. By expanding the membership of this pact, Grace expands and shifts the notion of "auto"biography. Who, exactly, in *The Diving Bell and the Butterfly* conveys Jean-Dominique Bauby's life? His *story* emerges from his autobiographical book, from interviews with friends and family, and from hospital records, but the performance of his life, more accurately, comes from a combination of those five positions Grace outlines. The film opens with a camera imitating the visual abilities of a man emerging from a coma and a voice-over that signifies his "true" voice (i.e., not the *authentic* voice that gargles in his throat, but an imitation of how his voice sounds in his head, if Jean-Do—as the protagonist is often affectionately referred to—were still able to speak aloud of a man who no longer speaks). Much filmic verisimilitude comes from the suspension of disbelief that any performance invites from audiences. However, in a visual medium more and more dominated by "reality," the fictionalized life still does—despite the crafted nature of cinema—invite from audiences the expectation of a narrating self, even when audience members recognize that the voice-over, as an example, could not likely be the actual historical person speaking.

In *The Autobiographical Documentary in America*, Jim Lane sets out the difference (in American documentary films) between the "autobiographical documentary" and the "autobiographical avant-garde" in "non-fiction" films. His aim is to distinguish between types of documentary cinema, and to explore notions of "subjectivity, reference, and the auto-documentary form" (4) that arise when filmmakers turn their cameras on themselves. His focus on the ways in which a film's approach to subjectivity, reference, and bio-depiction convinces audiences of the genuineness and accuracy of the projected protagonist is useful for my argument. Rather than relying on themselves as public figures, says Lane, documentarists "depend more on their interaction with historical events to achieve autobiographical authority" (4); in the same way, film directors creating biopics use the *idea* of their subject's interaction with historical events to achieve biographical authority. Indeed, as Lane concludes, "[T]he autobiographical documentary presents a tension between the cinematic accessibility of the autobiographical subject and the corresponding mediated status of the subject and the real" (192). Filmmakers rely on such tensions to depict a narrating individual, one who conveys a memoir of sorts—a history, a real life—even as the film itself entices its audience with novelistic techniques, with promises that it will not simply "document," but will provide the movie diversion of seeing through the eyes (or, in one case, the eye) of an actual person. Both Alejandro Amenábar's film about Ramón Sampedro's desire to kill himself, and visual artist and filmmaker Julian Schnabel's film about French fashion editor Jean-Dominique Bauby's post-life-threatening stroke, include visually stunning images—images that often contrast with the apparently "still life" of each film's protagonist. Both tell stories based on actual people, now deceased. Each makes use of visual composition, editing, lighting, camera angles, and so on[9] to position viewers within the eye-witnessing path of the narrator-character.

The Diving Bell and the Butterfly depicts Jean-Do's growing awareness that he must organize his idea of body around new criteria, and that he also needs to re-organize and re-categorize what he has previously thought of as his "life." Once the editor of *Elle* magazine, he fondly remembers his days of sexual promiscuity and social success. For nearly a quarter of the film, the camera's point-of-view is Jean-Do's, and audiences *see* what his character purportedly sees as he learns to adapt to a body he cannot command. Yet, as the film continues, the camera shifts from its exclusive position as the single eye of the protagonist to various shots that present Jean-Do being washed by hospital staff, waiting on the porch for visitors, wheeled along corridors, or spending time with his family on a nearby beach. The director, then, has made the decision to expand the visual scope of the film beyond the point-of-view of the protagonist but, as the narrative develops, this technique also distances audience members from that initial identifying-spectator position. The film conveys more than just the idea of how it feels to look with immobile and blurred eyesight; it also conveys Jean-Do's developing awareness and acceptance of his new physical reality. By positioning and re-positioning audience spectatorship, the director manages an identification that is more than mere character-recognition: the shifting point-of-view becomes a filmic device that entices viewers to follow Jean-Do's thoughts about his own body—*not* as he distances himself from his changed corporeality, but as he begins to "see" himself as *this* person who now lives in *this* body.

In the opening scenes, the camera mimics the blurred eyesight of someone who has suffered major corporeal damage. Jean-Do's entire body is paralyzed except for his left eye, and the muscles of that eye do not focus easily. Audiences experience a room through the visual stimuli of a roving camera, disembodied voices, and the effect of a blinking eye. Jean-Do narrates a perspective the intimate details of which the audience likely does not know, and the film promises to supply such intimacy. Thus, viewers "overhear" doctors say that the character has experienced a stroke and that he has been in a three-week coma. Although the narrator thinks he is speaking and responding to the medical staff, they do not react to his questions and comments, indicating that although *we inside his head* can hear him, none of the other characters can. As the opening scene continues, doctors, nurses, and medical therapists emerge as characters newly important to Jean-Do's post-stroke life (these characters, for the most part, are depicted as beautiful young women, perhaps to accommodate his lothario narrative). Surveying his situation, he says, "I'll be patient," claiming his new identity and reassuring himself and the audience of his willingness to live in this—what he hopes at the beginning of the film is a temporary—state. The film's projection of Jean-Do as roaming camera eye has a two-fold effect; the cinéma vérité technique introduces and reinforces the narrator's point-of-view but, as the film continues, the roving camera also visually enacts the male gaze: as a once-"normal" heterosexual male, Jean-Do is expected and *encouraged* to gaze at his (mostly female) caregivers and visitors.

In *The Sea Inside*, there is no welcoming of the in-between, no recognition that the protagonist, Ramón Sampedro, has *survived* a paralyzing diving accident that occurred twenty-eight years earlier. Instead, the film makes a capricious connection between disability and illness by, in effect, denying that a disabled person's identity can ever be healthy or whole. Amenábar's film endeavors to bring about viewer identification with the perspective of the disabled protagonist to the point of presenting his "death wish" as the only reasonable course of action. (For example, when picking Sampedro up for a court date, the driver of the van declares: "You're Ramón Sampedro, right? I was hoping I'd get to drive you, man!" His words reveal him as someone whose job entails conveying disabled people from one location to another; yet he is full of admiration for Ramón's suicidal intentions.) In the process, the film minimizes the socio-political contexts informing the protagonist's circumstances. Unusually, the film's point-of-view is focalized through a character who stays in bed, wishes to die, and views himself as a shut-in *because* he remains alive. Ramón interacts comfortably with his family, reads, and daydreams about his sexual prowess as an able-bodied man. But he refuses to consider his everyday existence as a form of "life." To Ramón, life is what he used to live when he was young and strapping. Not walking, not being able to approximate normative masculine conventions, is disability itself.

Ramón Sampedro's notion of self is either wrapped around a body that moves freely and strongly, as it did in his early twenties, or is permanently trapped in a body so useless that his only option is to die. The film's pro-euthanasia stance entices spectators to cheer for Ramón's "activism." In direct contrast, *The Diving Bell and the Butterfly* insists on chastising even the consideration of the thought of suicide. Early in the film, Jean-Do's speech pathologist demands, "How dare you?!" when he spells out the word "death." Although viewers may feel sympathetic toward Jean-Do's initial desire, the camera also lingers on Henriette's caring face and focuses on the considerate actions she performs for her client, leading viewers to experience and share her shock at his suggestion. Henriette's attitude stems from an adherence to Catholic dogma. Nevertheless, her reaction is not conveyed as dogmatic, but as a genuine (and growing) appreciation of what Jean-Do extends to her as a patient and as a man.[10] So when Jean-Do expresses the wish to die once—and early—in the film, he is effectively rebuked by his physical therapist. In this way, the film depicts Jean-Do as having confronted an obstacle in his imagination and, once past what Todd Davis and Kenneth Womack (2001) call the "ethical turn," he never revisits the idea.

Although Jean-Do is completely paralyzed except for one eyelid, he strives to connect with his estranged wife, with his friends, to flirt with his medical staff, and to write a book. Conversely, *The Sea Inside* rejoices *not* in the protagonist Ramón Sampedro's remarkable life (he is a writer and inventor, an involved uncle and caring son), but instead exclusively celebrates his efforts to *end* his life. His life, he says, "has no dignity." Paralyzed for nearly three decades, Ramón has spent his days in bed, physically cared for by his family. He composes poetry and invents a machine to assist his mouth with writing. Yet he believes his life has no purpose.

Linda, in *How Linda Died*, begins her treatment repeatedly asking "how" she will die and declaring that she "didn't want to linger as an invalid" (86). Yet, as her illness progresses (and she herself behaves in ways that, earlier in the narrative, she would have thought demonstrated a demeaning loss of physical control), neither she nor memoirist Frank Davey ever refer to her increasing symptoms as a form of past-her-due-date "lingering" again. Both Linda and Jean-Do transform and adjust their senses of self to fit within the bounds of what their bodies *can* do, rather than holding onto a nostalgic definition of life based on what their bodies *used to* be able to do. Though Jean-Do's key survival strategies—his memory, imagination, and creative talent—are infused with normatively organized desires premised on his success as a man, he uses them, however nostalgic they are, as a way of propelling himself into the future, *his* future. In contrast, Ramón, who is a quadriplegic, chooses to remain fixed in his bed for nearly three decades because accepting mobility with a wheelchair would be "accepting the crumbs of what used to be my freedom." Each of these narratives presents viewpoints that have dramatically distinct consequences for the rights and options of the disabled to witness and narrate their lives, and to have their lives witnessed, reviewed, and narrated by and through others.

In *How Linda Died*, Davey depicts his wife's last year and explores how her diminishing mobility influences the way he tells her story so that, in effect, the story organized around his wife's dying becomes his own. His role as spectator defines Linda's story not just as a remarkable narrative of a body growing exponentially unruly, but also as one of bereavement *before* the fact, of the telling of death by the still-living narrator. At times, Davey's memoir indulges in a narcissism of the healthy, yet he nonetheless manages to translate his personal account of Linda's life into one of his own role as bystander, participant, and spectator of her dying. Susanna Egan argues that most "death memoirs" (201) rely on the failing other to provide a narrative of an "undoing, and unbecoming" (245), nostalgically attempting to summarize the subject's life and disregarding the death itself. Instead, Davey renders Linda's dying in a way that challenges her life's outcome by focusing on her final year. This is not to say that biographers ignore the death of their subjects; on the contrary, biographers are meticulous about providing important dates such as birth and death, often listed on a page separate from the prose narrative. But rarely does a biography focus exclusively on the person who is dying, yet who is *not* telling her own story.[11]

Tracing the interpretive, pedagogic, and theoretical concerns of ethics in literary texts, Davis and Womack (2001) write:

> Part of being human involves the daily struggle with the meanings and consequences of our actions, a struggle most often understood in narrative structures as we tell others and ourselves about what has transpired or what we fear will transpire in the future [ix].

Each of these three texts—in the widest sense of Lejeune's autobiographical pact—proposes its protagonist as a realist character formation and expects audiences to react positively to such a mediated formation. *The Sea Inside* presents a "right to die" activism as if in support of disability rights, while hastily sweeping aside larger, more complex social issues impacting disabled people. Meanwhile, *How Linda Died* becomes—unwittingly—an argument *against* the "right" to die. The stereotypical point at which the "better off dead" notion usually claims a narrative is the very point at which this memoir convinces readers that Linda has made an "ethical turn." Davis and Womack argue that narrative itself can be "witness" to the representational truth of what happens in people's lives. Today, they argue, the "ethical consideration of a given work of literature ranges from the close reading of the text itself [...] to the ethical questions that the story raises in the reader's own life beyond the margins of the text" (x). The narrating character, Frank Davey, has no novelistic agenda other than to present diary entries concerning his wife's last year of life. Yet the story moves— as do he and Linda—from a determination at the beginning of the year to maintain "dignity," to an eventual celebration of the body's sensual demands.

Show-and-Tell

For the most part, the character of Ramón is humorless.[12] In contrast to Ramón, Jean-Do finds much about his new physical state to be amusing: when workers come to install a phone line, he laughs at their bafflement over how a man who cannot speak will make telephone calls. And when he imagines former acquaintances calling him a "vegetable," he wonders if he is "a pickle?" or "a carrot?" obviously enjoying the irony in how *un*vegetable-like his spirit continues to be, and choosing perhaps the most phallic of vegetables to represent himself. Later in *The Sea Inside*, Ramón lies in his bed and conjures an image of himself flying toward the coast. He does not inhabit a magical body so much as leave all notions of body behind. The camera follows his fantasy, imagining a bird's route to the salty water. In this fantasy, Ramón has achieved his ultimate desire: no present, no telling, no body. Ramón loves the ocean, yet hasn't visited it since his accident. He feels he is too much of a physical burden on his family, yet makes no effort to live on his own or to leave his room to go out into the world. He will not even go downstairs to debate a visiting priest, who is also paralyzed at the neck. This scene offers a parody of Roman Catholic doctrine, with the priest shouting up the stairs: "Freedom that costs a life isn't freedom," and Ramón shouting back: "A life that costs freedom isn't a life." Freedom, dignity, autonomy: for Ramón, these lofty terms, represented by his flying, all have to do with ambulatory mobility. He scoffs at using a wheelchair, detesting the very idea until he has the chance to go to court to argue for his right to be killed.[13]

Throughout, Ramón comes across as an attractive and compelling character. He is witty, well-read, intelligent, inventive, caring toward his family members, and fatherly to his nephew. Two women fall in love with him in the span of one year. One of them will ultimately help him achieve his goal of suicide, not because she wants to, but because he has told her that "the person who really loves me will be the one who helps me die. That's love." As a viewer, it is hard not to be swayed by such an articulate and eloquent character. He understands his own life better than anyone, and he has lived in a paralyzed body for a longer period of time than he lived in an able-bodied one. His single desire is so strong that one feels compelled to empathize with his ultimate goal.

The Sea Inside is organized around the notion that every individual has the right to choose his own life or death, and that archaic religious dogma should not prevent a man—for the notion of dignity and human worth is intricately tied to masculine pride and self-sufficiency in both films—from escaping a fate depicted as "worse than death."[14] The film reproduces in Ramón that monstrous hybrid: the disabled character who is both an erudite being misunderstood by those surrounding him and a monstrous beast who was once an intellectual, and who would obviously prefer to be dead rather than to carry on as a lesser being. Both *Sea Inside* and *Diving Bell* shift viewers' focus away from the power of the death drive to dissolve bodies coded as monstrous into a preferable nothingness and refocus, instead, on the everyday (and its pleasures); yet they remain implicated, imaginatively and politically, in regulatory norms of gender, age, and sexuality. In a chapter that critiques Hollywood disability clichés, Paul Longmore succinctly summarizes a century of disabled characters as physically reflecting a moral monstrosity. He demonstrates that not only do Hollywood films champion the supposed death wish of disabled characters (over America's high medical expenses of maintaining life), but also that disabled characters often "choose death themselves" (137) rather than continue an unbearable existence. In *The Sea Inside*, Ramón's loved ones castigate him when he talks about wanting to die. The understanding is that, despite those rows of able-bodied demonstrators on the court steps, it is always the disabled person who wishes death, and always his able-bodied loved ones who do not understand the monstrous nature of maintaining such a life.[15]

As with other narratives promoting what many people glibly term "euthanasia," *The Sea Inside* presents Ramón's paralysis as an obscene symptom of a horrific and debilitating illness,[16] an "illness" so drastic that he has been consigned to bed for three decades. But Ramón is disease-free. His fight is for a person other than himself to legally assist him with his suicide, an important distinction that no characters in the film ever make between the "right" to die and euthanasia. Not once in the film (nor in his actual life, for that matter) does Ramón Sampedro attempt to die by starvation. Paralyzed from the neck down, eating or not eating is a choice he makes multiple times every day. But dying, in itself, is not the point; rather, approval of the desire for death—approval that he and other characters believe will come through state-sanctioned third-person interventions—is Ramón's ironic raison d'être.

For Ramón, anything "less" than a body representing heterosexual male power and hegemonic stability is insufficient—is, in fact, deficient. His existence is trapped, Freud would say, in the throes of the "death drive" ("Beyond," 617). According to Freud, the death drive is not only a biological instinct, but is also so intertwined in the human psyche that responsiveness to it is automatic, offset only by the pleasure-seeking instinct. Freud's death drive, then, is a bodily instinct to return to the calm stasis that existed before birth (and, paradoxically, pre-corporealization). For Freud, the death drive explains why human beings feel compelled to repeat (through narrative or in dreams) traumatic events, even though these repetitions conflict with the bodily instinct to seek pleasure. The death drive is a mode of coping. Lying in bed, day after day, Ramón refuses any notion of physical Eros, longing instead for the nothingness he believes awaits him. Achieving this, for Ramón, would fulfill the only desire he allows himself, and the only desire denied him. Ironically, Ramón regards his life as more worthless than death because his body has unnaturally deviated from the very death he concludes should be its current condition. Although it is perfectly healthy, he deems his body to be deformed, grotesque, *sick*.

Patients in books and films often argue for the right to die when facing a terminal illness, based on the fact that death is imminent and that in their final few years or weeks (or days, or minutes), they will experience unmanageable, unimaginable, extreme, and/or inhuman pain. When Ramón demands a form of "euthanasia" based on the inhuman existence he feels he must endure, he equates disabilities—especially those depicting extremely limited mobility—with the powerful and evocative image of a dying body. In this way, the film trades on an implicit understanding that imminent death promises a much-deserved relief from unbearable life, and that visible disability necessarily implies that death is imminent.[17] In fact, Ramón's death is far from imminent, hence his need to petition for the right to hasten it. His argument is that ongoing life in a disabled body is worse than dying of a disease, any disease (he even jokes with Julia about smoking to bring about a quicker death). Both *Sea Inside* and *Diving Bell* shift viewers' focus away from the power of the death drive and refocus on the everyday and its pleasures, but both films remain implicated— imaginatively and politically—in regulatory norms of gender, age, and sexuality. In these films, notions of dignity and human worth are intricately tied to masculine pride and self-sufficiency.

How Linda Died

Davey writes his diary to record Linda's dying and his own coping. He is narrator and witness, caregiver and spectator. He is caregiver, narrator, participant and, strangely, biographer. In *How Linda Died*, readers are not going to "learn" how to cope with cancer; rather, this particular narrative presents the social terrain within which Frank and Linda negotiate their individual actions and reactions to her dying. This narrative, then, does not so much operate in the confessional mode of conjuring a so-called "self" as it does present a daily journal, the entries of which record everyday resistance to an obvious impending conclusion.

Both Linda's cancer and its treatment cause physical symptoms of illness: hair loss, weight loss, puffy face, leg weakness, and leukemia development.

And because it is a tumor attached to her brain, the cancer also steals her vocabulary, her ability to move certain parts of her body, her balance, her vision, and her ability to communicate with her family and medical team. In spite of being a character constructed within a narrative of ultimate death, Linda functions within the throes of Freud's death drive. Yet she is a character who adamantly resists any such "drive." Her death is both imminent and unpreventable, yet her instinct for pleasure remains potent. At times, Davey records her as "risking hope" (125), as having "guts" about dying (135), and as impatient to be "healed" (163). But she does not heal. The tumor grows, invading more of her brain, stealing more of her days. Hers is not a denial of the illness that gradually takes over her mind and body[18] but, rather, a stubborn reach towards the Eros that opposes the Freudian death drive. Always assured that she deserves the "good things" in life, Linda has consumed the best wines, hung the best carpets, displayed the best show dogs. After being given a life expectancy of about one year, she throws herself back into the life of pleasure that she and her husband had so assiduously built and maintained. She rearranges the kitchen so that she can more easily find ingredients and cooking utensils, and she indulges in elaborate meals accompanied by very fine wine. Paradoxically, Linda is exactly the character "type" that films display when they wish to present a formidable and remarkable hospitalized character who would rather be dead than accept permanent invalidism and physical dependency.[19]

In similar ways, the subject of Su Friedrich's autobiographical documentary, *The Odds of Recovery*, returns again and again to the sensual pleasure of her garden. William Wees, in his essay, "'Making it through': sickness and health in Su Friedrich's *The Odds of Recovery*," discusses how the garden serves as visual reference for narrative information or as visual counterpoint to the hospital's sterile surfaces and whining machinery. According to Wees, Friedrich's film invests "the garden imagery with both literal and metaphorical relevance to the film's dialectics of sickness and health, life and death" (Wees). Frank repeatedly tells the reader about Linda's fierce independence: for example, how "troubling" Linda's wish to keep her illness secret has become, or the incident when Linda continually tries, unsuccessfully, to "launch" herself from the bed all the while refusing the narrator's help (Davey 59, 218). She does not like to be helped; she does not like to be pitied; and she does not want to be needy, or reassured, or taken care of. Like Su Friedrich, Linda struggles to maintain citizenship in what Wees, following Susan Sontag, refers to as the "kingdom of the well" (Wees).

Adapting, once again, the phrase that McRuer adapts from Adrienne Rich, Linda's insistence on self-sufficiency and autonomy registers as a form of what I call *compulsory independence*. Repudiating any construction of herself as needy, Linda refuses to tell friends and family that she is sick, let alone dying, and does not allow her husband to discuss death. She clings passionately to self-sufficiency as confirmation that she is still alive and still very much in control. Visually compelling representations of such "compulsory independence" reinforce the disabled character as stuck between total self-sufficiency and absolute deterioration. At the same time, in a prose narrative that details virtually every aspect of Linda's physical "decline," her pleasure-seeking never waivers, never lessens. Her last year alive is one of determination, humor, intensity, purpose, and pleasure, as is her entire life.

Early in the memoir, Davey reflects that, for Linda, physical dependence is "perhaps even more of a disaster" than death (222). He documents Linda as announcing to her doctor that she doesn't want to "be a burden" by having the hospital put her on a respirator to extend her life (86). Such a sentiment not only fits her furiously autonomous character, but also reflects the fears and desires of many still-healthy readers: no, I don't want to be kept *artificially* alive; no, I don't want to *burden* anyone with my dying. Yet, as the narrative progresses, Davey details numerous occasions when Linda—while maintaining a forceful sense of independence and freedom—makes use of her surroundings and caregivers to enhance a life that has become, physically, more and more complicated. Some examples include: asking her husband to set the alarm clock so that she can tell when the angel food cake she is baking is ready (173); allowing her husband and children to set up an invalid bed table that was originally a dog-feeding table (238); and using the base of her wine glass as a spoon when it becomes too complicated to hold a glass of wine and cutlery at the same time (257). The "old Linda" (44) may well have been horrified to regard herself inelegantly spooning food into her mouth with the base of a wine glass, yet the ingenuity of her utensil vividly demonstrates Linda's voracious appetite—for food and wine, and for the days and minutes left to her; for the pleasures embedded in everyday physical yearnings and gratifications.

Dying to Be Told

At the beginning of *The Diving Bell and the Butterfly*, Jean-Do is a man who understands himself to have lost his sensual enjoyment, his sexual

measure, his culture itself. He constantly imagines and yearns for his girlfriend, Inès, who never visits. He longs to embrace his children and to
care for his father. The film offers a spectator's montage of his memories
with his children, with his lovers, at his job. In addition, audiences experience Jean-Do's (and others') repeated learning of the alphabet-dictation
his speech therapist has developed to aid his communication. She repeats
and repeats the French alphabet, from most-used letter to least-used:
"E-S-A-R-I-N…." She—and others—speak the letters of the alphabet in
this particular order, and they (and audience members) stare at Jean-Do's
left eye, waiting for him to blink a letter choice. As the camera closes in
on Jean-Do's one mobile eye, a single blink is recast as a climactic action,
the film relying on inner monologue and out-of-focus shots to convey the
internalized protagonist Jean-Do has become.

Diving Bell also cuts several times to the image of a deep-sea diver:
a man separated from the world by the ocean, encased within his diving
suit, the diving bell pulling him deeper. Director Schnabel chooses not to
repeatedly contrast this image with the other titular image that Jean-Do
Bauby-the-author used as his alternative self: able to roam his imagination
and the world as lightly and as delicately as a butterfly. The diving scenes
present audiences with visual evidence that Jean-Do has "decided to stop
pitying" himself and embrace the luxury of an imagination able to travel
anywhere, a body able to do anything. Rather, the visual stimulus is the
anticipated brush of eyelashes against camera lens. Putting aside his project of rewriting *The Count of Monte Cristo* (with the Count rewritten as
a contemporary female character), Jean-Do calls his publisher to continue
with the book deal, but proposes, instead, that he will compose and dictate
his autobiography. "A text doesn't exist until it can be read," he informs
his father in a flashback scene. The author-subject needs the reader; the
character-subject needs the audience. Rewriting a French classic was an
intriguing and playful option. Rewriting his own life onto the page, he now
understands, is the story that needs to exist through others' readings.

In her medical consultations, Linda seeks a cure or, at the very least,
treatment. Ramón believes the only "cure" for his disability is death, and
so denies himself any form of assisted living. And Jean-Do becomes the
speaking subject, the disabled writer who can compose his own story only
when he is literally frozen into the present. The difference is not merely
a semantic one between different conceptions of what it means to be
"cured," but indicates how narratives conflate representations of disability
with those of disease, often imposing ideas of disability as necessarily terminal and termination as necessarily desirable. Within such narratives,

the medicalization of disability points towards physical deviance; narratives of rehabilitation seek to "cure" difference. These cures—or, worse, the inability to "cure"—proliferate. Refusing to conform to other people's ideas of who Linda should be, to the construction of an ill woman, is one of the reasons Linda is such a compelling character, and why *The Sea Inside* spends so much time on Ramón's unique personality. Meanwhile, Jean-Do's individuality is entirely beside the point *until* he is paralyzed and his story is no longer a clichéd filmic tableau of yet another contemporary middle-aged lecher but, more and more, embodies this particular story about this particular life.[20]

Ultimately, *The Sea Inside*'s reliance on the ideology of individual autonomy entraps its protagonist. "Why can't I be like everyone else?" Ramón wails; "Why do I want to die?" The very fact that he *isn't* like anyone else, the film suggests, is what makes his case for suicide so undeniable. Ramón's battle for his legal death-rights in court includes only himself. He doesn't wish to discuss other quadriplegics, he insists, he's only talking about Ramón Sampedro. The film's representation of his disconnection from any social context serves to reinscribe him as a "normal" (read, able-bodied) man, but one who is perpetually damaged, suffering perpetual loss. Jean-Do, who has "Locked-in Syndrome," releases his imagination not so much *from* his body, as within it. Without the requirement to fulfill daily duties, Jean-Do devotes his time to composing small sections of his book. For hours, he "writes" words in his head, memorizes a full paragraph, then "dictates" (through their collaborative alphabet-listing) those words to the publisher's assistant. Several characters contribute to the making of the autobiography, but the film reassures audiences that the *story* surfaces from the imagination of the actual Jean-Dominique Bauby. The "reality" of his life expresses itself in the film when—post-speaking subject—audiences learn that Bauby died ten days after his book was published. The book, the "real life" *story*, is the pivotal moment in the film, even as a post-narrative addendum. Jean-Do, who has "lost" mobility, instead portrays himself as constantly within the swirl of what he has gained: floating through the ocean, socializing with Eugenie, the wife of Napoleon III, and the constant repetition of spoken letters, words, paragraphs, story. The legendary editor of *Elle* magazine has become a more legendary, more unique individual through auditory and representational depiction. In *How Linda Died*, Frank Davey negotiates medical services that have been weakened by late 20th- and early 21st-century neoliberal politics in Ontario, and his criticism of the medical system encompasses all cancer patients. The ingrained notion of individuality in *How Linda Died* demonstrates

Linda's disposition to adapt and change as her tumor grows. Frank Davey represents Linda's illness, then, as an individual tragedy, but also as belonging within and against a specific social context. Just as "disability" cannot entirely define or embrace numerous bodily realities, so too does the term "illness" fall short of encompassing a range of medical ailments and remedial disorders. Each of the primary characters I discuss in this chapter is attractive and compelling. One, entirely healthy, wishes for death; the second, hospitalized, literally struggles to compose himself; and the third, dying of cancer, grasps at every tidbit of life she can. Ramón portrays a character whose "use," in the film, is to preserve an ideology of superior masculinity and assumed wholeness. His "autobiography" falls within the biography genre that is familiar and easily contained. Linda, in dying, strikes at readers' appetites. Her story epitomizes the value of, and demand for, what is still her life, even as Frank is the character who seizes the first-person pronoun. And Jean-Do epitomizes the culture of change: his shift is not so much from able-bodied to disabled, as it is a profound conversion from superficial scoundrel to tender personality. Linda rails against the dying, and readers admire her fiery personality, wit, and determination. But it is Jean-Do who epitomizes the dream of marking one's own life as both history and art. The auto in bio, the self in my. "My first word is 'I,'" his voice-over recites, as he begins to get the hang of the alphabet-dictation-writing system his speech therapist has developed for him: "Myself." Within these three narratives, Jean-Do has "lost" the greatest mobility, yet Schnabel's film envisions him as throbbing within the jubilant swirl of all he has gained.

8

Where the Line Breaks

Disability in the Poetry of Roy Miki and Sharon Thesen[1]

What Poetry Is

What is, or might be, the role of disability in poetry? What is the "normal" body? Who gets to claim it? In what ways are marginalized and decentered bodies assigned the habitual role of alterity? To write about poetry through, within, and alongside disability studies is to open literary readings of disability to more than simply a fictionalized bodily reality; it is to examine fiercely held assumptions about normality, difference, and exclusion. Language takes a role in constructing and normalizing bodies, and in determining how conventional sentences or stanzas perpetuate a literal "normal standard" that readers may then respond to as if both bodies and poetics are, in some way, natural and fathomable.

One of my strategies for questioning the trope of belonging is to search for, research, play with, critique, puzzle over, rewrite, rethink, and reword the narrative poem, a form and a genre that remains generatively unstable despite—and possibly even because of—the recent attention drawn to it by certain writers and critics. Gertrude Stein famously begins an essay with the question: "What is poetry and if you know what poetry is what is prose" (125). Stein's words suggest doubt that a respondent can always successfully discriminate between the two. Marianne Moore suggests a similar genre instability when she notes in her essay "Subject, Predicate, Object" that "if what I write is called poetry it is because there is no other category in which to put it" (46). The categorization, then, becomes the form's naming, and how the words do or do not "fit" into particular categories likens literary writing to a typographical puzzle. Stein is asking not only about two supposedly separate modes of writing; she's also questioning where/how the separation between them is decided. Her question suggests doubt that a respondent can successfully discriminate between the two. This question of belonging asks which bodies—which words—hover over the border of belonging. Belonging, for poets, is a vexing notion: one always invokes the literary context of previous writers, at the same time as poets nudge the border which demarcates who may cross, who belongs. In this chapter, I examine the role language takes in constructing and normalizing bodies, and how normative sentences or stanzas perpetuate a literal "normal standard" that readers may then respond to as if both bodies and poetics are, in some way, absolutely natural and completely fathomable. I delve into the subject matter of certain poems, not simply to examine verse via its content, but to study the nature of its layered body metaphors, and to scrutinize identity poetics through invigorating recent disability theory.

Poets often invoke the language of limbs and enjambment, of breaks or the breath line, of feet, of oral storytelling. Thesen's short essay promises the body in all its poses and pangs. I shall examine the metaphorical language of poetry discourse, as well as turn to disability theory as a deliberate entry to the poetry of Sharon Thesen and Roy Miki, opening their poetics to a theoretical scrutiny that will allow me to read, as Thesen puts it, from "flesh to bone / moon to fingernail" (*Artemis Hates Romance*, 57), or as Miki puts it, from "desire's network" in order to "cross cultural heaps" (*market rinse*, n.p.).

I'm interested, then, in how Thesen and Miki address the role of the problem body: the uncomfortable or awkward body, the misplaced body, the irregular body. The notion that bodies can be or become "problems" depending upon the adjective thrust in front of the noun, maintains a focus on the corporeal reality of what certain bodies mean in the realm of normalizing implications. Reading Thesen and Miki is an extension of searching, researching, playing, critiquing, puzzling, rewriting, rethinking, and rewording what occurs in verse. Words by themselves don't belong to one genre, yet readers often assume that units of composition—such as the line or the sentence—do. But words are sneaky; whether as line, sentence, or otherwise, words cross borders, they tiptoe into rival camps, they traipse between one genre and another, refusing passports, scorning to "belong." Words belie their stanza breaks, their own prosthetic metaphors.

My project, in this chapter, is to read through these two poets via disability critique, while at the same time preserving their original poetic agendas, most of which have little or nothing to do with representing notions of disability on the page. In their oft-quoted book on disability and representation, *Narrative Prosthesis*, David Mitchell and Sharon Snyder argue that "disability pervades literary narrative, first, as a stock feature of characterization and, second, as an opportunistic metaphoric device" (47). They focus primarily on characterization in narrative, but I would like to draw their second assertion, the "opportunistic metaphoric device," into the realm of poetry. Thesen, in "Writing, Reading, and the Imagined Reader/Lover," tells readers of Prue Sarn, a character in a 19th-century romance novel, accused of witchcraft, in part because of her hare-lip. The hare-lip suggests to the other characters that her evil nature inside is reflected on her face. As Mitchell and Snyder point out, the more "romantic versions of disability emphasize stark contrasts between interior and exterior" (Mitchell, 109). But for Thesen—who gives a complicated and poetic reading of this character as punished for her reading skills, the outside *is* the inside: "[H]er mouth was the source of her misery" ("Writing," 68). Prue Sarn's words, the source of her power, dictate her appearance, and leave her isolated for a good part of the text. In Thesen's writing, Prue is feminine poetry and inventive distortion; thus Prue Sarn perpetuates both narrative and metaphorical roles, both literary flourish and rhetorical trope. She is metaphor for a woman judged on her integrity through her physical appearance. But she is also the embodiment of the spoken word, distorted through gender and disability and poetry.

One of the borders that fascinates me is the border that exists between bodies considered to be "normal" and those designated as "ab"normal. When people talk about the "normal" body, I know there's no such thing; but I know, as well, that the normal dictates the "ab." According to Lennard Davis, in *Enforcing Normalcy*, one way that "the category of disability defines itself [is] through an appeal to nationalism" (91). The disabled are not viewed as citizens in the same sense as the able-bodied who gaze at these "abnormalities." Davis joins such notions of citizenship to the historical eugenics that continue, in insidious ways, in contemporary language: "That the freak show begins in the same period as we have seen statistics and eugenics begin, indicates a change in the way people thought about the physically different" (91). The disabled body, reconfiguring itself in many ways, represents the problematic, the body that is too much body to ignore or overlook or *regard*.[2]

But *look*, rarely do readers see a disabled character front-and-center in a novel (unless the "theme" is overcoming difficulty), yet there s/he lurks: the next-door neighbor who uses a cane, the blind cousin, the ancient uncle, the retarded brother. Says James Porter: a "disabled body seems somehow too much a body, too real, too corporeal … it seems too little a body, a body that is deficiency itself, not quite a body in the full sense of the word, not real enough" (xiii). Disability in literature has been disproportionately under-represented at the same time that it has been excessively displayed. For the most part, disabled characters are minor figures, whose less-than-perfect bodies serve as a foil for the protagonist. In this way, characters portrayed as disabled perform the dual purpose of signifying a "lack" or character flaw which the protagonist must overcome, while at the same time disabled characters re-establish the wholesomeness and integrity of those key characters (and supposedly, the reading audience). In such narratives, disability figures as metaphorical emphasis for a specific moral impact.

"runs its tongue"

In a mid–1980s essay imagining the role of reader to her poetry, Sharon Thesen invokes the metaphor of the body to link her writing to the "inventiveness of distortions" ("Writing," 68). Her words, she argues, function "as momentum" and as "mandala" in order to look to "the other side" of the rest of the poem. "What does the beloved see?" asks Thesen, comparing her work to the mirrored body: "That face, those lines, that look" (69). The imagined reader as lover must invent the writing process as well as the story of entwinement. Step on a crack, break your mother's back. Break a leg. Break bread. Break prose. And the violence is so severe, so permanent, you invent verse.

Writing his own body into a ficto-critical foray on the body and "crippled poetics," Jim Ferris states in his essay "Enjambed": "[T]he body is not just an important image *in* poetry, it is also an important image *of* poetry (219). In other words, the body of the poem—whether sonnet or villanelle or limerick or prose poem—describes and defines its own form" (222). Thesen writes a line, threads the needle, and the eye breaks. I read across her sharp edges, and her shortest limbs break my rhythm. In her poem, "The First," the page stops, the words trip past and the reader trips at the end of the line, crutches flying:

> My arms feel unattached and threading
> even the largest needle
> I tremble and miss the eye [*The Good Bacteria*, 76]

Thrusting limbs and facial features and gender and skin and fingernails onto the page, the body of poetry perseveres. Writes Ferris: "If my meters are sprung, if my feet are uneven, if my path is irregular, that's just how I walk. And how I write" ("Enjambed," 228). As theorist *and* poet, as poet *and as poem.*

"To be a poet," writes Thesen in "What Poetry Performs," "especially a 'lady poet,' is in one sense to perform a spectacle of the ridiculous in public life" (*Po-It-Tree*, 20). Lady poets, Thesen suggests, are aligned with the childish, the sentimental, the feeble. A "lady" poet, like Prue Sarn, inhabits her gender as much if not more so than the role of Shelley's legislators. When Thesen calls lady poets "ridiculous," she invokes an idea of gendered gentility that represents the male poet as a desirable and enviable entity, and the female counterpart as a disgusting parody. Critic Sianne Ngai, in her *Open Letter* essay on "Disgust," is critical of the poetic embracing of "desire" as a trope for feminist writing, and proposes, instead, a poetics of disgust. The poetics of desire, she argues, led to a feminism dissipated as pluralism by the end of the 1990s.[3] The border between desire and disgust, then, is not only thin, but also one that relies on constantly reconstructing the difference between the two polar extremes. But what does it mean, in poetry, to align one's self with the disgusting? Where do the body's shortcomings *fall* on the page? Thesen, in "Magic," writes:

> Dyslexia
> lurks around the corner,
> can make you write backwards
> or not at all.
>
> The mind
> runs its tongue
> around itself, tries
> a phrase or two.
> Wonders
> if it came from the dyslexic
>
> …
>
> You may be a carrier &
> not know it.
> You may never write backwards
> or not at all
> & not know it [*Po-It-Tree*, 5]

Thesen connects the speaking body to the poetic language that makes use of the body. She writes the gendered and sexualized and awkward body onto the page: "Dyslexia / lurks … backwards / or not at all … carrier / & not." For the purposes of this chapter, I shall keep the subject at prosthetic finger's length; adhere to a theoretical stance that not only invokes disability theory to read poetry not overtly *about* disability, but also celebrates the *dis*-abled poem, toes its line-breaks. Or: lines its regular feet measurements into uneven, twisted, gorgeously disgusting toe-breaks.

Perhaps the line doesn't break, no matter how hard Thesen's lines smack against the implied right jagged margins, no matter how hard "dyslexic" cracks against the "back" of the line. Her stanzas reach forward, pulling the reader along, beckoning with section titles, page endings, more lines, more breaks, more punctuation. A codex diminishing towards its hind cover, a goddess who hates romance, a pose held too long, a Sunday pang. A monster attempting to complete itself. Monsters lurk in bedtime stories and under floorboards, and sometimes in (anti)-love poems. In "Jack and Jill," Thesen combines the lyric "you" with the monster as the embodied ennui that ails the persona:

> Your heart
> aching in your head
> I did not care about that.
> A monstrosity of boredom [*The Pangs of Sunday*, 4].

But Thesen does not simply gesture towards monstrosity as convenient metaphor. Jack's head aches because he has broken it on the "stones of the earth," on the "petrified heads of women / mouths agape" (13), love gone monstrously wrong, inside the petrifying process of patriarchy. Thesen's lines snap and scratch at the reader, unwilling to carry one thought farther than a few centimeters. Poetry that disrupts the line—at the same time as it invokes the line—ruptures the poetic structure, the stony edifice of the poem, ruptures the linear thinking that readers bring to each cowering image of not caring, of the body—mouth tight with not caring—trying to satisfy itself by the last line.

For Thesen, innovation means a breaking away from established conventions, such as sonnets or lineated blank verse, and also—physically—breaking away from the left margin each poem struggles to reinvent. Breaking away or breaking out implies defying the institutional, the ruled corridors and barred windows of the normative metaphorical corpus. Breaking out means limping towards a new rhythm, hobbling, hesitating through the ruptures, as in these lines from "Emergency":

> Human love
> is not so easy as speech
> will allow [*The Pangs of Sunday*, 113]

A gap just before speech, and a pang of physical disturbance, where "speech / will," broken as the line invites play. But what are the rules of these infinitely fracturing lines, in Thesen's poetry and as a tenet for most lineated poems? Is it ever possible to read her poetry in any way other than the projected linear? Do her line breaks, does her line breaking, reinforce the force of the line? In the "gala roses" section of Thesen's *Aurora*, her lines push to the end of the page, nudging the right margin, hinting at a prose poetry form that never quite emerges. In this piece, Thesen's sentences struggle against the sentence. As reader, I plan my route along edges and cracks in the prose sidewalk; as poet, she pencils in borders made up of words, only words, and we both cross over into blank space. Not because it is "new" or "white" or "virginal," but because the blank space is where the prose poem offers a *visible* margin, a territory (known or not) that hangs onto the edges of writing, clings to the edges of edges.

> Tone is something to take in the lake whose arms
> embrace peninsulas trees teepees canoes and strings
> of hung smoked fishes all in the museum The Museum [*Aurora*, 72]

The reader gets edgy when reading a prose poem, anxious, excitable, perplexed. Thesen's prose hangs about on the inside of this perplexing form, edging across whatever lines a poem insists upon/refuses, unsure and insecure, refusing the surety of either right-justified prose or lineated breaks.

Thesen's narrative pieces *and* her shorter lyrics veer away from line endings, from the enjambment that joins and closes the ceremony of the line, the final page next to the cover, the certain and the certified. She questions the metaphorical imperative (whose arms / embrace?) of "the museum" that introduces "The Museum," and grasps, instead, at the limping enticement of instability, hobbles on the phantom limb across the textured page, the "crannies, mosses, grasses, sedges" that make up "The Forests of the Taiga" (*A Pair of Scissors*, 6), or Mythology's "great dark that receives / with open mouth" (*Pangs of Sunday*, 117).

Thesen argues that "what poetry performs are the instincts of the rhythmic body—the body in time, the body as process, rhythm, and death" (*Po-It-Tree*, 20). The body's instincts, then, achieve rhythm no matter what the physical traits. The body "performs" not just gender, but undoing gender, not only form, but process; not simply disability metaphors, but enacted corporeal tales within a disability scope, a narrative that is at once poetic and counter-poetic, corporeal poem and metaphorical po-it-tree.

Break bread. Break a leg. Step on a crack, break your mother's back.

Break prose into bits and the violence is so severe, so permanent, we've tripped on poetry.

"unruly subjects"

In this section, I open Roy Miki's poetry to a theoretical scrutiny that will allow me to read what he describes as "desire's network" as well as its "cross cultural heaps" (*market rinse*, n.p.). Sharon Snyder and David Mitchell point out that "disability has been exclusively narrated as individual tragedy and deviance from bodily norms. As a result, humanities scholarship has only recently begun to understand disability as a foundational category of social experience, and a matter of symbolic investment" (*The Body*, 1). That symbolic investment is the approach to normative bodies traditionally taken in Western traditions of poetry (for example, in the blazon tradition of idealized beauty). Jennifer Bartlett, in the preface of the anthology *Beauty is a Verb*, asks what it means "to have a disability poetics?" (15). In the collection, she and her co-editors set out to explore "not only what it means to have a genre called 'Disability Poetics,' but to look at poetry influenced by an alternate body and how this intersection forms a third language" (15). By "third language," she intimates that disability and corporeal language extend beyond the convention—read metaphorical—body. I shall discuss Miki's poetry and poetics through a theoretical framework that reconsiders how certain bodies get represented (and accepted) as participating in the hierarchical world that fashions a normative center and peripheries of marginalization, while other bodies—by definition—are not represented in such a way. Stephen Kuusisto and Petra Kuppers claim: "Disability Studies is more than just a new subject area, an additional category of identity politics, a political claim. 'Disability' is not only a lived experience of individuality and difference, but it is also the hidden term, the shadow, behind many emancipatory politics" (74). It is telling that disability studies, still—in many academic, activist, artistic and other circles—needs defining as an entry point for cultural and literary analysis. At the same time, making a simple correlation between disability and analogous cultural indicators elides the problematic layers of representation. "[S]imply making the claim that disability is like race," maintains Cynthia Wu in her article on conjoined twins in 19th-century American literature "not only creates a white-centered model of disability while ignoring intersections of race and disability but, in some cases, replicates damaging images of blackness as they have existed historically in the white mind" (35).

Ellen Samuels, in speaking of disability as a category of Butlerian critical analysis, writes in "Critical Divides," that to articulate this category is still a radical endeavor. "Unlike other identity-categories such as gender, race, and sexuality, (dis)ability is not yet widely recognized as a legitimate or relevant position from which to address such broad subjects as literature, philosophy, and the arts" (58–59). Samuels asks: "[I]s there a fundamental dissonance between postmodern feminist body theory, as exemplified by Butler, and the existence/analysis of the disabled body?" (60). In her article, which attempts to read disability through Judith Butler's theories, the answer to Samuels's question, of course, is: yes, and no. As Samuels puts it: "[M]any of Butler's most compelling conclusions about how bodies are sexed can inform our analysis of how bodies are 'abled'; however, her work itself is en-abled by its own reliance upon a stable, functional body that is able to walk, talk, give birth, see, and be seen. When we utilize Butler's work without addressing these limitations, we incorporate the limitations into our own critique, and the problem compounds itself." (65) In *Bodies That Matter*, Butler expands her arguments about the performativity of gender in order, says Samuels, to "include other embodied social identities, most notably race" ("Critical Divides," 59). I wish to pose a similar question to Samuels here: Is there a fundamental dissonance between postmodern poetics (which encompasses the body's race, gender, and sexuality), and theories about the disabled body? One answer to the question of how disability theory can be useful in analyzing contemporary poetry is that poets and critics, in thinking about the Othered body, read (or reread) the poetic forms that encode disjunctive poetry through tactile embodiment. Even when poets do not directly address issues about, or situations representing, a specific disability, the ways they denote the trope of the body allows for discussions open to disability discourse.

I'm interested in how Miki addresses the role of the [adj.] body. The notion that bodies can be or become "problems" maintains a focus on the corporeal reality of what certain bodies mean in the realm of normalizing implications. My reading of Miki is an extension of searching, researching, playing, critiquing, puzzling, rewriting, rethinking, and rewording what occurs in his verse. What role, then, does language have in reconstituting and normalizing bodies, especially the body the poet works to reconstruct at the intersecting axes of race and gender? How do normative stanzas or broken lines or disjunctive syntax perpetuate or challenge the concept of an ideal body in a not-so-ideal world? or an abnormal body in a so-called normal world? How do poets "cure" metaphors of their able-bodied norms? How and why do poets continue to use "broken" as the ultimate metaphor for poetic language? My approach to these questions, turning to Roy Miki's poetry by way of recent disability theory, is deliberately awkward and clunky. With a few exceptions, Miki does not write specifically about the disabled body, but writes gendered, racialized, and poetic bodies onto the page. Few critics tend to think of disability theory as a way into his or others' poetry, unless it is specifically *about* disability. And most disability theorists still tend to turn to narrative in order to analyze and critique disability representations. So my "suturing" of disability theory to Miki's poetry is deliberate impairment rather than generalized cure. My reading of his work is disjointed—a method of un-jointing—and thus generates for me both the "routine enjambment" and "oblong resistances" (*Social Audit*, n.p.) that Miki's own work broadly embraces.

In an article on disability and poetry, Snyder and Mitchell write: "In literary studies, the effort to reread the canon through race and gender models simultaneously involves the revision of cultural expectations" ("Disability Haunting," 2). Among many other things, Roy Miki's poetry constructs identity (of race, of gender, of a myriad of "Othered" bodies) by way of body-text metaphors. His book *Surrender*, for example, presents a persona that is both cohesive narrator and partitioned teller. The persona's identity is not fractured so much as immeasurably layered, telling one story after another, each textual layer building upon or taking apart the previous layer. For example, the "material recovery" and "material recovery two" poems are separated by the poem "attractive," and the poem "surrender is a verbal sign" appears between "material recovery eight" and "material recovery nine." As such, the sequencing of recovery does not trace the progress of *cure*, but rather reveals the impact of the flawed notion of progress from one poem to another disparate one. The cumulative effect is to have the poems begin to present a manifold subjectivity that is sensation and speech and intellect and flesh and history and idea. In "material recovery eight," the persona instructs: "bank your memory" (80), an ironic command but also a play on the notion that memory can be contained, measured, *saved*. In delving into the poet's subject matter, I do not mean to rewrite his verse as plot-based, but rather to study its textually layered embodiment, and to consider what recent disability theory can offer to conceptualizations of identity in poetry. Snyder and Mitchell argue that as recent poets "contemplate the so-called broken condition of American experience, one might argue that only an earnest encounter with our attitudes toward broken-ness itself will suffice" ("Disability Haunting," 5). Just as Miki does not present a utopian wholeness as physical template in his poetry, so too do I wish to reconsider tropes such as broken and fragmented as offering predominantly a version of the body pathologized.

Often in narrative, the disabled character operates as a visually "deviant" body, through which to read duality: (1) the protagonist's character is then read as flawed (the blind friend indicates the main character is somehow willfully ignorant, etc.), and (2) he/r body at the same time is reinscribed as "whole." Miki, in his poetry and in his literary scholarship, exposes the social and symbolic prosthesis of a multitude of "adjective" bodies, and reinvests the colonized body as site for change and activism. Like the colonized body, the disabled body resists a categorization that not only exclusively situates it in the field of alterity, but also defines its role in literary studies as problematic. The problem body, in *Surrender*, is a critical and analytical category, as well as a poetical one. Many poets refer to their poetry as a corporeal extension of their thoughts (word made flesh) or language. In a talk on the book-writing progress, Erin Mouré says that in her "body of work over the years," she's pursued questions about what it means to love, to exist, to communicate. "In all this," she asks, "what is the place/role of the skin? Does the skin mark the body's limit?... Does the text act like a skin?" (26). That Mouré equates her desire to communicate with the text as membrane or crust indicates the connections she makes between writing as act and writing as textual artifact. Touch imparts and absorbs information; the body—full of noise and bustle—contradicts the vocabulary of singular containment, joins the vocabulary of marking (and demarcating) membership.

Thesen, for example, compares her writing to her material self: "Like my own body I know the geography, tendencies, and basic unalterable musculature of my own writing" ("Writing, Reading," 69). Roy Miki, in *Surrender* and *market rinse*, conjures this same geopolitical range to slip between the metaphorical and the literal, to theorize the movement of the poet's body through the social world, and to show how that world rewrites the body, of both reader and poet. But it is not enough to simply recognize that the textual body encompasses and projects actual bodies. Nor do Miki's poems. In *Surrender*, the poems bridle tongues (90), gesture toward the "marks and scars" one persona carries as "a witness for me" (118), champion "the unruly subjects" whose heartbeats lie doped up and bundled (94), each layered persona struggling against falling into the "category of the unmarked" (90).

Discourse surrounding corporeal difference and the ideal-body-now-flawed usually suggests a "progression" of literary anxieties and social concerns about the body and its normative target. Rosemarie Garland Thomson wishes to celebrate rather than regret the disabled body, turning away from language that situates bodies and their representations as within an uncomplicated normal-abnormal continuum. Furthermore, Garland Thomson says of the physically disabled body: "Constructed as the embodiment of corporeal insufficiency and deviance, [it] becomes a repository for social anxieties about such concerns as vulnerability, control, and identity" (*Extraordinary Bodies*, 6). When I read Miki's poems, I don't want to know or understand the narrative of abjected body become active. This "extraordinary" in Miki's poetry is the "poetic mutter stutter" of "cross cultural heaps" when "the lag body sighs" (*market rinse*, n.p.). The fervent self, stuttering across the words, intense, fierce, at odds with a world that judges "normal" as both necessary *and* possible. As in Miki's "kiyooka," I want poetry to "ambush" and "sputter" me, fold over meaning and content, expose the "dis sem blance" of "the utter & / outer skin." I want the poem to send me a sign "by priority post / if necessary," not because there is "no freedom / in this column / of print" (*Surrender*, 16), but because these specific words fit snugly between "material recovery two" and "material recovery three" (with another poem, "speed bumps," in between). The signifying trope is that the poem constantly and restlessly disassembles meaning, metaphor, and the *material* of recovery. In "material recovery eleven," Miki says, "it would be silly / (would it not?) / were it not / for the signage" (*Surrender* 119) as the poem signs itself off, ends within a quotation, "unrecorded" and "head long." Earlier in the book, Miki writes:

> "the   marks and scars I carry
>   to be a witness for me" [118]

His words imbedded within quotation marks indicate a prior authority, an oral statement, or simply emphasis; the reader is left to interpret these marks on the body. The scars not only metaphorically indicate a past injury, but here the "I" persona literally bears witness, holds onto and holds out the memory. The body, in the body of this poem, reads not only as material depository, but as sensual palimpsest: "the mellifluous gorge / on the path unrecorded" (*Surrender*, 119).

By writing lines that compose and animate my sense of sense, Miki's poetry uncovers underlying assumptions within the very language of syntax and line-break and stanza geography. Poetry that disrupts and ruptures the way I think. In the sort-of title poem of *Surrender*, "surrender is a verbal sign," the lower-case *i* "balks at its own groan," insists that the left-hand margin is as much a spoken cue as it is a visual one. A serial submission— a series of deferential resistances—the sections of the poem progress from number 1 to 15, the letter *i* shifting from speaker to identity to typographical guide to a divided version of "we." Moving from lamentations to formless vocables, the lower-case *i* of the first stanza makes room in subsequent stanzas for "the untold tale" that relocates a history "hampered" by nostalgia and belief (81). The so-called adjectivized body—that problematic corporeal reminder of who, exactly, is contained by a seemingly coherent "history"—that body waxes and wanes, never quite disappearing from the poetic page, but also not asserting itself entirely. In section 3, "the body" is passively "read by the brush of / leaves draped over the roadway" (82). Here the body is defined by manicured landscape, by the yearning for open fenders and fixed picnic benches. Whereas in section 6 the body is the body of the poem—a song sung by children that forces the plural "we" to "all fall down"—until the "you" and the *i* fall into "do do do" (84): is this a song or a suggestion? a rhyme or an imperative? a futuristic all-purpose pronoun or a petty joke? The "you" and the *i* do not meld so much as they recognize each other as formulations of language, of politics, of poetics. What Miki calls the "social graces" of "upper lower" (84) fixate the social body within the minutiae of the alphabet and its infinite arrangements. The "we" does not disappear from the poem any more than the body or the *i* does. The clamoring masses interrupt and shout and reminisce and fade out and fade in again: "where then do letters that / don't get inked get banked?" (87) one persona asks in the last lines of section 10. And section 11 begins with the ache not of the question unanswered, but for and against the "propped up syntax," for "restless / alphabets," and for the quotation marks around the "us," the stanza insists, "that is" (87). The poem doesn't answer its own questions, but invites readers to limp and stutter around, to search the poem's creases for more information, for candid doubt.

On the page, Miki speaks of stretched and splitting bodies, of split and competing personas, giving birth to themselves and each other. When the persona of "material recovery five" says: "i am in love with one sentence" (53), that sentence, somehow, fits into a world that views the *i* as both ubiquitous, singular, and ambiguous. In section "seven" of the longer poem "knocks at the door," Miki focuses attention onto the slippery inclusionary/exclusionary nature of the first-person singular pronoun by posing the *i* as hesitating behind billboards, just as "'we' all rushed..." and "'we' wanted to speak ..." (38). Readers are invited to both align and distance themselves from each appearance of another pronoun on the page, declining prohibition while at the same time reading themselves into (via recognition, rather than identification) the poem's "us / them" "we / i" "you / they," and even "i / I" clusters. By the end of the poem, only "registered" guests sit by the pool (38), while the pronouns chase after weather balloons.

Miki's poems surrender meaning, surrender form, and surrender into language. Each poem and its subsections suggest that the persona's drive to find (and possibly reject) a body will allow it to recognize and corroborate its own notational imprint as recovery and subversion. The lines turn into sentences and paragraphs, then abruptly veer off at jagged line breaks, refusing to look like either prose or poetry, refusing recognition, and refusing authorization from normative conventions of syntax and grammar. Miki stutters and stumbles, sprinkling a plethora of line indentations and breaks, tripping over the end of the page, falling out and falling away, fracturing the old, landing on his poetic ass, hesitating, hobbling through the ruptures, limping toward a new rhythm. Miki's poems do not fracture so much as they engorge: swelling the line with little regard for the metered, measured stanza, for verse conventions, or for the crescendo of enjambment (the body jammed up, the body's limbs striding forward and returning, the poem's lines holding hands and parting and rubbing up against the breaks, and breaking up).

>   lines   of
>   dis   content
>   to   doubt
>   this   line
>   slice   between (*market rinse*, n.p.)

The force of these unruly lines is such that they break from the sanctity of customary form. The persona cannot determine where, on the page, they belong. In the same way, the poem cannot settle into one formal structure, cannot limit itself to comfortingly or soothingly linear narrative progression. So too, readers of Miki's text are left with an array of points of identification in the text, none of them developing into the "plot" of unified identity. On these pages, the word "we" is comforting *and* frightening. Who is we when I or you or they exist outside the us?

The question of the "we" (with its prescribed and presupposed notion of unified affinity) leads me to questions of exclusionary politics, inclusionary poetics, and the "normal" methodologies of literary criticism. The adjective "abnormal," for example, as a grammatical depiction of the body, becomes quite appealing when coupled with "vowels"—what happens to "normal vowels" in this lexicon? And what might "deviant" vowels sound like? As my thinking changes about the body and the words poets use to invoke and contest it, my thinking also changes about how adjectives such as "abnormal" get subsumed into negative disability stereotypes. Government officials are "blind" to the truth, and the economy is "crippled" by global expansion, and everyone is "completely deaf" to reason. In "Prosthetic Politics" (in *Mannequin Rising*), he uses the image of crutches as prosthetic and poetic device to critique the idea of prosthetic devices. The opening line, "The power of crutches is so deceptive" (108), suggests that the deception is in the crutches as markers of bodily difference. Crutches can mean a sprained ankle or broken toe or ongoing disability. But like other prosthetic devices, viewers (and readers) gauge the import of crutches, decide what physical condition or status they indicate, then reassign them invisibility. The first line is followed by:

> Out of sight they bleed into the margins
> Out of hand they assemble the social scene
>
> As in this instance on the sidewalk
> note the pattern or the way the feet sashay [108]

The poem may claim that crutches are deceptive, but it also suggests that they provide methods to navigate through "flat" stairways or "unceremonial" crunch of the crutch pegs. Though the crutches are "out of sight" and in some ways "blind" viewers to the person using them, they are the visible markers that "assemble the social scene," that reveal the "deft / physical graces" defining one's access to each architectural and cultural "step" (108). And just as one can "give or take" effects of the body elsewhere in Miki's poetry—"give me body / take the gesture" (*market rinse*, n.p.)—so too do the politics of the disabled or injured body in "Prosthetic Politics" allow both speaker and subject to sashay off the page, to take a swaggering walk with dispossessed feet, to hear the missed beat of a meter, to ironically "go by the book" in order to gain "gaijin instability" (108) in this body, this poem.

9

Play the Facts and the Truth
Disability in Documentary Film

Truth to You

The short-lived North American television show *Lie to Me* featured a psychologist who exposes characters' deceptions by recognizing what he calls people's "universal" body signals. The premise of this detective drama is that all facial expressions and corporeal reactions to emotional stress are not only equal across cultures, but are identifiable signals that hide an inner "truth." In one episode, "Beyond Belief," an ex-member of a new-age cult constantly averts her eyes and lets her hair fall in front of her face which, to the show's protagonist, apparently demonstrates her obvious shame.[1] Regardless of racial, gendered, sexual, or linguistic backgrounds, characters on the show display "lies" on their faces and in their gestures, in a manner demonstrating what David Mitchell and Sharon Snyder reveal as narratives that propose physical "anomalies" to represent the normal gone awry (*Narrative Prosthesis*, 47–48). Despite what the ex-cult member says, her facial expressions and body language demonstrate to the psychologist and other scientists on the show that what she truly thinks and feels contradict her outward claims and demeanor. By ignoring or dismissing any gender, race, class, or cultural imprints, the premise of *Lie to Me* is that the human body can, indeed, tell the "truth"—primarily through its outward ability to represent inner turmoil.

In this chapter, I investigate how film viewers, especially documentary film viewers, attribute a similar kind of "truth" to a subject's body. The film I examine is the Canadian documentary *Citizen Sam*, in which film crews follow a mayoral candidate as he wheels through his campaigning days. My aim, in raising examples from popular culture, is to redirect

arguments about the "truth" of the body, examining the visual representation of "facts," a representation that underlies a somatic (and symbolic)
filmic truth that interests me here. What, in fact, is a *fact*? And how do
"facts" inform a viewer's acceptance of filmic authenticity and veracity?
And how do these facts betray the myriad ways we pronounce upon the
body?

James McEnteer observes in his book that explores the political evo-
lution of American documentary films over the second half of the 20th
century: "Documentary makers use actual people, settings, and situations,
rather than inventing their own" (xv).[2] This typical characterization of
documentary distinguishes non-fiction films from "fiction" movies. But
McEnteer goes on to caution against a too-simple definition when he says
(following and paraphrasing from Erik Barnouw's *Documentary: A History
of the Non-Fiction Film*) that "any claim to objectivity by nonfiction filmmakers is 'meaningless' because of the 'endless choices' they have to
make—from the topic, to individual shots, to the final order of edited
sequences" (xv). The range these choices cover exemplifies how much artistry goes into any documentary film. Canadian film critics Jim Leach and
Jeannette Sloniowski argue that in a documentary the "images on the
screen and their arrangement in the editing room must provide an external
and supposedly objective viewpoint on the film's subjects" (4). Viewers
do not necessarily demand absolute objective detachment, but the images
onscreen in a documentary film must adhere to a notion of independent
investigation. These are basic points; viewers are not unsophisticated
about how to read fashioned objectivity in visual form. Nevertheless, Jim
Lane argues that when filmmakers who are invested in the autobiographical mode turn the cameras on themselves, the projection of supposedly
candid subjectivity convinces viewers of the authenticity of the onscreen
protagonist (4). "By repositioning the filmmaker at the foreground of the
film, the new autobiographical documentary disrupted the detached,
objective ideal of direct cinema, which excluded the presence of the filmmaker, and the cinematic apparatus" (12). A similar elision of filmic construction occurs for viewers of the political documentary *Citizen Sam*.

In *Citizen Sam*, the projected points-of-view alternate between an
"along for the ride" camera-witness and a series of autobiographical personal addresses by "citizen" Sam, usually depicted as alone in his apartment. Sam Sullivan is a political hopeful who at times appears as the only
subject in front of *or* behind the camera.[3] *Citizen Sam*, a Canadian 2006
National Film Board documentary, was made by director Joe Moulins.
The film follows the 2005 Vancouver mayoral election, choosing as its

protagonist candidate Sam Sullivan, who ultimately wins the race. *Citizen Sam* offers almost entirely what one expects from a film that "documents" a political race: *in camera* meetings with campaign strategists, meet-and-greets with potential voters, debates with the opposition, and the obligatory "personal" scenes with wife or girlfriend. In addition, there are intimate scenes where it appears that no one is in the room with Sam as he speaks directly to the camera. Part confessional diary, these scenes offer to viewers the possibility of hearing—and seeing—the "real" behind the real. By speaking directly to the camera, with no one to overhear except viewers, the film suggests that Sam will reveal himself, strip away the public, authorized version and get to the private "truth" of who he is, what he represents.

There is a play on the title of the film with Orson Welles's *Citizen Kane* (1941) Both films present aggressive A-type personalities and promote and celebrate capitalist-minded individualists. Yet the notion of "citizenship" is problematic in *Citizen Sam*. Sam makes light of the public perception of his candidacy as aligned with marginal groups including the homeless: "People are shocked when they hear that, you know, I'm not some left-wing whiner that just wants everything given to me." On the way to an early-morning interview, Sam laughs at a wave he gets from a homeless man. Viewers are led to interpret Sam's laughter to mean that the homeless man wrongly assumed a body wheeling across the pavement in a wheelchair inherently signals a socially progressive politics. Sam's body and wheelchair, then, "campaign" for a certain position, while his words reject exactly that platform. Sam Sullivan's body, at this moment in his campaign, projects a particular message about disability, while he literally whisks away without talking to anyone but the camera. The scene thus challenges the broader epistemological assumption that the body is what Ludwik Fleck would call a "fixed and static" fact (*Genesis* 50), while Sullivan powers through the moment of failed social connection.

The (Un)Real Inside (Non)Fiction

In a 2010 article in the U.K.'s *Sunday Times*, Camille Paglia presents a vitriolic diatribe against singer Lady Gaga. Among her many complaints, she bemoans that Lady Gaga's lack of facial expression in her videos promotes in her fans personal fragmentation and "atrophied" voices, in which they "communicate mutely via a constant stream of atomized, telegraphic text messages" (Paglia). In a short online article in support of Paglia's opinion, blogger David Boles writes: "We read faces and bodies to receive unspoken clues about how people are feeling and what they're really thinking. The body does not lie—only the mind does—and removing access to our comprehension of the effective warning clues found in the physical realm wounds our ability to be seen, understood, appreciated, protected and preternaturally valued." Ironically, Boles cites Paglia in order to get at difficulties he experiences in teaching American Sign Language to undergraduate students. In an effort to celebrate the expressiveness of ASL, he aligns himself with a suspect argument: that the body needs to mirror the mind, that *not* projecting particular facial expressions associated with particular emotions leaves "kids today" with atrophied spirits (Boles). Not only does Boles reject, with Paglia, what she disparages as "mute" communication, but he also perpetuates European superstitions that emerged in the Middle Ages and persist in today's age of technology, about inalienable "truths" of the body: that its flaws and imperfections divulge higher meaning; in effect, that *the body cannot lie*. Boles's argument, like Paglia's, devolves into a worn "kids today" diatribe, lamenting days of yore before "technocracy" mediated bodily interactions. Bole attacks "kids" for experiencing the world via technology "through their hands and eyes," presumably a focus he should value as an ASL instructor![4]

When discussing the definition of documentary film with his students, film critic and teacher Henrik Juel admits that his students do "talk a lot about 'facts' and 'truth' as a necessary condition for non-fiction film" (Juel). To revitalize the discussion, Juel says, he asks if his cousin "can be justified in claiming that he is working on documentary films, when in fact what he does for a living is to install surveillance cameras at gas-stations and supermarkets. After all, this does seem to meet the criteria of representing reality, of filming without the use of actors, and recording as truthfully as possible what is actually there." At this point in the discussion, his students argue that they require from a film "some artistic point-of-view, a message of some sort." The facts, then, are not enough; the film—steered by the director—needs to navigate the facts in order to present a deliberate moral or ideological truth, or at the very least some demonstrable artistry beyond a twenty-four-hour static recording. "Recording reality," Juel notes, is "too vague a criterion" for what documentary films strive to achieve. A documentary film "is not a mere representation, but a willed presentation," he maintains. And that "willed presentation"—that director's cut of deliberate manipulations—is the artistic medium which viewers trust to view stylized fictional facts.[5]

Emerging around 1958, direct cinema (soon aligned with cinéma vérité) grew out of Québec and American documentary techniques (such as the hand-held camera, and synched sound and sight recordings outside the studios) that adopted the stance of an unbiased observer. By foregrounding the filmmaker, direct cinema autobiographies proposed a sense of "reality" wherein the principal filmmaker was not invisible, but was in fact the subject of the film. As Julie Rak points out in *Auto/biography in Canada: Critical Directions*, filmic autobiography is inherently "an interdisciplinary form." Rak wishes to emphasize the interdisciplinary nature of stories that rely on non-fiction "facts" and narrative strategies. Autobiography, Rak says, may draw from diaries and letters, sociology, photography, education, and anthropology (18–19). In film, the visual impetus is to observe—with an observing eye that constructs itself as scientific, or at the very least objective—the body as functional device of the viewing gaze. Audiences participate in the interdisciplinary evaluation of film in that the body is the subject, not simply the narrative surrounding the body. Mitchell and Snyder point out that disabled subjectivities exist in canonical narratives—from Aristotle to Nietzsche (*Narrative Prosthesis* 65–66). Portrayals of the body as able to outwardly represent inner turmoil or dis/order is an ongoing narrative strategy of truth-disclosure, especially in the cultural media of dramatic movies and documentary films. The fictions that may supplement the facts do not convince viewers that the subject being filmed is as constructed as protagonists in other movies; rather, the documentary focus on one particular body serves to aim a seemingly irrefutable and authentic factual story at the camera.

There may be no better example of manipulation than that found in a partisan political campaign, and films that document such events often strive to reveal or expose the various layers of political maneuvering. *Citizen Sam* offers an insider's view of a mayoral campaign in Vancouver, one that contested a number of political and social issues, including: the growing homeless and addict population, a sleazy history in previous mayoral races of partisan politics (Vancouver is one of the rare cities in Canada—certainly the largest—to conduct city elections by party, rather than by ward; one doesn't vote for a representative of one's community, but rather for one party over another), and—of course—the physical reality that a forerunning candidate moves about in a wheelchair, with a significant amount of footage spent on how that candidate appears to have trouble completing everyday tasks smoothly and without assistance. As the promotional material puts it, the film covers "from war room to bedroom," a catchy phrase that juxtaposes war and love, at the same time as it promises titillating glimpses into not only the public battle, but also the clandestine privacy of a would-be mayor. Thus Sam Sullivan's disabled body serves as "evidence" for certain policies during his run for election. Throughout *Citizen Sam*, the visible absence of camera crew, of any interviewer or director asking questions or leading conversations, allows viewers to focus entirely on Sullivan as the film's core, and on his body as the essential evidence that his physical reality is—in so many ways—his campaign.

Shortly after the opening credits, the film scrolls "Day 67" across the screen. At several points throughout the film, days continue to count down until the film ends four days after election day. For most of the film, the camera is set up, in direct cinema fashion, to act as an invisible recorder, there to "witness" the mayoral candidate's speeches, relentless campaigning, and political strategizing. In addition, Moulins's choice to shoot and package the film as a countdown suggests (albeit in reverse) linearity, a way of seemingly depicting the Vancouver election accurately through the day-to-day campaign, the details that drive the narrative to its ultimate conclusion (victory or defeat, vindication or condemnation, etc.). In maintaining this countdown strategy, Moulins's "invisible recorder" asserts objective reality but also purports to capture the subjective reality of Sam. Depictions of Sam Sullivan's private physical adjustments (traversing the city in his wheelchair, getting in and out of a bathtub, turning over in bed), allow viewers to glimpse "the unusual" body in action, at the same time as Sam's interspersed direct addresses to the camera invite an intimate acquaintanceship between subject and object of the film,[6] by relying on a filmic change-up that, ultimately, perpetuates normative narrative. In this way, much of the film concentrates on personal and intimate details of Sullivan's daily operations, often focusing on how a mayoral candidate who campaigns from a wheelchair must perform additional exertions. His personal "entries" interjected into a fairly straightforward documentary film narrative, convince viewers they are getting the "inside scoop."

In writing about television activist Pedro Zamora,[7] José Muñoz described what Zamora performs as a "Foucauldian ethics of the self" (143). "Within the structure of MTV," explains Muñoz, "Zamora performed his care of the self as a truth game that 'was for others,' letting them see and imagine a resistance to entrenched systems of domination" (144). This "game" took the form of the MTV reality show *The Real World: San Francisco*. Interspersed through the show, cast members "confess" to video cameras placed outside the community space. Muñoz notes: "These spaces of self-formation are, of course, highly mediated by MTV." As Jim Lane observes, "The autobiographical documentary presents an extraordinary site of subjective narration" (25). Whereas most cast members used the videos to weigh in on domestic squabbles, "Zamora used them as vehicles to perform the self for others" (Muñoz, 145). Of his shift from public speaking at high schools to appearing on a reality program, Zamora said, "I know that being on *The Real World* would mean exposing the most intimate details of my life on national television. How comfortable am I with that? Well, I do that through my job [speaking publically about being HIV-positive] every day" (in Muñoz, 150). Muñoz explains: "Zamora is willing to sacrifice his right to privacy because he understands that subjects like himself never have full access to privacy." And further, Muñoz argues that although "the dominant public sphere would like to cast him in the zone of private illness," such privacy is "always illusory" (150).

Muñoz contends (as does Zamora himself) that Zamora—as a queer, Latino, HIV-positive individual—in some way (through some pubic/private "truth game") *belongs* in the public eye. Rightly or wrongly, his private body speaks to public issues. *Citizen Sam*'s filmic construction is that Sam's body (and any private moments deemed particular to that body) belongs in the public eye. In Zamora's case, his private moment is by default a public one because of what his body already narrates on very first sighting, namely that he represents men who are HIV positive, Latinos, and queer men. As the political documentary was only released after the election (indeed, the final full scene in the film covers the night of election results), questions arise around who has access to those intimate video late-night entries. Further, the diary technique intimates that Sam is alone, that no one around him will view these "private" confessions: not his wife, not his opponents, not the voters, not the camera operator, not even the director; only the viewers.

The fiction of such access does more than create intimacy, it extends a titillating aura of illicit revelation. Sam declares in one of his private entries:

> I was on welfare, living in social housing, and I was just so disconnected from the community, from the world, from things that were happening.

Ah, the viewer might assume, now comes the core of his confession, as the dark lighting and quiet apartment suggest. Instead, "citizen" Sam turns from his personal life back to politician-speak: "This is an amazing system that we have: capitalism, democracy, the Western world. I wanted to be part of that system; I wanted to serve it in a way." As Sullivan waxes on about his tie choices, viewers understand his homily to be more of a "how I came to public service" announcement than the private and confidential information he promises to divulge. By speaking intimately with the camera in between more official campaign moments, Sam Sullivan sets viewers up to think that only "we" will hear the decisive truth about this overly honest political candidate. Exposing his non-public moments conveys a truthful and frank man, one willing to speak to a viewing audience outside the context of an electoral race. For Sam Sullivan, his private moments enticingly become public confession not only because he is running for public office, but because the body he constantly displays as a part of his campaign is a disabled one. So when Sam, within a moment of seeming intimacy, starts to speak his public agenda, viewers' expectations that this moment of confession—in which the private disability may disclose the truth of the public figure—are thwarted. To return to the homeless man who reads the mayoral candidate's body as offering a possible social alignment: Sam Sullivan's body, in this scene, reinforces a certain cultural assumption about what a disabled body *means*, at the same time as, for viewers at least, Sullivan's mind (expressed via his spoken words) thwarts those assumptions.

By dividing the film into segments where the candidate speaks directly to the camera, as if in a video diary, the director projects Sam Sullivan as not only the *subject* of the documentary, but as the *fact* of it. Giambattista Vico, in 1725, contradicts Descartes's stance that truth is absolute, observable, and separate from social construct. Vico suggests that truth emerges out of a form of creation, rather than from neutral observation. "For while the mind perceives itself," Vico says, "it does not make itself" (55), suggesting that there is no human truth prior to experience. And according to Mary Poovey, "[M]odern facts are assumed to reflect things that actually exist, and they are recorded in a language that seems transparent" (29). But what does such transparency communicate? As Sullivan "confesses" to the camera his fears over how he will run the campaign, and his glee at many of his once-enemies reluctantly shuffling to his side, viewers are reminded—again and again—that the political is personal, that Sullivan's efforts to stay a forerunner depend (as he puts it) on him learning to become a better "tap-dancer." He himself articulates corporeal metaphors that both invest in cliché and perpetuate normative images of the body and its physical movements. Does the facticity of the documentary film, then, lie less in the depiction of a race to become mayor and more in the depiction of a disabled man struggling through various political and personal minefields and conquests? Various of these appear in the film: Sullivan's insensitive lead opponent, his ways of dressing himself in the morning, his disclosure (prior to the election) that he gave crack and heroine to street people, and his final triumphant waving of the Olympic flag, by weaving his wheelchair around eight times in Turin.[8]

Like the plethora of disabled supporting characters in dramatic films, documentaries display disabled characters in various roles and narratives. In *Narrative Prosthesis*, Mitchell and Snyder argue that disability has been traditionally represented in film and literature as a "surface manifestation of internal symptomatology," a "surface manifestation" that predicts that the disabled individual in question has an "equally irregular subjectivity" (59). In plain words: a "twisted" body conveys a twisted mind; a "pure" body, a pure mind. In a way, this film offers what Eunjung Kim calls a "new physiognomy of documentary" (Kim e-mail). Its "newness" lies in how it attempts to *normalize* the character, rather than enfreak disability. The film projects (and perpetuates) an underlying conventional view that corporeality does, still, verify. In normalizing disability, *Citizen Sam* does not so much work against typical documentary conventions, but rather affirms them.

But what distinguishes *Citizen Sam* from other documentary profiles of public figures is the occasional scene in which viewers observe Sam performing evening ablutions in the bathroom, or morning scenes in which we see him bathing and dressing himself. These scenes are presented without voiceover commentary and serve no obvious purpose in depicting stages of a mayoral race. *Citizen Sam* lacks an omnipotent and omnipresent male narrator,[9] external to the subject. In his place audiences see only "Sam," a "regular" guy, performing "regular" activities, albeit with an "irregular" body. Visually, these telling scenes that foreground not only his body, but his daily manipulation of that body, function as truths or further confessionals about who Sam Sullivan "truly" is. Though determined to convey a sense of this candidate as complicated and physically different from most political contenders, the film at times seems to present Sullivan's body as object of a voyeuristic able-bodied gaze, constructing the viewer as safely situated within a domestic "normal." Charmaine Eddy once lightly quipped that *Citizen Sam* takes a "banal, then fetish / banal, then fetish" approach to its subject matter, offering a fairly conventional narrative of a political campaign, then interspersing those scenes with shots of Sullivan speaking directly to the camera about the "truth" of his body. Its fact is part of his campaign, garnering support from many disenfranchised members of the fractured Vancouver communities in a divisive mayoral race that sees an unraveling of Vancouver party politics.[10]

Sullivan's anti-government policies (he does not wish to maintain most social programs) was tempered by the constant display of his body—in and of itself—as representative of a marginalized group.[11] The film acknowledges, emphasizes, and constructs the "truth" of his body as needing the kind of attention not usually associated with victorious, commanding, political leaders. Yet Sam Sullivan manipulates not only his own physical vulnerability, but the vulnerable and proscribed bodies of disadvantaged constituents.[12] The film positions viewers as recipients of the "real" facts that preoccupy a disabled candidate.

There are Facts and There are FACTS

Simi Linton, in her memoir, *My Body Politic*, speaks about the transition into disability and its world. She became, she says, "an assemblage of body parts, notable only if they worked or not" (6). How the body does and does not "work" becomes the focus of many narratives about non-disabled young bodies that, like Linton's, shift into disability. Disability documentaries often center on one or more characters whose lives have become newly defined by disability, zooming in on the difficulty of maneuvering an unwieldy body, admiring the courage and determination such characters display. What non-disabled audiences believe to be the most important feature within any narrative about disability, according to Linton, is its genesis, that moment of transition, that irretrievable event that changed the character "forever" (*My Body Politic*, 110). In speaking of his own skiing accident (when he was nineteen), the now-mayoral candidate Sam Sullivan tells the camera:

> Really, I never did become Sam Sullivan again. The way I thought it through was I killed Sam. I figure, what would it be like if I *did* commit suicide? I imagined—graphically—ending it all, and that this is now a new person, with a new life.

Citizen Sam, then, is the figure who emerged from the metaphoric death of his former body. Of this film, Eunjung Kim has noted the following:

> A troubling notion in *Citizen Sam* is the fixation on independence (i.e., the camera's focus on Sam doing everything by himself regardless of how long and how much energy it takes) to establish the fact that he is an "able" citizen. This focus highlights how society values a certain "do it by myself" attitude, which assumes that able-bodied people do everything by themselves (especially those tasks of care labor, self-hygiene, and grooming). This test of independence is only given to disabled individuals, while many able-bodied citizens can pass without doing everyday body-sustaining labor by themselves [e-mail correspondence].

The "test" is as much about Sullivan's integrity as it is about his corporeal abilities. The positive focus the film takes in portraying Sullivan's physical movements testifies to his unwillingness to receive assistance from others, which distinguishes him from the image of weakness and neediness often imposed on disabled individuals who receive care. So how does the concentration on these scenes belie or sustain the idea of a film that offers audiences a behind-the-scenes "truth" about this one particular political candidate? How do the "facts" of health, fitness, disease, disability, gender, or economic position bear upon Sam Sullivan's mayoral campaign? What are the "facts" about this particular citizen that drew Moulins to this project? (And is it only Sullivan's role as disabled private figure that makes him so intriguing as public "citizen"?) And, finally, how is it that the physical body is a datum constant, no matter the inquiry?

In a 1935 treatise written in order to examine the development of progressive scientific research, Ludwik Fleck says that while philosophers "construe facts as something fixed and human thought as relative," facts are "changeable, if only because changes in thinking manifest themselves in changed facts" (50). As his editors put it, for Fleck, facts "are not objectively given but collectively created" (157). To Fleck, facts are collectively created, relational concepts "which can be investigated from the point-of-view of history and from that of psychology, both individual and collective" (83). So what happens to a scientific reading of the body, when every body does not conform to visual projections of normal? What is the "truth" of what viewers collectively accept as "fact"? How, indeed, does the notion of the factual inform and control the viewing of documentary film? Audiences leap from the specific scenes of body visualization in the film to visualizing (and re) the facts. Such leaps are especially useful in TV forensic shows, making the body an unequivocal carrier of what happens to it.[13] Facts are called upon because, as Fleck puts it, "[T]hinking is a supremely social activity" (98). Bodies appear fixed and static, and so too, then, does the thinking appear fixed and solid, when associated with bodies.

In his foreword to Fleck's book, Thomas Kuhn quotes a colleague's reaction to the book's title, *Genesis and Development of a Scientific Fact*: "A fact is a fact. It has neither genesis nor development" (viii). Peter Quartermain underlines the same point in his essay "Poetic Fact." Upon asking his brother, what is a fact, the brother replies: "Don't be daft! A fact is a fact! Trees are green! You're talking to me on the phone!" Quartermain concedes, tongue-in-cheek, "**A fact**, that is to say, **is true**. And yet of course my brother was mistaken—as he was telling me trees are green I was looking at a yellow one." When one examines the very notion of a fact (scientific, poetic, artistic), the word transforms from green to yellow and back to translucent: the real made tangible with words. The *act* of fact-making cannot be taken out of *fact*. What facts about disability say about disability is similar to what *Citizen Sam* claims: that certain bodies reveal a truth truer than any statement a political candidate (or character, or reality show contender) can ever make.

10

Sitting Pretty
The Politics of (Not) Standing on Ceremony

In Frances Hodgson Burnett's *The Secret Garden*, the character Colin Craven is confined to a bed his entire life, and only when newcomer Mary takes him to visit the secret, inner garden at his own home does he manage to get out of his wheelchair, stand, and walk. The children in the novel have an ambitious plan to help Colin recover entirely, so that when his father returns, he may run to him and his father will see "that he had a son who was as straight and strong as other fathers' sons" (183). When he first rises from his chair, Colin declaims to the neighbor boy, Dicken, about his ability to stand. Dicken responds: "I told thee tha' could as soon as tha' stopped bein' afraid" (169), perpetuating what critic Lois Keith argues are common literary representations of paralysis and the healing power of nature, each acting "as a literary device and as a metaphor for the power of self-will or faith to change the unacceptable" (Keith, 27).[1] Not only does Colin absorb the magic of the garden to cure his paralyzed and atrophied legs, but his new ability to stand, walk, and run indicate he has conclusively taken on his prescribed role to be a "proper" son,[2] to grow into and fully embrace his legacy. Angered by the hired man, Ben Weatherman, assuming he has "crooked legs" (Burnett, 167), Colin throws off the rugs covering his thin legs and stands "upright—upright—as straight as an arrow" (168). So dramatic and convincing is his erect standing that the hired man exclaims, "Tha'l make a mon yet [You'll make a man, after all]. God bless thee!" (168). As Keith points out: "When the children affirm that Colin is standing 'upright,' not 'crooked' and without a 'bent bone in him' ... they are not simply describing his physical condition; the language of 'straight' and 'bent' has clear moral implications." These implications

154

include honesty and trustworthiness, as well as heterosexual normativity,[3] all of which Colin must prove to himself, to others, and especially to his father, because his infirmity has de-masculinized him. "Throughout the period of Colin's illness his appearance is feminine and romantic but from the moment he stands up, he begins to become the 'real boy' his father never thought he could be" (Keith, 137). Only once he has left his wheelchair does Colin become the promising heir his father will embrace at the end of the novel.

In Joan Barfoot's novel *Critical Injuries*, the protagonist has a bullet lodged in her spine and spends most of the story supine on a hospital bed, waiting to see if she will ever walk again, or be forever paralyzed from the neck down. There is no nature-cure and no hope for spinal recovery, except through surgical intervention. In alternating chapters, Isla relates her life thus far, her trials with her children, her ex-husband, her job, her new husband. The narrators alternate between Isla and Roddy, the teenage boy who shot her during a robbery. In her chapters, readers slip through Isla's memories as she experiences them. Whenever the narrative reverts to a hospital scene, readers are as confined as Isla is, seeing only what she sees, feeling only her own frustration and sensory limitations. The novel chooses a "halfway" resolution, by having Isla end up in a wheelchair at the end. According to Lois Keith, in literature and in life, there have been three stock responses toward disabled characters (and people): 1) punishment, 2) pity, and 3) a push to "overcome" (15). And punishment, says Keith, is "inextricably linked to the idea of sin" (16) in many religions, and in Christianity through the succession of "sin, punishment, forgiveness and healing" (20). Barfoot plays with this notion of disability as punishment, as what Keith calls "a kind of life sentence for bodily impairment" (18) by contrasting Isla's physical confinement with Roddy's legal incarceration for the shooting. For Isla, "grace" has replaced the concept of God and—whether Isla walks again, whether Roddy deserves punishment or forgiveness—has to do with the ways in which each individual accesses the divine through physical suffering and personal atonement.

"Historically," say sociologists Barnes and Mercer in the introduction to their anthology, *Exploring the Divide: Illness and Disability*, "there was a trend away from judgments of social deviance rooted in religious criteria of 'badness' towards medical judgments of 'sickness'" (8). This trend—what disability scholars refer to as the "medical model"—shifted physically disabled bodies into the medical realm of illness and examination, and into what Foucault refers to as the "archaeology of medical perception," and created a social contract (aligning disabled and sick bodies, but also aligning the able-bodied with the healthy) that was difficult to resist: in the hierarchy of belonging, assuming the role of weak and vulnerable is a step up from embodying evil. By offering their symptoms to a physician's scrutiny, patients succumbed to the contract between the power of the medical establishment and the objective focus of their own bodies. Foucault argues that "up to the end of the eighteenth century medicine related much more to health than to normality; it did not begin by analysing a 'regular' functioning of the organism and go on to seek where it had deviated, what it was disturbed by, and how it could be brought back into normal working order; it referred, rather, to qualities of vigour, suppleness, and fluidity, which were lost in illness and which it was the task of medicine to restore" (*The Birth of the Clinic*, 35). At this point of Western history and emerging through the language of rationality, then, notions of health and normality converge. Before the 18th century, one could be abnormal and still healthy; suddenly, the two become synonymous in Western thought. "Nineteenth-century medicine," Foucault goes on to say, "was regulated more in accordance with normality than with health; it formed its concepts and prescribed its interventions in relation to a standard of functioning and organic structure, and physiological knowledge" (35). As scientific medical scrutiny became more and more prestigious in the 19th century, the medical structure of proposing a "healthy/morbid opposition," suggests Foucault, became established as the "medical bipolarity of the normal and the pathological" (35).[4]

Keith's triad of (1) punishment, (2) pity, and (3) noble triumph over disability, link easily with notions of (1) blame and, (2) gestures of charity, each one indicating a way of separating the disabled from the rest of society, setting up a hierarchy in which the disabled either deserve the "burden" with which they are inflicted or merit great sympathy for that burden. The third response (noble triumph) implies the possibility of cure, either through faith or individual resolve, thus encompassing the disabled into the greater society of which they are part, but only if they properly maintain what Talcott Parsons, in 1951, characterizes as the "sick role" (298–322). Parsons notes in his book analyzing broad patterns of Western civilization, *The Social System*, that sickness is a form of social deviance because it poses a threat to the "role performance" each of us is assigned—and, to a certain extent, embraces—by way of participating in social hierarchy. Unlike other deviant social roles (such as the criminal), Parsons argues that "the sick person is not regarded as 'responsible' for his condition, 'he can't help it'" (96). Such a role, argues Parsons, affords a citizen certain rights (for example, the sick person not being held responsible for being ill, and temporarily being "exempt" from social roles, such as working) and certain obligations (the sick person must try to get well). A "healthy" individual is temporarily shifted into the "non-participatory role" of ill person, as long as s/he agrees to these "contract" stipulations. The "sick role," then, allows an individual—for a short term—to abdicate from participation in economic productivity, etc. But within this model, "sick" and "disabled" often become conflated. In 1970, Constantina Safilios-Rothschild translated Parsons's argument onto a similar model of disability. The "disabled role," then, operates much like the "sick role" to account for individuals who—because of ongoing physical or mental disability—cannot participate in the same ways as those considered "full" societal participants (73). In order to be excused from normal societal roles, disabled individuals must accept some designation as sick. Thus certain individuals, though they may reject the "temporary abdication" of the sick role, must often perform and project roles wherein "fit," and "upright," suggest an identity reliant upon ideals of "decent" or "respectable."

Parsons was attempting to frame social scaffolding in which citizens can continue to access care and support within a nation, even as their bodies slip into the role often designated as extraneous to "full" citizenship. But as the role of "sick" conjoins with or merges into the designation "disabled," the "normal" citizens of the state often see the disabled/sick individual as breaking the contract to *recuperate*. A contemporary example is the case of Chris Mason, a British immigrant who was deported from Canada in January 2009, after becoming disabled while on the job in Winnipeg, Manitoba ("Canada Deports"). On January 27, 2009, Canadian parliamentary transcripts show the NDP parliament member from Winnipeg North, Judy Wasylycia-Leis, commenting that the present government (the Harper Conservatives) "has a tendency to use this section, section 38, of the [Immigration and Refugee Protection] act beyond its original intentions and to arbitrarily and unilaterally exclude persons living with disabilities" ("House of Commons Debates"). On the Council of Canadians with Disabilities (CCD) website, Vice Chair John Rae states: "The Immigration Act perpetuates long held stereotypical views of persons with disabilities as being less deserving and a burden on society" ("Immigration"). If the social agreement between healthy and sick involves co-operation and rehabilitation on the part of the sick individual, what does (or might) the social agreement entail between the disabled and the non-disabled? Tellingly, if the disabled person does not attempt to achieve "cure" (even if such a cure is impossible), that individual is often dismissed as non-patriotic, as non-participant, and in many ways as non-citizen.[5]

I do not wish to argue the problems with such hierarchical divisions (and there are obviously many). I wish, rather, to speak to the hierarchy itself, to the social mindset that creates different roles for different members (and, thus, perpetuates the notion of particular bodies having greater or lesser "value" than other bodies). In narratives pertaining to or reprising the construction of nation, there is a suggestion that the disabled individual's role is to either struggle toward cure, or passively accept lesser value as citizen within the nation. I'm thinking, for example, of Mitchell and Snyder, who make the claim that growing hostility toward biological diversity disseminates "an ideology of extinction disguised beneath rhetorics of assistance, support, and cure" (*Cultural Locations of Disability*, 33), Robert McRuer's argument about difference and belonging within the "cultural logic" of neoliberalism, that of "affirming and extending the immeasurable value of an increasingly global—and at times [… a] daringly anti-national—disability movement" ("Neoliberal Risks," 160), and Lennard Davis's extensive arguments surrounding the complex relationship between nation and class for deaf members of society.

As disability critics frequently point out, President Franklin Delano Roosevelt not only contracted polio when he was thirty-nine years old, but also spent most of his campaign and presidency in a wheelchair (except when he was standing with the assistance of braces designed to hold his legs rigid and, thus, his body upright). Although he could not walk, nor stand "on his own" at a podium, most of his media photos were staged (in ways that politicians cannot escape the media eye today) to conceal his disability. As the 2008 presidential election between Barack Obama and John McCain made clear, being healthy, youthful, and all-around able-bodied is an undisputed measure of political prowess.[6] Physical capacity, in subtle and not-at-all-subtle ways, denotes a candidate's capacity to "stand in" for the people (the party, the nation, etc.). Even in 1995, the very proposal to erect a statue of F.D.R. in a wheelchair caused consternation and protest.[7] Roosevelt, as an ultimate symbol of American national strength and vigor, *must* be depicted in a body that can "stand for" the people. To depict him in memoriam as "confined" to a wheelchair, not only shows off a body many perceive as weak or deficient, but also undermines the very metaphors which standing embodies. Although he was permanently paralyzed from the waist down, Roosevelt convinced those around him that, although unable to walk, he had begun the long road to recovery (successfully performing the role of an ill individual fulfilling the "contract" of recovery, even as such a recovery would have been extraordinary and improbable. Such a fiction enabled him to "stand" (to run) for office. When voters and campaign contributors met him early in his political career, he projected the image of a healthy vigorous man, on the road to (noble) recovery from a long convalescence. He repeatedly invoked (and relied on for his campaigns) the sick "contract" in that, although he was unable to walk or even stand, he was perceived as enthusiastically partaking in the hearty goal of recovery. The narrative he projected was the story of cure, and the end of that narrative was him, standing before the people as ultimate (and, thus, ultimately virile) leader.

The Men (1950) features Marlon Brando in his first movie role. Brando plays Ken (also going by the name Buddy), a World War II vet paralyzed from the waist down. He has been transferred from isolated treatment to a communal hospital situation, reluctantly joining other paraplegic vets. For the first half of the film, Ken tries to discourage his fiancée, Ellen (Teresa Wright), from visiting the ward, and insists that she break off their engagement completely. But she persists, even speaking to the ward's sympathetic Dr. Brock (Everett Sloane) about the likelihood of Ken's recovery. Again and again, Ken and Ellen are told that there is no cure for the paralysis, but at different points in the film, each believes such a phenomenon might occur. After much self-pitying and reluctance to join in the hospital's paraplegic community, Ken improves his attitude, seemingly accepts his situation, and embraces a future with Ellen.

In the film, each veteran character is perfectly disabled from the waist down (except for incidents of "the shakes," they have no ability to walk, twitch their legs, or feel anything), and perfectly healthy (in a youthful, fit, masculine kind of way) from the waist up. None of "the men" have been injured in any other manner than a bullet to the spinal cord below the C-7 vertebra (i.e., they are all paraplegics, none are quadriplegics), none of them walk in a spastic fashion, none hobble using braces (except when they're exercising). All, indeed, are in wheelchairs and—bucking a Hollywood tradition that persists to this day—none are ever "cured" of the infirmity that necessitates remaining seated.

In the scene that especially intrigues me, Ken prepares for his wedding day. This preparation takes the form of him doing physio exercises specifically to strengthen his leg muscles, as he is determined to stand while reciting his wedding vows. During a scene in the exercise room, one of the other patients asks Ken (as he pulls himself ahead using the parallel bars) if he's trying to "walk out of here." Ken replies, "No, but I'm going to be married standing up." There follows an exercise-montage scene where Ken devotedly pumps weights, climbs ropes, throws balls, does sit-ups, etc. To prepare for his wedding, Ken tries to balance without using his hands, his legs in braces, while a friend recites the wedding vows. During the wedding ceremony itself, Ken stands while his bride walks toward him, his fingertips lightly touching a wooden table before him. When the minister instructs the bride and groom to "join hands," Ken tries to hold Ellen's hands with both hands, thus letting go of the table. He is unable to maintain his balance and nearly falls, but his best man (the doctor) catches him. The scene cuts to alternating close-ups of Ken and Ellen's faces, both shocked by his inability to uphold the place of the groom. By rehearsing his standing more than he does his vows, and when he shows such bitter defeat at having swooned in front of his bride, Ken reveals his determination to at least *perform* the role of able-bodied masculinity. It is one thing to have to *be* in a wheelchair all the time, but another thing to have to *sit* in that wheelchair during the ceremony. Standing is a sign of respect and of manhood and so, for the duration of the ceremony, Ken plans to "master" the position that he, his guests, and his bride all want him to occupy.

Released in 1950, the film captures 20th- and 21st-century compulsory heterosexual anxieties that endure to the present. As a recent example, the Canadian medical drama *Saving Hope* features a paraplegic young woman (Zoe Cleland)—seemingly realistic about her disability and future with a wheelchair—but who nevertheless remains determined to "walk down the aisle" on her wedding day. The episode includes the requisite lecture to family about "supporting" her ambitions,[8] and a prosthesis device (exoskeleton legs) that—even after she dislocates her shoulder and is thus unable to continue her physiotherapy—allows her to "walk" (A Simple Plan"). Ideas and ideals behind standing itself, and how a character's (dis)ability to stand, participation in rituals through physical signification, or preferences to sit encode not only notions of able-bodiedness and the normal/abnormal binary, but also invoke intense passions about gender roles, nationalism, patriotism, and citizenship.

People rise to their feet when they hear their national anthem, especially when that anthem is played at a ceremonial event. To do so is regarded as participation in national identity, good citizenship, and a show of respect. In his short story "Joe the Painter and the Deer Island Massacre," Thomas King conveys the particularities of his narrator's best friend, Joe. Set in a small town in California, Joe speaks too loudly, greets people with comments about their private lives, clears his nose vigorously on the streets ("like shooting beans through a straw" [98]), and has an excess of civic pride. He stands at the country fair when they play the national anthem. "He'd even stand when they played it on television" (99); he even stands when they play the Canadian national anthem. "Come on," Joe urges the narrator as the two watch a baseball game on TV, "stand up and get your hat off, those folks got feelings too you know" (100). The expectation is that—except when watching television—all will stand, except those who *cannot*: the too young, the old, the infirm, and the disabled. Standing, then, is only expected from the so-called "able-bodied" members of the community, citizens who are strong (or independent) enough to rise to their feet using their own bodies and healthy muscles.[9] But what does it mean when one chooses *not* to stand, *not* to rise to the occasion? To many, remaining seated when formal occasion demands that one rise (during weddings, national anthems at hockey games, when royalty enters the room, etc.) is a sign of contempt, either for the individual being honored or for the occasion itself. In this chapter, I focus specifically on notions of mobility (and, in particular, upright mobility) as a means of assessing and giving value to particular bodies. I examine how definitions of citizenship lean towards the non-disabled, the young, the masculine, and other "normative" depictions of what it means to live within a body that has been inscribed by the nation as much as by race, class, and gender.

When I was growing up in Alberta, morning elementary school assemblies began with a formal, group address to the flag. Shortly after the bell rang and we'd all taken our seats, a teacher or principal asked us to stand and recite: "I salute the flag, the emblem of my country; to her I pledge my love and loyalty." Although absolutely no one could tell if we mouthed the words, or replaced the official words with choice selections of our own, it was obvious if any single kid in the assembly refused to stand, either from objection, from laziness, or out of disrespect. Standing denotes respect. Kids in wheelchairs or with crutches were not admonished when they continued to sit. In churches, babies and elderly parishioners may continue to sit when the minister enters, or during hymns. But for a "normal" person, for a seemingly able-bodied person to choose to remain seated once an officiate has announced, "All rise," indicates a profound act of disrespect or contempt for the occasion, for the authority leading the event, or for any local politics surrounding the moment. I am interested in such resistant politics, as they give the individual a route to express disapproval or distrust or disdain, without having to *do* anything: without having to stand and be heard, without having to call attention to oneself, without having to speak or act or even move—just sit there, and become a radical dissident.

I am also interested in the idea behind the (non)action; namely, that sitting is—in and of itself—a fundamental "anti" statement. Anti-speaker, anti-politician, anti-nationhood, *anti-* to whatever the "pro"s are standing *for*. I am interested in examining the experience and meaning of sitting for those citizens who identify as disabled and for those allies who ceremoniously sit with them.

I here present a short anecdote from my academic institution. A few years ago, I was a member of the disability studies committee at the University of Windsor, whose main task was to begin and maintain a disability studies program, to create more connections with disabled students at the university as well as with people within the disability community. To launch the program, we invited the lieutenant governor of Ontario, David Onley, to attend the ceremonies. Subsequently, we invited him to join us for lunch, after which he gave a talk to students enrolled in the program. Most of us gathered in the banquet room before the lieutenant governor joined us. We chatted about various things while we waited, including the introduction one member of the committee was to make at his talk. She rehearsed in front of us, and we told her what a wonderful job she'd done. But I thought I should speak up about one issue. "It's great," I said, except you end with: 'Please stand and welcome the Honorable…' and since I'm not going to stand, I'm wondering if you could leave that part out or change it to, "Please stand or otherwise show respect for…" I had hardly finished when the other committee members broke in with questions and (horror-stricken) rebukes. Why was I not going to stand? The Honorable David Onley was a representative of the queen, how could I *not* stand? etc., etc. I explained that, despite what many of them believed, I was *not* not standing out of protest (OK, a little out of protest, I'm from western Canada; we don't assign great value to the monarchy as a minor political deity), but in solidarity with people who cannot stand, and are thus viewed *either* as (a) making a harsh statement that they may not wish to make, *or* (b) are re-relegated into that "less than full citizen" role because, for them, not standing is "excused" or "forgiven" because of disability. This is a role similar to the "sick role" Parsons outlines, and calls for a similar "sanctioned deviance" of societal norms. To show respect, you *must* stand, unless there is something physically "wrong" with your body. In which case, just sit there, quietly, without calling attention to yourself (and accept the quick glances at your body and prosthesis from other audience participants reassuring themselves that, indeed, your sitting is a matter of impairment, not of choice).

I could go on (and on) about how hard it was to convince my colleagues to give even the barest of credit to my argument. I could mention that the lieutenant governor himself gets around in a wheelchair. I could regale you with two hilariously condescending e-mail reprimands that I received from one of the (male) committee members the following day. But as shocked as I am that members of a committee whose entire focus is disability issues would express astonishment at the *possibility* of sitting during a ceremonial occasion, I am more shocked that raising one's body—still—connotes the image of admiration and appreciation. Disability or disrespect. Disability *and* disrespect. This is an issue, in part, of transferring ideas about what the body *can* do into what the body *should* do, and what the body *should* do into what the body *should be able to do*. What does it mean, in a larger social context, to be "excused" from standing because one's body has been designated as incapable of "standing up" for the occasion? If one cannot stand for ceremony, one certainly cannot stand up for oneself. Or for anyone else. Excused, but not valued. Incorporated, but written into the margins.

To return to my discussion of how one does or does not put legs to use in formal tribute: sitting denotes passivity, or protest, or illness. One sits because one cannot stand, or one may join a sit-in to express protest. Whereas to sit as an active *choice*, as vehemently *for* something (i.e., sitting to demonstrate respect for the lieutenant governor), seems an oxymoron; a metaphor bent backwards. How, then, do such metaphors not only generate what Johnson and Lakoff, in their book *Philosophy in the Flesh*, call a "conceptual mapping" (66), but also generate and establish a set of axioms which articulate the body's thresholds as innate and valid (as opposed to invalid)? The assessment of wine based on whether or not it "has legs" has morphed into a metaphor for superior accomplishment or economic success ("That film has legs!" to cite but one example of the phrase). The preponderance of body parts to indicate something has value gestures to the body as a positive gauge or piecemeal judgment. (For example, when one has a "nose" for the truth" one can "sniff out" a good idea or a bad egg, and it is one's physical attributes that lead to such conclusions, not just one's intellect.) Though few realize the metaphor of "that (blank) has legs" comes from wine,[10] anyone who hears the phrase immediately recognizes it as one indicating a positive attribute. "Having legs" is good. Not having legs, obviously, indicates a negative: i.e., the inability to stand up for oneself or to stand tall, to stand in tribute to give a standing ovation, or to stand in for.

When Canadians sing the lyrics to the national anthem that include the following chorus lines, "Oh Canada / We stand on guard for thee," few question that "standing" for one's country is an honor. In the English language, the proverbial phrases "stand on one's own two feet" and "stand up

for oneself" metaphorically imply that one's ability to literally stand upright
is connected to one's abilities to successfully navigate the social relationships of everyday life. Indeed, such phrases suggest that *standing* somehow
indicates independence, confidence, attractiveness, and even pride ("stand
tall"). In *Metaphors We Live By*, Johnson and Lakoff argue that metaphors
are not merely rhetorical turns of phrase, but rather the ways in which
language constructs our perception of the world. In May 1997, John Howard, at the time the prime minister of Australia, gave the opening address
at a Reconciliation Convention in Melbourne. In that speech, he declared
that "true reconciliation must come from the hearts and minds of the
Australian people" and that "in facing the realities of the past, however,
we must not join those who would portray Australia's history since 1788
as little more than a disgraceful record of imperialism, exploitation, and
racism" (qtd. in "TimeToGoJohn"). In effect, his words not only denied a
long-overdue apology (since delivered by Prime Minister Kevin Rudd in
February 2008), but also dismissed official acts of violence and cruelty as
historical and as a mere "blemish."[11] At that convention, Aborigine delegates famously stood and turned their backs to John Howard. No such
political response had ever been recorded in Australia's history. Much of
the disappointment delegates expressed was at Howard's failure—in
addressing Australians at such a crucial convention—to officially recognize and apologize to Australia's Aborigine people for past atrocities. As
he had throughout his term as prime minister, Howard "stood firm"
behind his party's status quo stance.

What's interesting to me about this example, is it is the only one I
have found where people stood to demonstrate protest. The audience reaction in this case was not to sit in protest, but use the action of standing
so as to then face away from the politician. With this one exception, the
idea of the "sit-in" has conjoined with the ideals of rising from one's seat
to indicate support for the status quo. I am not primarily interested in
discussing the actions of people who, by sitting through a formal occasion,
recognize and re-inscribe the notion of standing as a sign of deference. I
am interested in the choice to *not* stand as an action that can also denote
respect and reverence, but that is often not recognized as denoting such.
In an immediately infamous web video, a teacher, Stuart Mantel, in New
Jersey, pulls a chair out from underneath his student, Jay, who refuses to
stand during the playing of the national anthem. The teacher can be seen
and heard yelling at all the students to "stand and keep [their] mouths shut."
When he directs his anger at Jay, Jay says he does not have to stand; Martel
then yanks away the chair, forcing Jay out of it. Perhaps predictably, the

school suspended the student who recorded the incident on his mobile phone, but did not discipline the teacher. Reports one online journal, "Jay said that he didn't have any political reasons for his refusal to stand but that he wanted to sit because he feels it is his right to do so and that right was being threatened by Mantel" ("Teacher"). In part, says the student, he chose to sit not so much to protest his national anthem, but as part of a strategy to make a record of his teacher's aggression and volatile nature. In other words, political activism, but not Political activism. Responses to the various postings of this video have asked about whether—if the student in question had been disabled—the teacher would have had the same feelings of justification in violently removing his chair, how pulling the chair out might actually contribute to a disability, and whether sitting through America's national anthem executes the same dissent as sitting through the pledge of allegiance. For this student, sitting to show disrespect for his teacher (and to provoke a furious reaction on the part of his teacher), can be read as similar to the Australian aborigine delegates' reaction to Prime Minister Howard.

In another student-related anecdote, in 2009 a ten-year-old boy in Arkansas, Will Phillips, refuses to stand and pledge allegiance to the flag at his elementary school until the federal government recognizes gay marriage. Despite being ridiculed and physically harassed by classmates (repeatedly calling him a "gaywad"), Phillips determines to persist in his active sitting until the Supreme Court changes its marriage laws. As a child, he has no voting rights, no legal venue for showing his displeasure at politicians' platforms and party decisions. But he is versed in the language of civil disobedience, and understands that—despite his age—he has the ability to participate (ironically by a show of non-participation) in the political process. Phillips feels not only disquiet about his nation's refusal to grant equal rights to all its citizens, he also feels optimism about the power of the individual "standing up for" what s/he believes. Again and again, to reporters amused by the story, he says he will continue his protest until "there really is liberty and justice for all" ("Gaywatch").

When one stands, especially in respect for a religious symbol or for an emblem that represents nation, one is ironically presenting oneself as both subordinate and dominant. Colonized nations and members of the U.K. stand for the queen to show respect, and to demonstrate a healthy subservience. To remain sitting, then, conveys an equally two-pronged message: that the citizen who does not stand is both an ineffectual and insubstantial citizen, *and* obstinately rejecting participation by refusing to recognize the stylized gravitas of the moment. One claims power, then, through the ritualized performance of offering oneself up to power. That a disabled character or person is automatically read as less powerful than an able-bodied person also, in part, shows that such characters *cannot* stand; unlike able-bodied characters who are ready and willing and able-bodied and prepared to stride forward into whatever the situation demands, a disabled character is relegated to occupying the position of being both discourteous and incapable.

Afterword: Not
Assisted Suicide, Yet!

As I complete final edits on this book (February 2015), Canada's Supreme Court, on appeal from a case in British Columbia, resolves to legalize physician-assisted suicide. The title of my afterword plays on the title of the activist group, Not Dead Yet. Founded in 1996, the Not Dead Yet organization in the United States champions the rights of disabled people, most prominently opposing laws permitting euthanasia and assisted suicide. According to their website: "Not Dead Yet demands the equal protection of the law for the targets of so-called 'mercy killing' whose lives are seen as worth-less" (Not Dead Yet website). The name of the organization comes from a line in the 1975 film *Monty Python and the Holy Grail*, spoken by a plague victim being prematurely carted off. Given laws that have passed in Europe, and most recently in Canada, that sanction an individual's "right to die," my title is an (admittedly nasty) tongue-in-cheek retooling of that same, frantic, character plea. In this afterword, I offer an analysis of the larger neoliberal discourses that pervasively and prevalently make "common sense" out of a narrative of euthanasia, in couching that narrative as giving freedom and liberties to individuals who would otherwise suffer at the hands of systems that ignore their individual rights. As I have argued throughout this book, it is the very multiplicity of media—film, poetry, billboards, newspaper articles and opinion pieces, medical and juridical institutional responses—that cumulatively shape contemporary social and political discourses.

The Canadian Supreme Court ruling states that the "prohibition on physician assisted dying infringes the right to life, liberty and security of the person in a manner that is not in accordance with the principles of fundamental justice" (*Carter vs. Canada*). The ruling identifies an explicit subject; namely, the "competent adult person who (1) clearly consents to the termination of life, and (2) has a grievous and irremediable medical condition (including an illness, disease, or disability) that causes enduring suffering that is intolerable to the individual in the circumstances of his or her condition" (*Carter vs. Canada*).

Around Canada and other parts of the globe, liberal-minded thinkers celebrate this decision, and social media floods with celebratory comments, such as "Kudos to the Supreme Court" ("Woodrow Pelley") and "Finally! Now suffering people can choose to die with dignity!" ("Theresa Marie"). Contrast this casual approval with the myriad of (mostly ignored) criticisms from disability-rights groups who view this decision as dangerous and even hazardous to the lives of Canada's most vulnerable citizens. For example, an Angus Reid poll conducted in 2014 reveals that 37 percent of Canadians "strongly approve" of physician-assisted suicide, and 42 percent "moderately approve," whereas 8 percent "moderately disapprove," and 10 percent "strongly disapprove" (Angus Reid). Yet as the poll questions become more specific, support dwindles. For example, 82 percent of Canadians support physician-assisted suicide for a patient with a terminal disease, but only 35 percent support a patient's desire to die if that patient has multiple conditions such as arthritis and diabetes (Angus Reid).

Were the Supreme Court ruling based solely on the final month or two in the lives of terminally ill people (those already diagnosed as explicitly having less than eight weeks to live), far fewer voices would raise objection to the court's decision. But the inclusion of virtually all people with disabilities and of anyone who feels (or is made to feel) an intolerable suffering, shifts the focus on a "right" to die free from pain, to one in which disabled people (as well as elderly people or anyone living with chronic disease) are put into a position where their situation is *already* understood as unbearable, as representing a somehow "undignified" existence. The very language itself (dignified versus undignified) speaks to the ways that illness and disability are conceived by many to convey a constructed identity based on an ignominy. Implicit in such language is the outlook that individuals with disabilities somehow live a humiliating or degrading life, a life understood as fundamentally abject, and that arouses pity and fear within the larger social community. Thus, the very existence of people with disabilities challenges the stability of what is (or is perceived to be) normal.

In her article "The Specter of Vulnerability and Disabled Bodies in Protest," Eunjung Kim looks at *Kandahar*, a film about a Canadian woman's return to Afghanistan to search for her amputee sister. Kim argues that the very designation of vulnerability is a category that functions as a means of making subjects vulnerable. Speaking of risk within the context of Afghan refugees, Kim quotes Benjamin Reiss, who says that while risk as a statistical category "rationalizes and objectifies problems," the concept of vulnerability is "relational and flexible." Kim points out that "vulnerability operates via hierarchical constructions of differences" (139). In other words, "vulnerable" as a category re-inscribes difference, and reads anyone portrayed within the corporeal Other category as assumed to be weak, defenseless, exposed. Michael Davidson says that negative categories create a "stigma of dependency," which, in turn, lead to barriers obstructing disability rights (*Concerto* 225). Claiming vulnerability does, in effect, operate as a divisive category. Within that film (and other narrative modes), depictions of vulnerability perpetuate the construction of audience members as normal, or at least "safe" from the dangers such a film projects. But more than invoking the normal/abnormal ableist gaze, Kim argues that such depictions characterize disability as especially vulnerable and in need of protection, and that "viewers become emotionally-driven surrogate protectors" (141). Kim's article focuses on depictions of non–Western disabled characters, often presented as spectacles of war or global poverty. Yet her arguments encompass and embody various minority groups, especially as humanitarian organizations constitute vulnerable people as needing aid. "Statements such as 'the vulnerable are hardest hit' and 'we are all vulnerable,'" Kim points out, "are rarely made by those who typically are labeled vulnerable, and thus they tend to mask embodied disparities and geographical specificities as they are used to forge alliances" (143). In the Canadian context, for example, the voices of the supposedly most "vulnerable" populations, such as disabled people, tend only to be quoted when they shore up support for the larger discursive strategies that label them as "victimized."

Responding to Canada's Supreme Court decision, Nancy Hansen writes: "I have four university degrees, am very happily married with a great job, and I have a disability. Yet, whenever the topic of assisted suicide comes up I feel vulnerable." Sad that any person needs to cite a list of accomplishments in order to convince the majority of readers that her life is much more than only her disability. But interesting that even someone employed as a university professor feels susceptible and exposed by a law purportedly designed to protect people's rights. Hansen goes on to remark: "It is strange how one has to deal with a lot of obstacles to obtain access to or qualify for basic supports and services like transportation and wheelchairs—yet the path to assisted death is so unobstructed" (Hansen), echoing the sentiments of the following political cartoon by activist Amy Hasbrouck[1]:

Why is it that public opinion rests so solidly on the notion that disabled people should be "allowed" to die? Heidi Janz says that the Supreme Court's decision is tantamount to saying to a vulnerable population: "We won't do anything to help you LIVE, but now, we're prepared to hasten your death" (qtd. in Chua). In Canada, roughly 16 to 30 percent of Canadians have access to palliative care. But because in the disabled community it's only about 5 to 10 percent, Janz argues that this lack of access makes the division between care and suicide much more stark: "This decision removes rather than provides any incentive to improve access to palliative care for people with disabilities."

There is a neoliberal undercurrent that shapes the discourse of disability in current North American culture. Self-regulating citizens know they must be productive in what is a competitive environment and, as neoliberalism demands, resources must be routed to this goal. The disabled person is often seen as a drain on resources (often expressed through the examples of: the financial resources of the government; emotional and social resources of family and friends; physical resources of the individual); in such discourse, having the "right" to choose to end your life is couched as "choice" rather than systemic pressure. Even as stories emerge of occasional models of disability "success," such as Stephen Hawking, who fits the paradigm of contributing to wealth and knowledge capital, "despite" his disability, this option to choose death insidiously positions disabled people as represented through the voice of victimized individuals relentlessly awaiting relief in death. Paul Longmore points out that "legalizing *physician*-assisted suicide" means it takes place "within the context of a health care system" (178, emphasis mine); problematically, such a context offers institutional legitimacy and medical sanction.

Repeatedly, discussion of laws about a person's "right" to choose death, circle around notions of individual freedom and choice. But many factors—including economic pressures—restrict choice. John Kelly, director of Second Thoughts: People with Disabilities Opposing the Legalization of Assisted Suicide, said in his testimony delivered in 2012 to the state of Massachusetts that, with "assisted suicide, self-determination becomes a slogan, not a reality." Novels, films, and even poetry depicting disability or illness all too often represent a disabled or ill character as an individual facing a choice of extremes: intolerable life or a hastened death. For example, *The Right to Die*, a 1987 made-for-TV film, features Raquel Welch as a successful psychologist diagnosed with ALS who struggles with her illness but ultimately asks her husband to help her die. And in *My Sister's Keeper* (both film and novel), eleven-year-old Anna is originally conceived as a tissue and organ donor for her older sister Kate, who has leukemia. In seeking legal emancipation so that she can refuse further medical procedures, Anna is ultimately "helping" Kate, who just wants to die. These are but two examples of the diverse media that proliferate narratives about a dying patient who wishes to end pain and suffering. But, as John Kelly succinctly argues, "[T]he fact is that we *already have* self-determination, as we can refuse any and all lifesaving treatment. Gone are the days of unnecessary invasive treatments. People can have an advance directive, they can choose someone to make decisions if they can't. And you have the right to pain relief, all the way up to palliative sedation, which in effect lets you die in your sleep" (Kelly).

On February 6, 2015, the Supreme Court gave the Canadian government one year to pass a physician-assisted suicide bill into law.[2] The Netherlands decriminalized euthanasia in 2002, and so perhaps provides a broader example for this discussion. Acknowledging the complicated emotions that figure into people's decisions to request an assisted death, Winston Ross writes in *Newsweek*: "The Dutch don't require proof of a terminal illness to allow doctors to 'help' patients die. Here, people can choose euthanasia if they can convince two physicians they endure "unbearable" suffering, a definition that expands each year." The article quotes Theo Boer, professor of ethics at the Theological University Kampen in the Netherlands and a former euthanasia supporter: "I like autonomy very much. But it seems to have overruled other values, like solidarity, patience, making the best of things. [...] Killing yourself is the end of autonomy" (qtd. in Ross). This understanding of the individual as autonomous-above-all permeates representations of the "right to die" in popular media. Most frequently in the movies, once-independent men become permanently disabled, and must fight friends, family, and the medical system for the "right" to die. (*The Sea Inside, The Switch, Whose Life Is It Anyway?* to name only a few). What makes their autonomy so precious seems to rest primarily on how much they have lost in the process of becoming a member of a marginalized group. In *The Switch*, Larry McAfee (Gary Cole) only comes to realize that he accepts life once he has convinced his friend to install a "kill" switch that he can operate with his mouth. Another popular theme that other pro-euthanasia films focus on is the disabled character whom a loved one cannot "bear" to see disabled. In *Act of Love*, a man shoots his brother who has become a paraplegic after a motorcycle accident, and is acquitted of the murder. In *One Flew Over the Cuckoo's Nest* one of the other inmates famously kills off the protagonist, Randle McMurphy (Jack Nicholson), because he has become brain damaged from electroconvulsive therapy. And *Million Dollar Baby* features a boxer, paralyzed during a fight, whose trainer suffocates her as an "act of mercy." True, at first Maggie's (Hilary Swank) trainer, Frankie (Clint Eastwood), argues against such an action, but as Lawrence Carter-Long points out in an article on this film and *The Sea Inside*, "Frankie's opposition to Maggie's deathwish is portrayed not as a moral stand, but rather a moral failure; a weakness" ("Better Dead Than Disabled?"). By the end of the film, Frankie has "overcome" his weakness to kill his scrappy protégée.[3]

The image of the "rugged individual" is one that permeates most textual or filmic narratives. As I wrote in chapter 3, David must die in Earle Birney's eponymous poem because to live as "less" able than his former self is presented as unimaginable. In taking on this thorny issue of individual rights versus communal good, Catherine Frazee points out,[4] "We know that private acts have public consequences. To frame the issue at stake in this debate as one of individual liberty and choice diverts attention from the deeper question of how our laws and social policy respond to human vulnerability and decline." Frazee, spokesperson for the Council of Canadians with Disabilities (CCD), speaks what for many able-bodied people is unimaginable; namely, that "the slings that lift us, the tubes that feed us, the instruments that fill our lungs with air and empty our bladders of urine are understood as tools for living, rather than as markers of spoiled life." Often, when people talk about "dying with dignity" they suggest that "living with indignity" is the unbearable cross. Frazee tries to show that tubes and medication and other prosthetic devices do not mark what Erving Goffman calls a "spoiled identity"; rather, they are the tools of regular life. They are the clothes that people wear, the cars people drive, the utensils people use to eat, the chairs upon which people sit (whether with wheels or stationary), etc., etc. In other words, human beings make the world accessible through innumerable tools and instruments and gizmos that we fashion for our bodies. Some bodies need more tools than others, some bodies need labyrinthine tools for intense periods of time. And some bodies need awkward and clunky and gauche tools, which can also be beautiful. Jim Ferris says that he loves taking his brace off at the end of the day. But he also says, "One of my favorite moments in the day is when I put my brace on" (Ferris, 229).

In contrast, the film *AfterLife* (2003) depicts endearing, selfish, rude, and very funny Roberta (Paula Sage), a young woman with Down syndrome. The film mostly centers on what an enjoyable (for the audience, at least) irritant Roberta can be for her career-oriented reporter brother (who pursues a story about a man "treated" at a euthanasia clinic, who may not have been legally fit to make such a decision). Near the end of her own life, Roberta's mother (Lindsay Duncan), decides to poison them both. The mother has been diagnosed with terminal cancer, and does not think her daughter can survive on her own. But Roberta learns of her mother's plan, and forestalls the poison. The film is much more nuanced and plot-driven than my short summary here, nevertheless it does—in this scene—seem to provide two options for characters: choose death or choose life. But Roberta's mother, assuming her daughter is too "vulnerable" to face a life on her own, elects to decide for Roberta (and to only kill herself in accompaniment to killing her daughter).

Ross notes in his *Newsweek* article on legalized euthanasia, "In light of the Dutch experiment, critics say there is no way to legalize assisted suicide without accepting the risk that vulnerable people will be pushed to their deaths—by the health care system, by their own guilt or by abusive family members or caregivers." Belgium, too, legalized euthanasia in 2002, principally for "unbearable physical suffering" though the law did not restrict the practice to terminal patients. In 2013, the Senate extended the laws to include terminally ill children and patients with dementia. By 2009, Belgian physicians could not agree on the definition of euthanasia. One survey asked physicians to define euthanasia, according to their own practices. According to data examined by Irene Ogrizek, "In one scenario, a terminally ill patient explicitly asked for and was given a lethal injection. 20% of physicians failed to define this as euthanasia and 30% did not realize the procedure had to be reported to the Federal Control and Evaluation Committee." Ogrizek reports that in Belgium, more and more nurses perform euthanasia procedures, while in Holland, according to Ross, 4,829 people in 2013 chose to have a doctor end their lives—"triple the number of people who died this way in 2002." For a few years after the law changed, the number of euthanasia cases declined, then the statistics began to climb, at an average jump of 15 percent every year. Says Ross about a key factor for the increase: "It's getting easier each year to qualify for euthanasia. In the beginning, most of those eligible were terminally ill. Now doctors are helping people die if they no longer want to bear depression, autism, blindness or even being dependent on the care of others" (Ross). Back in Canada, Christine Kelly and Michael Orsini point out that the 2015 Supreme Court ruling "reminds us of how disability, dependence and bodily difference continue to challenge common conceptions of social justice to the point of erasure" (Kelly).

In Canada and the United States (and also other parts of the world, though the divide has not been as polarized, elsewhere) the "right to euthanize" supporters and detractors tend to follow political party lines. For these reasons, Longmore advocates distinguishing the "disability rights position from that of the right-to-life movement" (177). In the United States, many Republicans and far-right Christian groups vocally demonstrated or petitioned against any court decision to remove Terri Schiavo's feeding tube.[5] In Canada, many Liberal Party and NDP supporters consider the 2015 Supreme Court decision as a blow against right-wing thinkers. Say Kelly and Orsini, "Liberals who think the Supreme Court decision is solely about compassion for the less fortunate, those with irremediable illness, are contributing to a long-standing tradition of relegating disability to the political margins." That people's beliefs about issues as important and serious as terminal illness, persistent vegetative states, palliative care, and long-term disabilities are reliant on party-line-loyalty is unfortunate to say the least, and verging on the grievous at worst. Writing an article about political scientist Brendan Nyhan, Maria Konnikova cites his many studies that reveal that—even when presented with science and facts—people often won't change their minds about important issues (in the case of Nyhan's current study, whether or not to vaccinate their children). Nyhan concludes, says Konnikova, that "[w]hen there's no immediate threat to our understanding of the world, we change our beliefs. It's when that change contradicts something we've long held as important that problems occur." What intrigues me most about Konnikova's article is that what Nyhan calls "false beliefs" (not merely errors, but a "lasting state of incorrect knowledge") are most often dearly held when considered as ideological knowledge. For example, "Strong partisanship affected how a story about climate change was processed, even if the story was apolitical in nature." In other words, "[T]he cross-party, cross-platform unification of the country's élites, those we perceive as opinion leaders, can make it possible for messages to spread broadly" (Konnikova). Nyhan hopes to change people's perceptions about scientific facts through approaching their ideas at an emotional level (mostly through self-affirmation exercises). Given the nuances of the Angus Reid poll about physician-assisted suicide, perhaps, in Nyhan's terms, if people stop "feeling" that developing or acquiring a disability is an "immediate threat" then such figures may shift.

By concentrating on disability aesthetics in this book, I hope to also promote an awareness of social engagement and social justice. As Paul Longmore argues it, disability studies "has been conceived as a bridge between the academy and the disability community" (223). Roland Barthes, in 1957, speaks of the petit-bourgeois as "a man unable to imagine the Other," and thus relegates all sense of the Other into sameness. In terms of disability, then, the non-disabled remains the norm, while any and all disabilities reside in the margins, ultimately reinscribing that very norm. This normalizing of the Other, says Barthes, is because "the Other is a scandal which threatens his essence" (151). Such scandalous risks, it sometimes seems to me, provoke cultural tensions, and from such tensions emerge politics and activism. And art.

In this book, I have attempted to read disability through literary and filmic narrative, through conventional and disjunctive poetry, and through cultural texts such as advertisements, photographs, cartoons, and blog postings. How disability navigates the world (and how the world understands disability) continues to be an emotionally charged issue, one that reveals itself through cultural chronicles. For this reason, parsing text matters tremendously, as does rights activism in the "real" world. The body *does* speak, and how it speaks, through which media, and how we pay attention to all that the body can tell, speaks to what I wish to achieve in this book. The urge to "adjectivize" the body endures: the aging body, the female body, the Chinese-Canadian body, the lesbian-butch body, etc., and such tagging does allow for important identity groupings. But the [adjective] body needs also to be her body, your body, our body, and not just some Other body. With this book I hope to reconsider, to re-evaluate, and to redraw what disability is, how it matters, and how to embrace its splendid manifold commonality.

Chapter Notes

Introduction

1. "2manypetz" writes: "If you just visit a hospital like Sick Kids in Toronto…"; "Ann" writes: "I saw a program about a boy in India…"; and "Danty" writes: "Poor little thing!"

2. A pivotal book in the history of disability theory is Erving Goffman's *Stigma: Notes on the Management of a Spoiled Identity*. Goffman describes stigma as the process by which people with bodily differences become excluded from various dominant groups. He includes in his discussion a "wide range of imperfections" and details how such spoilage often includes "desirable but undesired attributes" such as his example of a blind woman being asked to endorse a perfume, to emphasize the olfactory sense (5).

3. For more recent characterizations of the social model, see Barnes and Mercer (*Disability*, 14), Goodley ("Learning Difficulties"), and Siebers (*Disability Theory* 73–75).

4. See footnote 11, in Chapter 10, where I touch on evaluations of disability as blemish when elided with issues of racial identity.

5. Indeed, since 1988, in the category of Best Actor, fourteen out of twenty-seven Academy Awards have gone to able-bodied actors playing ill or disabled characters, with Tom Hanks winning twice (Moyer).

6. When Tod Browning's *Freaks* (which featured actors who had worked in sideshows) was first released, many movie houses quickly stopped showing it or refused to show it at all. The main characters—all disabled actors—were *not* absurd, but sympathetic; *not* adorable, but often powerful. The film depicts evil "normal"-bodied characters and victimized "freaks" (with a horror-revenge ending), leaving little room for audience members to identify with (and thus situate their own bodies within) a "correct" moral extreme.

7. For a further explication of this term, "problem body," see my *Tessera* introduction, as well as the co-written introduction with Sally Chivers to our co-edited anthology, *The Problem Body: Projecting Disability on Film*.

Chapter 1

1. Although modest compared to most mainstream films, *The Saddest Music in the World*, Maddin swoons, was to be made with: "a $3.5 million budget, a twenty-four-day schedule, and real movie stars" (*The Village Voice*).

2. Maddin filmed *The Saddest Music in the World* entirely with a combination of hand-held cameras, including Super 8, 16mm, and with many of his actors receiving camera credit. Maddin also relied on push processing to increase the grain, iris shots to evoke silent film techniques, and two-color Technicolor (or "Melancolour," as he terms it). Maddin eschewed using contemporary special effects (for example, when filming Lady

Port-Huntley's amputated legs), because he regards such "digital effects as grotesque artifacts of the present" (*The Village Voice*).

3. The film's portrayal of the music contest parodies the Eurovision Song Contest, a long-running annual competition among countries of the European Broadcasting Union, in which each country may submit a single song that will be performed on live television. Commencing in 1956, it is one of the longest-running television shows in media history, and also one of the most-watched programs in the world. According to Matthew Murray, the Eurovision song contest show is "viewed by 600 million people in 35 countries" (quoted in Raykoff and Tobin, xvii). The contest commends a series of components, say Raykoff and Tobin, including "fast pace and catchy rhythms," an "appealing dance routine," and costumes (xviii), all major elements in *The Saddest Music*'s finale number. In contrast to Maddin's film, where Canada loses after only one round, the inaugural 1956 contest was won by Switzerland, the host nation for that year. Even though audience members cannot vote for their own nation's efforts, the inaugural contest evoked the ideals of national allegiance inflamed at a moment when people still grieved war losses and held nation-centered grudges amplified over two world wars.

4. Lee Easton and Kelly Hewson succinctly describe and analyze the casting of the various national musicians: "Maddin cast his national musicians from actual groups who were in Winnipeg performing at the folk music festival. What this means is that the stereotypical quality of the national groups' musical numbers is not as parodic as we might think, and/or the groups think they have to be parodic to distinguish and make a spectacle of themselves" (235). The levels of staging are multiple: Maddin casts "real" folk musicians to satirize a musical contest in which a "director" such as Chester Kent exploits and restages nationality as both central (he constantly highlights music from identifiable ethnic origins) and unimportant (in his finale he has the contest entrants from India performing as Eskimos).

5. Narcissa has no memory of Roderick or of their son, and first appears as Chester's paramour. When she first speaks, it is in response to Fyodor demanding to know if she's an American. Lee and Hewson point out that her reply: "I'm not an American, I'm a nymphomaniac," aligns notions of nation, feminine (excessive) sexuality, and the pathologized body (229–30). In addition to her amnesia, she also claims to follow the counsel of her tapeworm, suggesting she experiences a combination of mental, emotional, and physical malaise.

6. One exception in such mass media portrayals is the 2007 ad by SoBe drinks, that shows a young athletic man removing part of his leg and inserting cans of Arush into a prosthetic slot, as if replacing batteries; the product was discontinued in 2009.

7. In her pivotal article on the role of gendered bodies in genre film, Linda Williams makes note of the "long-standing tradition of women's films measuring their success in terms of one-, two-, or three-handkerchief movies" (27).

8. I analyze the film version of Bauby's autobiography in Chapter 7.

Chapter 2

1. I have written briefly about this film elsewhere; see my "Punching Up the Story" article.

2. I speak further to how the body's flaws and imperfections supposedly indicate factual meaning, in Chapter 9.

3. Perhaps even less explored are issues of disability passing for disability (when people feel the need to heighten or diminish one disability to receive requisite attention for another).

4. Keyes published this story in 1958, and subsequently expanded it into a novel by the same name in 1966. A film based on both story and novel, *Charly*, came out in 1968.

5. David Mitchell and Sharon Snyder argue extremely skillfully, in *Narrative Pros-*

thesis, that the disabled character in film and literature functions as a prosthetic device. Within narrative, the disabled character acts narrative prosthesis for the (usually) non-disabled protagonist.

6. Siebers proposes this term principally to suggest the filmic depictions of disability that feature a non-disabled actor "playing" disabled (what Frances Ryan calls "cripping up" and what S.E. Smith calls "cripface"). But I find "disability drag" to be a fitting term, here, in that Charlie's co-workers accept and befriend him because they understand his increased intelligence to have been a temporary and artificial performance.

7. Cal Montgomery mentions the same quandary in the article "A Hard Look at Invisible Disability," and further mentions "the person who uses a wheelchair to get into the library stacks, but then stands up to reach a book on a high shelf" (Montgomery web), generating what Ellen Samuels calls the "disbelieving gaze" ("My Body, My Closet" 254, fn42).

Chapter 3

1. I speak more of the metaphorical consequences of "broken" poetics in Chapter 8.

2. This poem has been published many times. It was included in Birney's book, *David and Other Poems*, which won the Governor General's Award for Best Poetry Book in 1942.

3. In my afterword, I speak further on disability activism, such as the "Not Dead Yet" movement whose members dispute and oppose euthanasia dogma.

4. Published in several of Birney's books, frequently read on the radio, and wildly anthologized, "David" has also been popularly reprinted in school textbooks across Canada.

5. I do not wish to argue that Birney should have (somehow retroactively) written a "politically correct" hero, or a poem that in some way nods to the 1940s disability concerns. Rather, I investigate the notion of the physical ideal as *always* represented as desirable, better, and even as somehow attainable. What is it about the structure, social setting, timing, and storyline within "David" that leads to an ending where the hero is "better off dead"? Despite its poetic and metaphorical flourishes, Birney's poem retains a narrative realism, a poem where "how it ends" matters as much as how readers reach that ending.

6. Interestingly, although the poem reads as an anti-war statement, it does not (as Birney's poem does) suggest that the character would have been better off dying in battle. As anti-war testimonial, the poem aims to convince young readers never to go to war in the first place. Depicting a glorious dying would perpetuate the noble appeal of war this poem opposes. The war—that battlefield moment when the body shifts from abled to dis-abled—does not appear in the poem. There is only pre-war innocence and perfection, and postwar stagnation and decrepitude.

7. Although the poem appears to warn young men of war's dangers, the poem puts all onus for the decision to enlist on the young wretch. His legs weren't broken due to any mention of a surprise bombing, for example, so much as they were discarded: carelessly, thoughtlessly, unthinkingly.

8. When sexism and disability conflate, it is difficult, sometimes, to read the prominent prejudice. Readers may indeed feel that a young, vibrant woman's life would also be "wasted" in a wheelchair. However, because of the complicated layers of patriarchal-instituted gender roles, a woman's "purpose" to fulfill her heteronormative functions of pleasing her mate and ensuring procreation, might in some ways "salvage" her plotline.

9. The women present in his nightmare now control sexuality and subjectivity. Their "I"s pass by his lacking body, and move on to choose another, more normal male specimen. Through his injury, he has lost the patriarchal subject-position to own the male gaze and watch girls dance or holds their waists. His disabled (and in many ways queered) body has made him less "male" even, than female characters.

10. Robert McRuer talks about a cultural context in which homosexuality can be

"cured" (13) and "proper" heterosexuality "healed" (*Crip* 14) by explicitly celebrating and invoking examples of monogamy and healthy, natural marriages.

11. Both homosexuality and disability have a history of being analyzed as illnesses, despite historical medical evidence that also refuted such diagnoses. The former has a history of being designed as mental illness, while the latter has been configured within medicalized discourse as physical difference that—through enduring bodily diversity—often signifies sickness or disease.

12. Although angry in this correspondence, Birney, at other times, seems quite amused by readings of the poem with himself as the Bobbie figure. In an interview with Peter Edwards, about ten years later, he says, "There are a lot of literal-minded people," but adds that, for most readers, "Literature is literature" (129).

13. Owen was himself injured in war, and died in action in November 1918.

14. For fun reading around poetry as both grueling and cheeky, see Charles Bernstein's marvelous book of essays, *Attack of the Difficult Poems: Essays and Inventions* (Chicago: University of Chicago Press, 2011).

15. When asked, in a 1956 interview, what approach he would suggest to people who say they cannot understand his writing, even after they read it two or three times, Faulkner replied: "Read it four times" (Faulkner, web).

16. Indeed, the poem title on the facing page reads: "next top model," referring to a popular TV show, but also critiquing the idealizing of female bodies to the point that they appear undernourished and emaciated.

Chapter 4

1. Despite these "ordinary" scenes, the film does play on the conjoined twins' ability to experience each other's sensations—such as when Daisy is aroused by Violet kissing her fiancé—exaggerations and ruses that are usually referred to as "gaffs" in sideshow terminology.

2. And apparently desirable: "In the eyes of men she had gone from being pretty to perfect."

3. Who confesses that he "needed someone to look in the eye" sometimes.

4. Interestingly, though film audiences see the performers eating, walking about, doing laundry, etc., *Freaks* never displays the actual sideshow performances that emphasize the sideshow "freakish" bodies.

5. This process of erasure is similar to the way, in Dempsey and Millan's film, that the female body with no brains is transformed into a headless freak, as she represents a patriarchal ideal of femininity that the film extends to its extreme.

6. The sideshow acts in the novel are discouraged from wandering through the towns they visit until the last day of the circus, because the manager does not want them showing themselves and losing potential business. "Absolutely no freebies" (130) is his decree.

7. Wiseman inserts the violence of a pogrom subtly into what appears to be a comical tale of two special people finding one another. Despite the horrors of the plague, the image of the village idiot Golgol, beckoning bandits to "Kill Jews! Kill Jews!" (18) as they shoot bullet after bullet into him remains the most horrific image of Danile's bedtime tale.

8. The story of her parents' marriage and subsequent rescue of their town is so important to Hoda that she assumes everyone else will share her pride and joy. A crucial turning point in her life comes when, at school, she offers this story as a gift to her classmates, and is not only ridiculed and dismissed by the teacher, but so humiliated that she does not return (94–97).

9. Although Rahel and Danile are terribly poor, they have a rich uncle in Winnipeg who "everyone knows" refuses to help them at all. It is to spite this rich man that many

of Rahel's neighbors hire her as a charwoman. For the most part, they "did not like the idea of a Jewish woman hiring herself out to do what they considered to be demeaning tasks" (8), yet they revel in the niece of this rich man so demeaning herself.

10. The opposite, in fact, is true, as it is this very "abnormality" that has led her to the life she now leads. Had she been born "normal," she would never have married Danile, never borne Hoda, and not settled in the New World, family life intact.

Chapter 5

1. In similar ways, technological advances often become the target for ongoing societal ills, both metaphorical and actual. As a germane example, the rise of the "anti-vaccination" movement (particularly in North America, but also across other "developed" countries), reveals fears that some parents have about potential side-effects. The rhetoric of the past ten years tends to center on whether or not giving children vaccine shots will "cause" autism. As Anne Thériault puts it in her blog, *The Belle Jar*, "[R]egardless of whether or not vaccines cause autism, our entire conversation surrounding them is completely ableist." Vaccination opponents believe that medical advancement—giving shots to children in order to prevent disease—may cause disability (which they read as illness). For those in the anti-vaccination camp, one risks acquiring one kind of "disease" in order to prevent another. But as Sarah Kurchak succinctly puts it in *The Archipelago*, "[W]e're facing a massive public health crisis because a disturbing number of people believe that autism is worse than illness or death." Both sides of the argument, then, rely on autism as a key debating factoid. These two bloggers wish to change the conversation. They both argue that vaccination does not lead to autism, but rightly point out that beginning and ending the conversation with this fact only puts emphasis on autism as an "undesirable" outcome.

2. Lacan, first translated into English in 1977; Foucault, in 1973.

3. For example, many adults became deaf by catching scarlet fever as children; subsequently, all trace of that childhood disease has disappeared. Yet many scientists and physicians maintain the rhetoric of cure even when approaching someone who most likely considers h/er so-called "illness" to be, instead, membership in a recognizable community.

4. Falling into this rhetoric of cure, Christopher Reeve—perhaps the most famous celebrity to dramatically shift from an able body to a disabled body—achieved repeated media attention for his dedication to "finding a cure"; again, despite not actually having contracted a lingering sickness from his accident, but attempting to "cure" his disability via a nostalgia that defined his former able body.

5. Surreptitiously, the company's vice president, Harvey Stumm, goes to the office on weekends and after midnight simply to keep up with the plethora of electronic memos that come in daily. Stumm has the power to fire Chalmers when it appears he is not keeping up with his own e-mails, yet he himself must bring his wife to work after hours (253–57) because the politics of the company motto is that it is governed and managed by all its subordinates, and so Stumm must maintain a position that upholds his status as a superior who never falls behind in his paperwork.

6. Bauman and Murray quote a similar anecdote in their essay on the topic of "deaf-gain" (255, fn1). Davidson critiques the term "deaf gain" in his forthcoming essay, "Cleavings: Critical Losses in the Politics of Gain," where he argues for the "critical potential of 'loss' for the purposes of gain" (unpublished, 12).

7. In another sense, people "lose" their minds—"I just lost it today"—indicates an *excuse* for exhausted, bizarre, or even careless behavior.

8. For more on Parsons and the sick role, see Chapter 10.

9. CAMH is Canada's largest mental health and addiction teaching hospital and one of the world's leading research centers in its field.

10. I do not wish to suggest that Joy/Hulga believes herself to be unattractive because she has an artificial leg; rather, her recognition of standard beauty ideals leads her to discard conventional images and labels of femininity. In fact, she herself is protective of her prosthesis, and usually in a way that presents her character as aligned with masculinity: "[S]he was as sensitive about the artificial leg as a peacock about his tail" (192).

Chapter 6

1. In fact, my nephew began to assert unambiguous ideas about gender portrayal in picture books, even those fantasy stories that challenge certain everyday norms (i.e., in stories about aliens or talking animals), while still maintaining visual conventions of a nuclear family. If, for example, I read that the mother was going off to work, when the story depicted a green three-eyed alien holding a briefcase, my nephew would adamantly insist that the character was "the PAPA!"

2. I argue that my nephew experienced such acute anxiety over a sudden necessity to designate his classmates as either/or when he had never previously needed such category divisions, partly because such gender separation is unimportant for most members of my family, but also, perhaps, because in Mandarin—my sister-in-law's first language and a language that all their children speak—pronouns are not gender-specific. But I do not insist on using my nephew's growing discomfort around gender-identification as either the example of one that suggests a larger rule for all Canadian children; nor can I assume his experience as necessarily unique.

3. Shildrick herself claims psychoanalysis as a strategy for uncovering "the psychic work that supports the cultural imaginary, both as it operates through individuals and as it symbolizes the normative structuring of society" (83).

4. I make reference to their definition in Chapter 2.

5. There is a generally unacknowledged dependency around the subject of infants. Few would argue that a typical baby is disabled, yet in terms of Lacan's mirror stage, the child is so dependent that it doesn't know itself.

6. This normative construct is almost the opposite of Lacan's approach: that one begins as fragmented, then develops the illusion of wholeness.

7. Lacan is speaking about the relationship between human beings and their own bodies in terms of social practices; however, he goes on to use, as an example, small children who play at ripping apart dolls, indicating the ritual practice of taking a supposed "whole" body, and rendering it into pieces.

8. Said one of Latimer's lawyers, Ed Greenspan, at a press conference in January 2001: "This is simply a most tragic case of a man who loved his child too much" (in Hunter, A13).

9. Wong says she took an amniocentesis test even though there was a 5 percent chance of miscarriage, because she was a "thirtysomething female" and therefore "high risk" for having a Down's Syndrome baby. By citing this personal anecdote in the context of an article about Tracy Latimer's murder, Wong implies that—had the doctor actually confirmed her own worries about her fetus—she would have made the choice to terminate the pregnancy; moreover, that choice would have been based on the perceived flaws of her fetus, not because of her reluctance to become a parent.

10. I do not wish to invoke ongoing abortion debates into this discussion, except to note that many feminists who are also disability activists have shifted the argument with their refusal to devalue disability. As Susan Wendell says, the debate deepens when individuals insist on "questioning the consequences of reproductive technologies and abortion policies for everyone with a disability" (*Rejected Body*, 153). She goes on to summarize various positions in the succeeding three pages.

11. I am uncomfortable with the adjectives usually preceding depictions of people with disabilities (for example, "severe," "extreme," "mild," or "challenging") and find that

they warrant closer scrutiny. Not only do descriptions of people with disabilities usually concentrate solely on the disability, but such adjectives also impose an assessment of the disability intensity that supports a medical diagnosis for what is often an ongoing way of being. I here retain the term, but with added emphasis to indicate how such adjectives label people, not only by their disability, but also by how conspicuous the disability appears to the non-disabled.

12. For an extended evaluation of this argument see, Paul Darke's essay on the film *Whose Life is it Anyway?* in *The Problem Body: Projecting Disability on Film*. In my afterword, I discuss legal declarations to do with this issue.

13. Fred Wah has written about the concept of mixed race as a negotiation of the "in-between" within the Canadian construction around the hyphen. See especially his critical article "Half-Bred Poetics" in his book, *Faking It* (71–96) for further discussion of mixed race as a negotiation of the "in-between" and of the Canadian identity hyphen.

14. Most disjunctive poets embrace notions of a fragmentary subjectivity. For example, in her critical essay "On *A Frame of the Book*," Erin Mouré writes: "If everything is a fragment, if the brain works in 'fragments,' then we no longer need this word that reflects a nostalgic possibility of a wholeness" (27).

15. I do not wish to simply privilege the experiential over the metaphorical. But in its very title, this historically entrenched and suggestive book presents ways of encountering the city through the body's senses, as opposed to viewing its façade while secured within a fast-moving vehicle. Nevertheless, such an approach presupposes a subject who functions as an able-bodied biped.

16. In Updike's story, a teenage boy working at a convenience store serves three teenage girls, dressed only in bathing suits. When the manager chastises them for not dressing appropriately, the clerk takes off his apron and quits, hoping to impress the trio, only to discover they have already left the store.

17. Similarly, in the Tara Mateik video, *Toilet Training*, one speaker remarks: "When you mark a W or an M on a bathroom door, it does not function as a lock." The video primarily concerns access to public bathrooms for transgendered people, but has interesting implications for the ways that gender-segregated bathrooms also restrict disabled users.

Chapter 7

1. While many serious illnesses cause lifelong disability, an incautious conflation of illness with disability collapses distinctions and allows the one type of body to be read entirely as the other. For further discussion on illness and disability crossovers, see Chapter 5.

2. In my afterword, I speak of the goals and objectives of "Not Dead Yet" activists.

3. The book also serves as a contrast to the two filmic depictions of caregivers as young, entirely able-bodied, female, and well.

4. In *Bending Over Backwards*, Lennard Davis calls attention to "the routine use" of commonly used phrases such as "turn a deaf ear" or "morally blind," and pejorative references in print to "lame" ideas (38). As I mentioned in the introduction, Simi Linton discusses disability terms and their metaphorical impact within various discourses in *Claiming Disability* (see, in particular, pp. 16–17).

5. Disability scholars have condemned such a conflation in many ways. Mitchell and Snyder (*The Body and Physical Difference*) point out that "the ill body and the disabled body are culturally distinct entities" (37). Other theorists, however, continue to construct disability and illness as physically linked and theoretically connected.

6. McRuer invokes Adrienne Rich's terminology of "compulsory heterosexuality" to argue that "the system of compulsory able-bodiedness, which in a sense produces disability, is thoroughly interwoven with the system of compulsory heterosexuality that produces

queerness: that, in fact, compulsory heterosexuality is contingent on compulsory able-bodiedness, and vice versa" (*Crip*, 2).

7. In Edelman's argument, the heterosexual reproductive model socializes all to produce (or desire to produce) "the child" as an ideological formation of the future. Edelman goes on to critique and celebrate the paradoxical role assigned to homosexuals within this model. His argument is useful to me here, as he demonstrates that stigma can be strategically embraced, especially within what he calls the "social order's death drive" (3).

8. Besides the various re-spellings of "auto/biography," "(auto)biography," etc., Egan gives a further list of "auto" terms: Jeanne Perreault's "autography," Audre Lourde's "biomythography," Michel Beaujour's "autoportrait," Françoise Lionnet's term for Zora Neale Hurston's work as "autoethnography," Thomas Couser's "autopathography" (164), and Nancy Miller's "autothanatography" (15).

9. In Bauby's book (1997), sound is both distorted and exaggerated because of his condition (99–100). Much of the focus on his hearing and speech (he spends his birthday reciting the entire alphabet [40–41]) on the page is redirected into visual cues onscreen.

10. In the film, Jean-Do gently ridicules how Henriette encourages her fellow parishioners to pray for him whereas, in the textual autobiography, Bauby writes that such emotional attention, although mostly "unremarkable" in terms of physical results, lifts his spirits and has a direct connection to his body (12–13). He also says that once his daughter sends up her prayers every evening, "I set out for the kingdom of slumber with this wonderful talisman, which shields me from all harm" (13). At the same time, for much of the film, the female nurses and therapists come across as a bevy of helpmeets, women Jean-Do *could* fall for or flirt with or pursue sexually, were it not for his present situation. Such depictions of professional workers register considerable nostalgia for the formerly able-bodied, sexually powerful Jean-Do.

11. Egan provides a long list of autothanatographies wherein an author tells of he/r own imminent demise. But in *How Linda Died*, the story of the end of the subject's life is seen only through her husband's and caregiver's perception.

12. In the scene I discuss next, where he rages against outdated church rhetoric, the humor is directed *at* the priest, as opposed to the amusement either character might feel for the other. Ramón says at one point in the film that he considers himself a vegetable; to follow such logic, he must also consider the quadriplegic priest to be one, too.

13. The film makes much of Ramón's insistence—when he does, finally, leave his home to argue his case in court—that he not simply plunk himself into a "ready-made" wheelchair, but that he supervise his father and nephew as they modify the chair according to his specifications. Such a scene implies that other wheelchair users do not have the inventive impulse to cater to their "impaired" needs, but must accept a pitiful situation, regardless of its inadequacy. This not only disregards the fact that most wheelchair users customize their chairs, but it also suggests that only a willful character such as Ramón Sampedro has the determined individuality to fight for "what's right," and that his strength of character with respect to the right to die is exemplified by his imaginative creativity with respect to individual mobility.

14. The phrase "a fate worse than death" appeared about two centuries ago to describe a woman who has been raped or whose honor has been wrested away from her body; interestingly, the phrase is most often used in contemporary times either ironically, or as a description of a disabled patient whose body can no longer perform an expected masculine role.

15. As I have pointed out, only Ramón's family members truly believe he is making a mistake in taking steps to end his own life. In particular, his brother and sister-in-law express, respectively, anger and grief at the thought of Ramón carrying through with his plans. Late in the film, his brother argues that, indeed, the family members have become "slaves" to Ramón, and it is *because* of this miserable truth that Ramón must continue to live. The circular argument, then, is that Ramón is a burden that—because the brother

and family have sacrificed for that burden—must continue to live to justify their sacrifices. Ramón's sacrifice, in effect, releases his entire family from the cycle.

16. As the film plays and replays the scene of Ramón's diving accident, the narrative suggests that his paralysis is a symptom resulting from an interrupted "normal" trajectory of death. He dives, he breaks his neck, he feels the pull of death, and then a hand drags him out of the water. When Ramón commits suicide, the film repeats the exact same shot of him drowning, but this time no hand intervenes to halt his "natural" flow towards death.

17. Julia, the lawyer character in the film who has the degenerative and terminal illness CADASIL, confesses to Ramón that she "can't take it anymore; this isn't a life," and resolves to join him. When she does not show up on their appointed date and the film ends with the scene of Julia so cognitively debilitated that she can no longer remember Ramón, the implication is that (unlike Ramón) Julia has missed her chance to die "with dignity." Here, the conflation of illness with disability is especially insidious in that Julia embodies both: her illness causes disabilities, but also *prevents* her from fulfilling her original (and thus depicted as her "true") desire to end her life.

18. In fact, early in her diagnosis, Linda insistently demands that the doctors answer her questions: "What's going to happen to me?" (Davey, 81), and, "How am I going to die?" (86).

19. For a particularly saccharine example, see John Badham's *Whose Life Is It Anyway?* (1981), and Paul Darke's essay detailing his key argument that demands for demedicalization often conflate with claims against keeping disabled patients alive (97–107). In speaking of that same film, Paul Longmore writes that he and "disabled friends have had people say to us, '[I]f I were you I'd kill myself'" (*Why I Burned My Book*, 121). Films that propose the nobility of a disabled character "fighting the man" in order to be allowed to die often perpetuate the idea that a life lived at any level other than fully-abled participation is not worth much. Few of those people Longmore quotes are, I believe, actually urging Longmore or his friends to commit suicide as much as they are declaring their own panic about the possibility of facing what they assume is an either/or "choice."

20. Jean-Do constantly jokes that *if* he were able to move, he would re-establish his Casanova role. In the visual field of the film his observation is emphatically empowered: the highly sexualized point-of-view shots of the women who visit him perpetuate the dominance of his (extremely heterosexual) male gaze. Whereas the ongoing joke in *The Sea Inside* is the same one, but inverted. Ramón insinuates that he is looking up women's skirts or that they flirt with him endlessly, or that he will go to bed with them: the film's "punch line" is the suggestion that such conduct on his part is preposterous.

Chapter 8

1. Roy Miki is a Vancouver-based poet, active in the Japanese-Canadian community and who fought hard—and successfully—for redress from the Canadian government for the internment of Japanese-Canadians during World War II. He has published four books of poetry, including the 2001 Governor General's Award for poetry winner, *Surrender*, and numerous critical works. Sharon Thesen is a British Columbia poet with over a dozen books of poetry; in 2000 she won the Pat Lowther Memorial Award for *A Pair of Scissors*.

2. *Regarding* leads into a tangent I have not room enough to explore, here, and I highly recommend Rosemary Garland-Thomson's book, *Staring: How We Look*, for the myriad ways she analyzes the ableist gaze upon the disabled body, and the diverse ways that disabled people, characters, art representations, etc., look, and look back.

3. Ngai's essay delves into the notion of "disgust" as a counter to the so-called poetics of "desire." Her essay is exciting for its turn from the libidinal economy of jouissance, but fails to recognize disability theory as an existing rubric under which her discussion would well be placed.

Chapter 9

1. Contrast this "universal" response and interpretation to Rupert Ross's example, in his book *Dancing with a Ghost*, of First Nations defendants in Canadian sentencing hearings, who avert their eyes, because "sustaining direct eye contact was frequently considered rude" (4). Ross speaks not only of cultural differences, but about how assumptions of sameness create divides. In the northern Ontario communities he writes about the "proper way to send someone a signal of respect was to look down or to the side" (3). Whereas "the messages received by non–Native court personnel were exactly the opposite ones. Their inclination was to interpret such respectful glances as evasive, and often even indicative of an admission of guilt (4).

2. Setting up documentaries in this way invites the viewer into a role similar to that of the psychologist in *Lie to Me*. Like the protagonist, viewers throughout a film search characters' facial expressions and other physical features as a way to observe manifested truths.

3. Although the filmmaker is Joe Moulins, and Sam Sullivan acts entirely as subject and is not credited with co-directing or co-producing, at times he addresses the audience as if he is alone. This autobiographical effect may emerge from the confessional technique I discuss in the following paragraph, but is just as likely a dramatic technique that Moulins creates by setting up the equipment so that Sullivan can, at times, video himself without the presence of film technicians.

4. For more discussion on the contemporary evaluations of the body that—through technoculture—convey legal certainties, see Katja Franko Aas's article about new technologies that investigate, and also come to conclusions about, somatic identity. Speaking of the example of UN surveillance of Afghan refugee border crossings, Aas writes, "Bodies, fused with the latest technologies, are proving to be vital to contemporary governance" (144). The article focuses on the body as a source of information and identification, and asks important questions about how the body has been wrested from its social context, yet is still—and, perhaps, even more—able to discharge forensic information.

5. Juel's students seem unwilling to recognize or allow for the possibility that surveillance cameras may also be constructed, deliberate, and willed. Indeed, the very circumstances of a public that accepts permanent cameras capturing moments of their existence shopping or driving or going to school or taking money from a bank machine, puts pressure on the idea of an impartial recording.

6. Aas, in arguing how bodies have become "unique tokens of identification" (145), asserts that "the human body is always treated as an image of society" (155), in that the "rituals of bodily control" (whether they be habits of eliminating dirt, or official methods of preventing unwanted outsiders from joining a particular membership) determine who belongs on which side of the "us/them" divide.

7. Pedro Zamora was a Cuban-American performer who worked as an activist to change people's perceptions of HIV and AIDS and who turned to television to reach a larger audience. He died in November 1994. Muñoz argues that Zamora's work was for "*potentially* politicized queers and Latinos; for a mass public that is structured by the cultural forces of homophobia and racism; for those who have no access to more subculturally based cultural production and grassroots activism" (146).

8. Such a scene overlaps with viewers' concurrent memories of news coverage from the time, adding to the truth value of the film by invoking this particular historic moment as supporting reference.

9. In writing about John Grierson, whom many consider to be the founder of documentary film, Jim Leach and Jeanette Sloniowski write that even though the process of "arranging (editing) the images itself provides a kind of commentary on their meaning, the Griersonian documentary employed a (male) commentator whose omniscience and invisibility gave him the authority of 'the voice of God.' The commentary was usually pre-scripted and the images filmed (or selected from stock footage) and arranged to support the argument" (5).

10. Sullivan's win is arguably tied to the subsequent loss of the Non-Partisan Association political party.

11. Indeed, the "fact" that Sam Sullivan bought drugs for street people comes up as a repeated political blunder that he must constantly address, and yet he also uses it to successful political ends, as an example of his connection to downtrodden citizens.

12. During the campaign, Sullivan often exposes his own physical abilities in order to align himself with the vulnerability of particular constituents, all the while offering his "suicidal-to-triumphant" accomplishments as political fodder.

13. One example is the American television program *Bones*, in which crime evidence is often microscopically inscribed onto the remains of the victim.

Chapter 10

1. Keith later states: "The children's faith [in *The Secret Garden*] is not in 'God's plan' but in the power of the self to evoke 'good thoughts' and thereby make good things happen" (135). Burnett herself followed both Theosophy and Spiritualism, especially after the death of her first son, at age sixteen.

2. The garden not only cures physical ailments, but psychological ones. Both the protagonist, Mary, and her new friend, Colin, have bad tempers and need to learn how to behave properly—Mary as a good girl should, and Colin as an heir to wealth and privilege. Interestingly, once Mary is "cured" of her assertive and forceful nature and Colin can walk upright, Mary literally disappears from the text—the last chapter is all about Colin's reunion with his father; Mary has no lines and is barely mentioned. For a further feminist reading of the ending of *The Secret Garden*, see Elizabeth Lennox Keyser's "'Quite Contrary': Frances Hodgson Burnett's *The Secret Garden*" in *Children's Literature*, Vol. 11, 1983, 1–13.

3. Even though "bent" as slang for homosexual emerged in the 1970s, it has been used, along with "crooked," as pejorative to indicate anyone considered a "criminal," a drunk, or "spoiled" since as early as the 1550s. See *The Oxford English Dictionary*: www.oed.com.

4. I speak more on Foucault and *The Birth of the Clinic* in Chapter 5.

5. In her memoir, *My Body Politic*, Simi Linton (paraplegic from a car accident) writes that she told her mother that "the quest for a cure didn't interest [her]" (69). Later in the book, when she interviews for a job teaching a course on sexuality at a nearby college, she is startled when her interviewer, Chair of the occupational therapy department, touches her thigh and wheelchair, and then speaks to her as if she is a patient seeking medical advice (157).

6. About his decision to release a 1500-page medical report about the state of his physical and mental health, presidential candidate John McCain said, "[P]eople were spreading rumors that I was crazy and disabled both" (Simon). Even as McCain hoped such an extensive report would "prove" his physical and mental capabilities, much was made of his age (he was seventy-two in 2008) and lengthy medical history by Democrats, reporters, and political analysts.

7. Lennard Davis describes how, when the memorial to honor FDR was being constructed, disability-rights activists protested the lack of a sculpture depicting (or even referencing) Roosevelt in a wheelchair. Although some mention of Roosevelt's disability was included textually when the monument was dedicated in 1997, the memorial committee opposed any visual representations of FDR in any way other than "intact and normal" (*Enforcing Normalcy*, 98–99).

8. Dr. Joel Goran (Daniel Gillies) inverts the expected medical advice when he lectures the father about how he must "accept" his daughter as she is; not, ironically, as a disabled person, but as a person who has mobility ambitions beyond the life the father thinks his daughter should "settle" for.

9. Although those who use such prosthetic devices as crutches or leg braces are also included in the range of citizens who "can" stand, the prosthetics themselves often draw particular attention to the user, making the very act of standing into a category that divides the "normal" viewers from the "abnormal" spectacle.

10. The "legs" in question are also sometimes called "wine tears," by experts, which maintains within the metaphor a link to the corporeal body, but is a less-used term, perhaps because "robust legs" is a more powerful image than "crying wine." The metaphor, ironically, is often divorced from its context (the "legs" in question refer to the lines that run down a wine glass and indicate its level of alcohol) whereas the metaphor of the metaphor simply announces that for something to "have legs" is a positive and desired attribute.

11. In a YouTube video highlighting this speech, Howard goes on to say, "Such a portrayal is a gross distortion and it deliberately neglects the overall story of great Australian achievement that is there in our history to be told and such an approach will be repudiated by the overwhelming majority of Australians who are proud of what this country has achieved, although inevitably acknowledging the blemishes in its past history." Judith Brett, analyzing John Howard's 1997 Reconciliation Convention speech in this YouTube video, points out that—by choosing the word "blemish" to minimize the impact of the historical damage—Howard not only minimizes the Australian nationality as one that was built on the murder and persecution of aborigines and on the disposition of land, but he also inadvertently brings attention to the skin, to different-colored skin. Says Brett, "Here is a prime minister denying that race relations are at the heart of some of Australia's most intractable problems ... at the same time that he's using a word that draws attention to skin color. Blemishes are on skins ... but blemishes are also on reputations.... There were actually people here with the wrong skin color when we got here.... In this choice of the word 'blemish' we were seeing the return of the repressed in Howard's public discourse. He was, by using that word, he was admitting the very thing he was attempting to deny" ("TimeToGo").

Afterword

1. The drawing depicts a woman in a wheelchair, facing two doorways. The one with the sign, "Suicide Prevention Program," has only stairs leading to its entrance; the other, with the sign, "Assisted Suicide" has only a ramp to its entrance.

2. On April 14, 2016, the Liberal government of Canada set out to recognize "the antonomy of persons who have a grievous and irremediable condition that causes them enduring and intolerable suffering" by putting forth a bill for those wishing medical assistance in dying. Much to the chagrin of those in support of "right to die" legislation, the bill also included language that protected "vulnerable people" from being induced to end their lives, and "to avoid encouraging negative perceptions of quality of life of persons who are elderly, ill or disabled" (Bill C-14). The bill still needs to go to a committee for further study, and then goes to the House of Commons for a vote.

3. John Hockenberry, in his review of *Million Dollar Baby*, calls such an ending "crip ex machina" theatrical convention to specifically signal a Hollywood film that ends with the disabled character choosing suicide. Similarly, Jay Dolmage suggests the phrase "dis ex machina" (56) to signal a narrative that concludes with disability cure (or even admission that the character has been "faking" disability).

4. Frazee writes this opinion piece nearly a year before Canada's Supreme Court Decision, as a response to a Toronto lawyer's open letter about his ALS and choice to go to Switzerland to terminate his life.

5. Terri Schiavo was a Florida woman who suffered brain damage as a result of heart failure in 1990. In 1998, her husband, Michael Schiavo, petitioned the courts for the right to end Terri's life, battling her parents, Mary and Robert Schindler, who fought to keep Terri alive, for more than seven years.

Works Cited

Aas, Katja Franko. "'The Body Does Not Lie': Identity, Risk, and Trust in Technoculture." *Crime, Media, Culture* 2:2 (2006), 143–58.

Act of Love. Dir. Jud Taylor. NBC. September 24, 1980.

AfterLife. Dir. Alison Peebles. UK: Gabriel Films, 2003.

Angus Reid Institute. "Most Canadians support Assisted Suicide, but Under Which Circumstances Reveal Deeper Divides?" November 25–28, 2014.

Associated Press. "New Miss Wheelchair Crowned After Dispute." *USA Today*, April 6, 2005.

_____. "Six-legged Calf wins Swiss Hearts." *The Guardian* online; Yahoo! News, March 29, 2012.

Barfoot, Joan. *Critical Injuries*. Toronto: Key Porter Books, 2001.

Barnes, Colin, and Geof Mercer. *Disability*. Cambridge: Polity, 2003.

_____, eds. *Exploring the Divide: Illness and Disability*. Leeds, UK: Disability Press, 1996.

Barthes, Roland. *Mythologies*. Translated by Annette Lavers. London: Grenada, 1973.

Bartlett, Jennifer. "Preface." *Beauty Is a Verb: The New Poetry of Disability*, edited by Jennifer Bartlett, Sheila Black, and Michael Northen. El Paso, TX: Cinco Puntos, 2011, 15–17.

Bauby, Jean-Dominique. *The Diving Bell and the Butterfly*. Translated by Jeremy Leggatt. New York: Knopf, 1997.

Bauman, H-Dirksen L, and Joseph J. Murray. "Deaf Studies in the 21st Century: 'Deaf-Gain' and the Future of Human Diversity." *Disability Studies Reader*, 4th ed. New York: Routledge, 2013, 246–61.

Beach, Christopher. *ABC of Influence: Ezra Pound and the Remaking of American Poetic Tradition*. Berkeley: University of California Press, 1992.

Beard, William. "Maddin and Melodrama." *Playing with Memories: Essays on Guy Maddin*. Edited by David Church. Winnipeg: University of Manitoba Press, 2009, 79–95.

Being There. Dir. Hal Ashby. USA: United Artists, 1979.

"Beyond Belief." *Lie to Me*. Toronto: Global Network, November 17, 2010.

Birney, Earle. "David." *The Collected Poems of Earle Birney: Volume 1*. Toronto: McClelland and Stewart, 1975, 107–13.

Bogdan, Robert. *Freak Show: Presenting Human Oddities for Amusement and Profit*. Chicago: University of Chicago Press, 1990.

Boles, David. "Camille Paglia Scolds Lady Gaga's Nattering Vagina." *Celebrity Semiotic*, September 16, 2010.

Brinkema, Eugenie. "Browning. Freak. Woman. Stain." *The Cinema of Tod Browning: Essays of the Macabre and Grotesque*. Edited by Bernd Herzogenrath. Jefferson: McFarland, 2008, 158–73.

Brown, Ian, with Robert Adams, Jeannie McFarlan, and Michael Winter. "Talking Books." *This Morning*. CBC National Radio, January 28, 2000.

Brueggemann, Brenda. "On (Almost) Passing." *Lend Me Your Ears: Rhetorical Construc-tions of Deafness*. Washington: Gallaudet University Press, 1999, 81–99.

Brune, Jeffrey A., and Daniel J. Wilson, eds. "Introduction." *Disability and Passing: Blur-ring the Lines of Identity*. Philadelphia: Temple University Press, 2013, 1–12.

Budde, Rob. *Misshapen*. Edmonton: NeWest, 1997.

Burnett, Frances Hodgson. *The Secret Garden*. Manchester: World International, 1989.

Burton, Robert. *The Anatomy of Melancholy*. Edited by Floyd Dell and Paul Jordan-Smith. New York: Tudor, 1938.

Butler, Judith. *Gender Trouble*. New York: Routledge, 1990.

"Canada Deports Chris Mason Because He Has a Disability." *A Voice of Our Own* 27:1, January 2009.

"Cane and Able." *House, M.D.* Fox Network, September 12, 2006.

Carter vs. Canada. Judges: McLachlin, Beverley; LeBel, Louis; Abella, Rosalie Silberman; Rothstein, Marshall; Cromwell, Thomas Albert; Moldaver, Michael J.; Karakatsanis, Andromache; Wagner, Richard; Gascon, Clément. Case no. 35591; citation: 2015 SCC 5: February 6, 2015.

Carter-Long, Lawrence. "Better Dead Than Disabled?" *Satya*, March 13, 2005.

_____. "I Am Disabled and I Am Proud." *Ollibean*, November 8, 2013.

Case, Mary Anne. "Why Not Abolish the Laws of Urinary Segregation?" *Toilet: Public Restrooms and the Politics of Sharing*. Edited by Harvey Molotch and Laura Norén. New York: New York University Press, 2010, 211–25.

Chivers, Sally. "The Horror of Becoming 'One of Us': Tod Browning's *Freaks* and Disa-bility." *Screening Disability: Essays on Cinema and Disability*. Edited by Anthony Enns and Christopher Smit. Lanham, MD: University Press of America, 2001, 57–64.

_____, and Nicole Markotić, eds. *The Problem Body: Projecting Disability on Film*. Colum-bus: Ohio State University Press, 2010.

Chua, Jane. "Assisted Suicide: Physicians Want More Palliative Care As Well." CBC News online, February 6, 2015.

Church, David, ed. *Playing with Memories: Essays on Guy Maddin*. Winnipeg: University of Manitoba Press, 2009.

Citizen Sam. Dir. Joe Moulins. Canada: NFB, 2006.

Couser, G. Thomas. "Autopathography: Women, Illness, and Writing." *Women and Auto-biography*. Edited by Martine Brownley and Allison Kimmich. Wilmington, DE: Scholarly Resources, 1999, 163–74.

"CTV News." CTV National News Broadcast, February 8, 2000.

Darke, Paul. "No Life Anyway: Pathologizing Disability on Film." *The Problem Body: Projecting Disability on Film*. Edited by Sally Chivers and Nicole Markotić. Colum-bus: Ohio State University Press, 2010, 97–107.

Davey, Frank. *How Linda Died*. Toronto: ECW Press, 2002.

Davidson, Michael. "Cleavings: Critical Losses in the Politics of Gain." Unpublished essay, 2015.

_____. *Concerto for the Left Hand: Disability and the Defamiliar Body*. Ann Arbor: Uni-versity of Michigan Press, 2008.

Davies, Alan. "A Course in Melancholy." University of Windsor: September 19, 2011.

Davis, Lennard. *Bending Over Backwards: Disability, Dismodernism & Other Difficult Positions*. New York: New York University Press, 2002.

_____. *Enforcing Normalcy: Disability, Deafness and the Body*. London: Verso, 1995.

Davis, Todd, and Kenneth Womack, eds. *Mapping the Ethical Turn: A Reader in Ethics, Culture and Literary Theory*. Charlottesville: University of Virginia Press, 2001.

Dead Ringers. Dir. David Cronenberg. Canada: 20th Century Fox, 1988.

Dempsey, Shawna. "On Becoming Fatale." Manitoba Writers' Guild Conference, Win-nipeg: October 2, 1993.

Diehl, Charlene. "Making a Problem of the Problem Body: Guy Maddin's *The Saddest*

Music in the World." Film and the Problem Body Conference. University of Calgary: January 28–30, 2005.

Doane, Mary Ann. "Film and the Masquerade: Theorizing the Female Spectator." *Screen* 23:3–4 (September/October 1982): 74–87.

Dodson, Will. "Tod Browning's Expressionist Bodies." *Quarterly Review of Film and Video* 31:3 (January 2014): 231–39.

Dollar, Ellen Painter. "'Inspiration Porn' Objectifies People with Disabilities." HuffPost TED Weekends, July 11, 2014.

Dolmage, Jay Timothy. *Disability Rhetoric.* New York: Syracuse University Press, 2014.

Easthope, Antony. *The Unconscious.* London: Routledge, 1999.

Easton, Lee, and Kelly Hewson. "'I'm Not an American, I'm a Nymphomaniac': Perverting the Nation in Guy Maddin's *The Saddest Music in the World.*" *Playing with Memories: Essays on Guy Maddin.* Edited by David Church. Winnipeg: University of Manitoba Press, 2009, 224–38.

Eddy, Charmaine. Personal conversation, Peterborough, September 23, 2010.

Edelman, Lee. *No Future: Queer Theory and the Death Drive.* Durham, NC: Duke University Press, 2004.

Edwards, Peter. "Politics and Poetry: An Interview with Earle Birney." *Queen's Quarterly* 90:1 (Spring 1983): 122–31.

Egan, Susanna. *Mirror Talk: Genres of Crisis in Contemporary Autobiography.* Chapel Hill: University of North Carolina Press, 1999.

Farrant, M.A.C. "Studies Show/Experts Say." *And Other Stories.* Edited by George Bowering. Vancouver: Talon, 2001, 145–55.

Faulkner, William. "The Art of Fiction No. 12." Interview by Jean Stein. *The Paris Review* (1956, reprinted 2013).

Ferris, Jim. "The Enjambed Body: A Step Toward a Crippled Poetics." *The Georgia Review* 58:2 (Summer 2004): 219–33.

Fiedler, Leslie. *Tyranny of the Normal: Essays on Biothics, Theology & Myth.* Boston: David R. Godine, 1996.

Fleck, Ludwik. *Genesis and Development of a Scientific Fact.* Edited by Thaddeus Trenn and Robert Merton. Foreword by Thomas Kuhn. Chicago: University of Chicago Press, 1979 [1936].

Forrest Gump. Dir. Robert Zemeckis. USA: Paramount. 1994.

Foucault, Michel. *The Birth of the Clinic: An Archaeology of Medical Perception.* Translated by A. M. Sheridan. New York: Random House, 1994.

_____. *Power/Knowledge: Selected Interviews and Other Writings 1972–1977.* New York: Pantheon, 1980.

Frank, Arthur. *The Wounded Storyteller: Body, Illness, and Ethics.* Chicago: University of Chicago Press, 1997.

Frazee, Catherine. "A Respectful Postscript to Edward Hung's End-of-life Letter." *Toronto Star*, March 30, 2014.

Freaks. Dir. Tod Browning. USA: MGM, 1932.

Freud, Sigmund. "Beyond the Pleasure Principle." *The Freud Reader.* Edited by Peter Gay. New York: Norton, 1920; 1989, 594–626.

_____. "Creative Writers and Daydreaming." *The Standard Edition of the Complete Psychological Works of Sigmund Freud: Introductory lectures on psycho-analysis (parts I and II).* Translated by James Strachey and Anna Freud. London: Hogarth, 1962, 141–55.

_____. "The Dissolution of the Oedipus Complex." *On Sexuality*, Vol. 7, Penguin Freud Library. Translated by James Strachey. Edited by Angela Richards. Harmondsworth: Penguin, 1976, 313–22.

Gamman, Lorraine, and Margaret Marshment. "Introduction." *The Female Gaze.* Seattle: Red Comet, 1989.

Garland-Thomson, Rosemarie. "The Case for Conserving Disability." *Bioethical Inquiry* 9 (2012): 339–55.

_____. *Extraordinary Bodies: Figuring Physical Disability in American Culture and Litera-ture.* New York: Columbia University Press, 1997.

_____. *Staring: How We Look.* Oxford: Oxford University Press, 2009.

"Gaywatch." *Daily Show.* USA: Comedy Central, November 19, 2009.

Gill, Michael. *Already Doing It: Intellectual Disability and Sexual Agency.* Minneapolis: University of Minnesota Press, 2015.

Gillespie, Nancy. Private correspondence, October 27, 2011.

Goffman, Erving. *Stigma: Notes on the Management of Spoiled Identity.* New York: Touch-stone, 1963.

Golden, Christopher. "On Tod Browning's *Freaks*." *Cut!: Horror Writers on Horror Film.* Edited by Christopher Golden. New York: Berkley Books, 1992.

Goldwyn, Robert. "Deformity and the Humane Ideal of Medicine." *The Tyranny of the Normal.* Kent, OH: Kent State University Press, 1996, 85–88.

Goodley, Dan. "'Learning Difficulties,' the Social Model of Disability and Impairment: Challenging Epistemologies." *Disability & Society* 16:2 (2001): 207–31.

Grace, Sherrill. "Performing the Autobiographical Pact: Towards a Theory of Identity in Performance." *Tracing the Autobiographical.* Edited by Marlene Kadar, Linda Warley, Jeanne Perreault, and Susanna Egan. Waterloo: Wilfrid Laurier University Press, 2005, 65–80.

Greville, Fulke. "Mustapha." *Selected Poems of Fulke Greville.* Edited (and introduction) by Thom Gunn. Afterword by Bradin Cormack. Chicago: University of Chicago Press, 1968.

Grosz, Elizabeth. *Jacques Lacan: A Feminist Introduction.* London: Routledge, 1990.

Hansen, Nancy. "Better Dead Than Disabled, I Don't Think So!" *UMToday.* Winnipeg: University of Manitoba news blog, February 13, 2015.

Hawkins, Joan. "'One of Us' Tod Browning's *Freaks*." *Freakery: Cultural Spectacles of the Extraordinary Body.* Edited by Rosemarie Garland-Thomson. New York: New York University Press, 1986, 265–76.

The Headless Woman. Shawna Dempsey, and Lorri Millan, writers and directors. Win-nipeg/Vancouver: Finger in the Dyke Productions, 1998.

Hobbs, Allyson. *A Chosen Exile: A History of Racial Passing in American Life.* Cambridge: Harvard University Press, 2014.

Hockenberry, John. "And the Loser Is." *Beyond Chron: The Voice of the Rest.* February 21, 2005.

Hostert, Anna Camaiti. *Passing: A Strategy to Dissolve Identities and Remap Differences.* Translated by Christine Marciasini. Madison, NJ: Fairleigh Dickinson University Press, 2008.

"House of Commons Debates." *Parliament of Canada.* Hansard: "40th Parliament, 2nd Session, #002: January 27, 2009.

Hunter, Ian. "A Quality of Mercy for the Mercy Killer." *The Globe and Mail.* January 19, 2001, A13.

"Immigration." Council of Canadians with Disabilities website, March 23, 2012.

The Intouchables. Dir. Olivier Nakache and Éric Toledano. France: Gaumont, 2011.

Jensen, Dean. *The Lives and Loves of Daisy and Violet Hilton: A True Story of Conjoined Twins.* Berkeley: Ten Speed Press, 2006.

Johnson, Mark, and George Lakoff. *Metaphors We Live By.* Chicago: University of Chicago Press, 1980.

_____. *Philosophy in the Flesh: The Embodied Mind and its Challenge to Western Thought.* New York: Basic Books, 1999.

Johnson, Mary. *Make Them Go Away: Clint Eastwood, Christopher Reeve, and the Case Against Disability Rights.* Louisville: Advocado, 2003.

Juel, Henrik. "Defining Documentary Film." *P.O.V.* 22. December 2006.

Keith, Lois. *Take Up Thy Bed and Walk: Death, Disability and Cure in Classic Fiction for Girls.* New York: Routledge, 2001.

Kelly, Christine, and Michael Orsini. "Assisted Suicide and the Erasure of Disability." *Winnipeg Free Press*, February 10, 2015.

Kelly, John. "With assisted suicide, self-determination is just a slogan." *Not Dead Yet: The Resistance*, March 29, 2012.

Keyes, Daniel. "Flowers for Algernon." *The Science Fiction Hall of Fame, Volume One, 1929-1964*. Edited by Robert Silverberg. New York: Tom Doherty, 1970, 502-27.

Kim, Eunjung. Personal correspondence, November 24, 2010.

_____. "The Specter of Vulnerability and Disabled Bodies in Protest." *Disability, Human Rights and the Limits of Humanitarianism*. Edited by Michael Gill and Cathy J. Schlund-Vials. Farnham, Surrey: Ashgate, 2014, 137-54.

King, Thomas. "Joe the Painter and the Deer Island Massacre." *One Good Story, That One*. Toronto: HarperCollins, 1993.

Kittay, Eva. "Thoughts on the Desire for Normality." *Surgically Shaping Children: Technology, Ethics, and the Pursuit of Normality*. Edited by Erik Parens. Baltimore: Johns Hopkins University Press, 2006, 90-110.

Konnikova, Maria. "I Don't Want to Be Right." *The New Yorker*, May 16, 2014.

Kurchak, Sarah. "Vaccines Don't Cause Autism. But Even If They Did, Is Being Like Me Really a Fate Worse Than Death?" *The Archipelago*, February 6, 2015.

Kuusisto, Stephen. *Planet of the Blind: A Memoir*. New York: Dell, 1998.

_____, and Petra Kuppers. "Auto-Graphein or 'The Blind Man's Pencil': Notes on the Making of a Poem." *Journal of Literary & Cultural Disability Studies* 1:1 (Spring 2007): 74-80.

Lacan, Jacques. "Aggressivity in Psychoanalysis." *Écrits: A Selection*. Translated by Alan Sheridan. London: Routledge, 1977, 7-22.

_____. *Quarto* (Belgian Supplement to *La lettre mensuelle de l'École de la cause freudienne*), 1981, no. 2. Translated by Jack W. Stone, 1-6.

_____. *Seminar III: The Psychoses*. Translated by Russell Grigg. New York: Norton, 1993.

_____. *Seminar XVII: The Other Side of Psychoanalysis*. Translated by Russell Grigg. New York: Norton, 1991.

Lane, Jim. *The Autobiographical Documentary in America*. Madison: University of Wisconsin Press, 2002.

Larriere, Claire. "The Future of the Short Story: A Tentative Approach." *The Tales We Tell*, 195-99. Edited by Barbara Lounsberry. Westport, CT: Greenwood, 1998, 195-99.

Lars and the Real Girl. Dir. Craig Gillespie. USA: MGM, 2007.

Leach, Jim, and Jeannette Sloniowski, eds. *Candid Eyes: Essays on Canadian Documentaries*. Toronto: University of Toronto Press, 2003.

Lejeune, Philippe. "The Autobiographical Pact." *On Autobiography*. Minneapolis: University of Minnesota Press, 1989, 3-30.

Lightman, Alan. *The Diagnosis*. New York: Pantheon Books, 2000.

Lindemann, Kurt. "'I Can't Be Standing Up Out There': Communicative Performances of (Dis)Ability in Wheelchair Rugby." *Text and Performance Quarterly* 28:1-2 (2008): 98-115.

Linton, Simi. *Claiming Disability: Knowledge and Identity*. New York: New York University Press, 1998.

_____. *My Body Politic*. Ann Arbor: University of Michigan Press, 2007.

Livesay, Dorothy. Correspondence with Earle Birney. Dorothy Livesay Papers. University of Manitoba Archives. Mss. 37, Box 47, Folder 69. Special Collections.

_____. "The Documentary Poem: A Canadian Genre." *Contexts of Canadian Criticism*. Edited by Eli Mandel. Chicago: University of Chicago Press, 1971, 267-81.

L.N. "The Circus Side Show." *New York Times*, July 9, 1932.

Longmore, Paul. *Why I Burned My Book and Other Essays on Disability*. Philadelphia: Temple University Press, 2003.

MacCormack, Patricia. "Posthuman Teratology." *The Ashgate Research Companion to*

Monsters and the Monstrous. Edited by Asa Simon Mittman, with Peter Dendle. Surrey: Ashgate, 2012, 293–311.

Maddin, Guy. *From the Atelier Tovar: Selected Writings.* Toronto: Coach House, 2003.

_____. "Sad Songs Say So Much: A Shooting Journal." *The Village Voice,* May 6, 2003.

Mar Adentro (The Sea Inside). Dir. Alejandro Amenábar. Spain: Eyescreen and UGC, 2004.

Markotić, Nicole. "Introduction: 'Coincidence of the Page.'" *Tessera* 27 (Winter 1999): 6–15.

_____. "Punching Up the Story: Disability and Film." Introduction, *Canadian Journal of Film Studies/Revue canadienne d'études cinématographiques* 17:1 (June 2008): 2–10.

McCulloch, Sandra. "Ozzy Osbourne Latest Album Features Song Inspired by Story of Robert Latimer." *Calgary Herald,* May 22, 2010.

McEnteer, James. *Shooting the Truth: The Rise of American Political Documentaries.* Westport, CT: Praeger, 2006.

McIntire, Gabrielle. "Toward a Narratology of Passing: Epistemology, Race, and Misrecognition in Nella Larsen's *Passing.*" *Callaloo* 35:3 (2012), 778–94.

McMillan, Ross. *The Saddest Characters in the World: The Cast of* The Saddest Music in the World. Dirs. Caelum Vatnsdal and Matthew Holm. DVD extra. 2003.

McRuer, Robert. "Compulsory Able-bodiedness and Queer/Disabled Existence." *Disability Studies: Enabling the Humanities.* Edited by Sharon Snyder, Brenda Brueggemann, and Rosemarie Garland-Thomson. New York: MLA, 2003, 88–99.

_____. *Crip Theory: Cultural Signs of Queerness and Disability.* New York: New York University Press, 2006.

_____. "Neoliberal Risks: *Million Dollar Baby, Murderball,* and Anti-National Sexual Positions." *The Problem Body: Projecting Disability on Film.* Edited by Sally Chivers and Nicole Markotić. Columbus: Ohio State University Press, 2010, 159–77.

Memento. Dir. Christopher Nolan. USA: Newmarket Films, 2001.

The Men. Dir. Fred Zinnemann. USA: United Artists, 1950.

"Mental Illness and Addictions: Facts and Statistics." Centre for Addiction and Mental Health (CAMH), 2012.

Miki, Roy. *Mannequin Rising.* Vancouver: New Star, 2011.

_____. *market rinse.* Calgary: disOrientation Press, 1993.

_____. *Social Audit.* Calgary: No Press, 2007.

_____. *Surrender.* Toronto: The Mercury Press, 2001.

Million Dollar Baby. Dir. Clint Eastwood. USA: Warner Bros., 2004.

Milne, Tom. "The Real Avant Garde." *Sight and Sound* 32:3 (Summer 1963): 148–52.

Mitchell, David, and Sharon Snyder. *The Body and Physical Difference: Discourses of Disability.* Ann Arbor: University of Michigan Press, 1997.

_____. *Cultural Locations of Disability.* Chicago: University of Chicago Press, 2006.

_____. "Disability Haunting in American Poetics." *Journal of Literary & Cultural Disability Studies* 1:1 (Spring 2007): 1–12.

_____. *Narrative Prosthesis: Disability and the Dependencies of Discourse.* Ann Arbor: University of Michigan Press, 2000.

_____. Private e-mail to the author, March 20, 2015.

Montgomery, Cal. "A Hard Look at Invisible Disability." *Ragged Edge* 22:2, March 2001.

Moore, Marianne. *The Complete Prose of Marianne Moore.* Edited and Introduction by Patricia Willis. New York: Viking Penguin, 1986.

Mouré, Erin. "On A Frame of the Book." *Tessera* 27 (Winter 1999): 25–31.

Moyer, Justin. "Welcome Eddie Redmayne: Since 'Rain Main,' Majority of Best Actor Oscar Winners Played Sick or Disabled." *Washington Post,* February 23, 2015.

Mulvey, Laura. "Visual Pleasure and Narrative Cinema." *Screen* 16:3. (1975): 6–18.

Murphy, Robert F. *The Body Silent: The Different World of the Disabled.* New York: W.W. Norton, 2001.

Muñoz, José. *Disidentifications: Queers of Color and the Performance of Politics.* Minneapolis: University of Minnesota Press, 1999.

My Sister's Keeper. Dir. Nick Cassavetes. USA: New Line Cinema, 2009.

Ngai, Sianne. "Raw Matter: A Poetics of Disgust." *Open Letter: A Canadian Journal of Writing and Theory* 10:1 (Winter 1998): 98–122.

Norden, Martin. *Cinema of Isolation: A History of Physical Disability in the Movies.* New Brunswick, NJ: Rutgers University Press, 1994.

Not Dead Yet: The Resistance. April 27, 1996.

Nussbaum, Susan. *Good Kings Bad Kings.* Chapel Hill, NC: Algonquin, 2013.

O'Connor, Flannery. "Good Country People." *A Good Man is Hard to Find.* New York: Harcourt Brace, 1983, 169–96.

_____. "Writing Short Stories." *The Art of Short Fiction.* Edited by Gary Geddes. Toronto: HarperCollins, 1999, 365–73.

The Odds of Recovery. Dir. Su Friedrich. UK: Downstream Productions, 2002.

Ogrizek, Irene. "Buffet Liberals and Champagne Charlies." *The Practical Leftist*, December 15, 2013.

Oliver, Michael, and Bob Sapey. *Social Work with Disabled People.* London: Macmillan, 1983.

One Flew Over the Cuckoo's Nest. Dir. Miloš Forman. USA: United Artists, 1975.

Owen, Wilfred. "Disabled." *The Poems of Wilfred Owen.* Edited by Jon Stallworthy. London: Hogarth, 1983, 152–53.

Paglia, Camille. "Lady Gaga and the Death of Sex." *The Sunday Times*, London, UK, September 12, 2010.

Parsons, Talcott. *The Social System.* London: Routledge: 2005.

Peranson, Mark. "Introduction: 'The Great Pretender.'" *From the Atelier Tovar: Selected Writings.* Toronto: Coach House, 2003, 9–13.

Pevere, Geoff. "Guy Maddin: True to Form." *Playing with Memories: Essays on Guy Maddin.* Edited by David Church. Winnipeg: University of Manitoba Press, 2009, 48–57.

The Player. Dir. Robert Altman. USA: Avenue Pictures, 1992.

Poovey, Mary. *A History of the Modern Fact: Problems of Knowledge in the Sciences of Wealth and Society.* Chicago: University of Chicago Press, 1998.

Porter, James. "Introduction." *The Body and Physical Difference: Discourses of Disability.* Edited by David Mitchell and Sharon Snyder. Ann Arbor: University of Michigan Press, 1997, xiii–xiv.

Price Herndl, Diane. "Disease Versus Disability: The Medical Humanities and Disability Studies." *PMLA* 120:2 (March 2005): 593–98.

"Puerto Rican Day." *Seinfeld.* NBC. May 7, 1998.

Quartermain, Meredith. *Vancouver Walking.* Edmonton: NeWest Press, 2005.

Quartermain, Peter. "Poetic Fact." Talk at University of Windsor: Oct. 26, 2010.

Rak, Julie, ed. *Auto/biography in Canada: Critical Directions.* Waterloo: Wilfrid Laurier University Press, 2005.

Ran. Dir. Akira Kurosawa. Japan: Herald Ace, 1985.

Raykoff, Ivan, and Robert Deam Tobin, eds. *A Song for Europe: Popular Music and Politics in the Eurovision Song Contest.* Hampshire: Ashgate, 2007.

Razack, Sherene. *Looking White People in the Eye: Gender, Race, and Culture in Courtrooms and Classrooms.* Toronto: University of Toronto Press, 1998.

Reimer, Nikki. "fist things first." (Chapbook) Vancouver/Windsor: Wrinkle Press, 2009.

_____. *[sic].* Calgary: Frontenac Press, 2010.

The Right to Die. Dir. Paul Wendkos. NBC. October 12, 1987.

Robbins, Tod. "Spurs." *Olga Baclanova: The Ultimate Cinemantrap*, April 6, 2004.

Robertson, Lisa. *The Weather.* Vancouver: New Star, 2001.

Ross, Rupert. *Dancing with a Ghost: Exploring Indian Reality.* Markham, ON: Octopus, 1992.

Ross, Winston. "Dying Dutch: Euthanasia Spreads Across Europe." *Newsweek*, February 12, 2015.

Rottenberg, Catherine. "Passing: Race, Identification, and Desire." *Criticism* 45:4 (2003): 435–52.

Rubin, Jeffrey. "Foreword." *Women with Disabilities: Essays in Psychology, Culture, and Politics*. Edited by Adrienne Asch and Michelle Fine. Philadelphia: Temple University Press, 1988.

Ryan, Frances. "We Wouldn't Accept Actors Blacking Up, So Why Applaud 'Cripping Up'?" *The Guardian*, January 13, 2015.

The Saddest Music in the World. Dir. Guy Maddin. Canada: IFC Films, 2003.

Safilios-Rothschild, Constantina. "From Disability to Rehabilitation: The Disabled Role." *The Sociology and Social Psychology of Disability and Rehabilitation*. New York: Random House, 1970: 73–78.

Samuels, Ellen. "Critical Divides: Judith Butler's Body Theory and the Question of Disability." *National Women's Studies Association. NWSA* Journal 14:3 (Fall 2002): 58–76.

_____. "My Body, My Closet": Invisible Disability and the Limits of Coming-Out Discourse." *GLQ: A Journal of Lesbian and Gay Studies* 9:1–2 (2003), 233–55.

Le Scaphandre et le papillon (*The Diving Bell and the Butterfly*). Dir. Julian Schnabel. France: Pathé Renn Productions, 2007.

Sedgwick, Eve Kosofsky. *Epistemology of the Closet*. Berkeley: University of California Press, 1990.

Shaviro, Steven. "Fire and Ice: The Films of Guy Maddin." *Playing with Memories: Essays on Guy Maddin*. Edited by David Church. Winnipeg: University of Manitoba Press, 2009, 70–78.

Shildrick, Margit. *Dangerous Discourses of Disability, Subjectivity and Sexuality*. Belfast: Queen's University Press, 2009.

"Show Stoppers." *American Horror Story: Freak Show*. USA: FX, January 14, 2015.

Siebers, Tobin. *Disability Theory*. Ann Arbor: University of Michigan Press, 2008.

Simon, Roger. "McCain's Health and Age Present Campaign Challenge." *Politico* 44: January 24, 2007.

"A Simple Plan." *Saving Hope*. Canada: CTV, February 4, 2015.

Smith, Angela M. *Hideous Progeny: Disability, Eugenics, and Classic Horror Cinema*. New York: Columbia University Press, 2011.

Smith, Laura, Pamela F. Foley, and Michael P. Chaney. "Addressing Classism, Ableism, and Heterosexism in Counselor Education." *Journal of Counseling & Development* 86:3 (Summer 2008): 303–09.

Smith, Mark. "Grotesquerie is Merely a Sideshow in *Freaks*." *Los Angeles Times*, October 30, 1995.

Smith, S. E. "Where Are All the People with Disabilities?" FWD: feminists with disabilities for a way forward, October 24, 2009.

SoBe drinks advertisement, June 22, 2007.

Sontag, Suan. *Illness as Metaphor*. New York: Vintage, 1979.

Stein, Gertrude. "Poetry and Grammar." *Look at Me Now and Here I Am: Writings and Lectures 1909–45*. New York: Penguin, 1990.

Stork. Francisco X. *Marcelo in the Real World*. New York: Scholastic, 2009.

Straw, Will. "Reinhabiting Lost Languages: Guy Maddin's *Careful*." *Playing with Memories: Essays on Guy Maddin*. Edited by David Church. Winnipeg: University of Manitoba Press, 2009, 58–69.

The Switch. Dir. Bobby Roth. USA: CBS. January 17, 1993.

Tate, Claudia. "Nella Larsen's *Passing*: A Problem of Interpretation." *Black American Literature Forum* 14:4. (Winter 1980), 142–46.

"Teacher Caught on Tape Pulling Chair from Under Student Refusing to Stand for National Anthem." *The Daily Irrelevant*, February 20, 2005.

There's Something About Mary. Dir. Bobby and Peter Ferrelly. USA: 20th Century-Fox, 1998.

Theresa Marie. Comments under: "Supreme Court Strikes Down Canada's Assisted Suicide Laws." Global News online, February 8, 2015.

Thériault, Anne. "Vaccines Don't Cause Autism, But That's Not the Point. Stop Being Ableist." *The Belle Jar*, February 5, 2015.
"These People Describe the Taste of Foods to the Blind and It's Beautiful." ClickHole, April 1, 2015.
Thesen, Sharon. *Aurora*. Toronto: Coach House, 1995.
_____. *The Good Bacteria*. Toronto: Anansi, 2006.
_____. *A Pair of Scissors*. Toronto: Anansi, 2000.
_____. *The Pangs of Sunday*. Toronto: McClelland and Stewart, 1990.
_____. *Po-It-Tree: a selection of poems and commentary*. SFU chapbook, 1992.
_____. "Writing, Reading and the Imagined Reader/Lover." Special Issue of *La Nouvelle Barre du Jour. Tessera* (Spring 1985), 67–74.
Thompson, Gary. "Film Portrays the '60s as Tale Told by an Idiot." *Philadelphia News*, July 6, 1994.
"TimeToGoJohn#9." *YouTube*. Online video. Posted October 9, 2009.
Tobin, Jean. *Creativity and the Poetic Mind*. New York: Peter Lang, 2004.
Toilet Training: Law and Order in the Bathroom. Dir. Tara Mateik. USA: Sylvia Rivera Law Project, 2003.
Travers, Peter. "Forrest Gump." *Rolling Stone*, July 6, 1994.
"Treehouse of Horror XXIV: Freaks, No Geeks." *The Simpsons*. USA: FOX. October 6, 2013.
Trueman, Terry. *Stuck in Neutral*. New York: HarperCollins, 1999.
Turan, Kenneth. "Simple Lessons from 'Gump': Turning a Particularly Harebrained Lens on Some Turbulent Decades." *Los Angeles Times*, July 6, 1996.
Verghese, Abraham. "Crashed." *The New York Times Books*, September 9, 2000.
Verhaeghe, Paul. "From Impossibility to Inability: Lacan's Theory on the Four Discourses." *The Letter: Lacanian Perspectives on Psychoanalysis* 3 (Spring 1995): 91–108.
Vico, Giovanni Battista Giambattista. *Vico: Selected Writings*. Cambridge: Cambridge University Press, 1982.
Wah, Fred. *Faking It: Poetics and Hybridity*. Edmonton: NeWest Press, 2000.
Warner, Michael. *The Trouble with Normal: Sex, Politics, and the Ethics of Queer Life*. New York: Free Press, 1999.
Watson, Leon. "Udderly Cured! Lilli the Cow with Six Legs Has Successful Surgery to Remove Extra Limbs." *Daily Mail* online, July 24, 2012.
Wees, William. "Making It Through": Sickness and Health in Su Friedrich's *The Odds of Recovery*." *Jump Cut: A Review of Contemporary Media* 54, Fall 2012.
Wendell, Susan. *The Rejected Body: Feminist Philosophical Reflections on Disability*. New York: Routledge, 1996.
Whose Life Is It Anyway? Dir. John Badham. USA: MGM, 1981.
Wilkinson, Joshua Marie. "On Poetry and Accessibility." *Evening Will Come* 27, March 2013.
Williams, Linda. "Film Bodies: Gender, Genre, and Excess." *Genre, Gender, Race, and World Cinema*. Edited by Julie Codell. Malden: Blackwell Publishing, 2007, 23–37.
Wilson, Daniel J. "Passing in the Shadow of FDR: Polio Survivors, Passing, and the Negotiation of Disability." In *Disability and Passing: Blurring the Lines of Identity*. Edited by Jeffrey A. Brune and Daniel J. Wilson. Philadelphia: Temple University Press, 2013, 13–35.
Wine, Bill. "*Forrest Gump* in IMAX." CBSPhilly, September 4, 2014.
Wirt, John. "At 20, Endearing 'Forrest Gump' Makes Another Run." *The Advocate*, October 14, 2014.
Wiseman, Adele. *Crackpot*. Toronto: McClelland and Stewart, 1974.
Wong, Jan. "What Parent Can Tolerate a Child in Unremitting Agony?" *Globe and Mail*, January 19, 2001, A4.
Wood, Neil. "UPDIKE." *As I Die Lying*. MA thesis: short stories. University of Windsor. 2009, 50–61.
Woodrow Pelley. Comments under: "Assisted Dying: Elation and Alarm at Top Court's Ruling." *Ottawa Citizen* online, February 6, 2015.

"Would You Tell Your Manager You Had a Mental Health Problem?" Centre for Addiction and Mental Health (CAMH), January 26, 2015.

Wu, Cynthia. "The Siamese Twins in Late-Nineteenth-Century Narratives of Conflict and Reconciliation." *American Literature* 80:1 (March 2008): 29–55.

Young, Stella. "I'm Not Your Inspiration, Thank You Very Much." TEDxSydney, April 2014.

Zackodnik, Teresa. *The Mulatta and the Politics of Race.* Jackson: Mississippi University Press, 2004.

Žižek, Slavoj. *How to Read Lacan.* New York: Norton, 2006.

Index